Family, Bureaucracy, and the Elderly

Family, Bureaucracy, and the Elderly

Edited by Ethel Shanas and Marvin B. Sussman

Duke University Press   Durham, N.C.   1977

© 1977 by Duke University Press
L.C.C. card number 76–4319
I.S.B.N. 0–8223–0365–5
Printed in the United States of
America by Kingsport Press

Contributors to this Volume

Michael Anderson is reader in sociology at the University of Edinburgh where he has been a member of the faculty since 1967. His main research activities have focused on the sociology of nineteenth-century Britain, and particularly on marriage and patterns of primary relationships. He is the author of *Family Structure in Nineteenth Century Lancashire* and editor of *Sociology of the Family: Readings*. His current research employs a 2 percent sample from the enumerators' books of the 1851 Census of Great Britain and is concerned with a detailed analysis of the social structure of Britain in 1851. He is also working on a book on the development of the family since the eighteenth century.

Kurt W. Back is James B. Duke professor and chairman of the Department of Sociology as well as professor in the Department of Psychiatry at Duke University. He is the author of *Beyond Words, The Story of Sensitivity Training and the Encounter Movement* and *Slums, Projects and People: Social Psychological Problems of Relocation in Puerto Rico*, as well as the coauthor of a number of other volumes. Professor Back, who served as guest investigator at Rockefeller University and visiting scholar at St. John's College, Cambridge, England, has written a number of articles and chapters in books in the field of gerontology.

Vern L. Bengtson is associate professor of sociology at the University of Southern California and chief of the Laboratory for Social Organization and Behavior at the Andrus Gerontology Center. He is director of the Study of Socio-Cultural Contexts of Aging and of the Study of Generations and Mental Health. He has been involved in research concerned with cross-cultural patterns of adaptation to retirement, intergenerational continuity in values and behavior, adult socialization, ethnic variations in needs related to aging, and attitudes and stereotypes regarding aging. He is author of *The Social Psychology of Aging* and editor of *Youth, Generations, and Social Change*.

K. Dean Black is at the Institute for Computer Uses in Education at Brigham Young University. He was formerly in the Sociology Department at the University of Southern California and in the Andrus Gerontology Center.

Juanita M. Kreps is vice-president and James B. Duke professor of economics at Duke University. Her publications include *Lifetime Allocation of Work and Income*, 1971; *Income, Employment, and Retirement Problems of the Aged*, 1963; and *Technology, Manpower and Economic Policy*, 1966. She has also coauthored a leading text in introductory economics and in labor economics. Professor Kreps was the 1975 president of the Southern Economic Association and holds a presidential appointment on the National Commission for Manpower Policy. She is a member of the Board of Directors of the New York Stock Exchange and a trustee of College Equities Retirement Fund.

Joep M. A. Munnichs is reader in psychogerontology at Nijmegen University (the Netherlands) and director of the Nijmegen Gerontological Center. He is the author of *Old Age and Finitude* and together with colleagues in West Germany and the United States is the coeditor of the cross-national study, *Adjustment to Retirement*. He is now working on a book on dependence in old age.

Paul M. Paillat is head of the Department of Social Demography of the National Institute of Population Studies (INED) in Paris. He is responsible for the institute's surveys on the conditions of life and the needs of the aged in France. Trained in political economy and public law, Dr. Paillat has served as rapporteur for a French Special Study Committee on the Aged and participated in the preparation of the V and VI French Plans. He has been chairman of a United Nations Expert Group on Aging and in 1974 was elected chairman of the French Society of Gerontology. He has been chairman of the International Demographic Terminology Committee supervising the revision of the *Multilingual Demographic Dictionary*. He is also a chevalier of the Légion d' Honneur and a chevalier of the Ordre National du Merite. In 1975 he was appointed scientific adviser to the National Foundation of Gerontology (Paris).

Jerzy Piotrowski is professor at the Institute of Philosophy and Sociology of the Polish Academy of Sciences in Warsaw, in the Independent Research Unit in Family Sociology. His main fields of interest are in family sociology and social policy, especially the changing social roles of men and women and family problems in later life. His book, *The Place of Old People in Family and Society* (in Polish), received the 1974 prize in sociology of the Polish Academy of Sciences. Professor Piotrowski was the 1975 president of the Polish Gerontological Association, and has served as chairman of the Section on Family Sociology of the Polish Sociological Association, vice-president of the Committee for Family Research of the International Sociological Association, and chairman of the East European Regional Group of Family Sociologists.

Leopold Rosenmayr is professor in the Department of Sociology of Vienna University and director of studies in social science on aging of the Ludwig Boltzmann Institut für Altersforschung, Vienna. He has studied and taught in the United States and in France and has served as a consultant and expert for the Council of Europe and for many other international organizations. He has been a member of the Executive Committee of the International Sociological Association and has served as president of the Austrian Sociological Society. Professor Rosenmayr has published widely on the sociology of both aging and youth. He is coauthor (with Eva Köckeis) of a major study of the family in old age, *Unwelt und Familie Alter Menschen*, and (with Hilde Rosenmeyer) of *Gerosociology, Propositions for a New Theoretical Foundation* and author of the handbooks on *Youth* and on *Aging* (*Handbuch der empirischen Sozialforschung*, ed. R. König).

Ethel Shanas is professor of sociology at the University of Illinois at Chicago Circle and professor of Health Care Services at the University of Illinois at the Medical Center. Her special interests are in the social and psychological aspects of aging. She is the author, coauthor, or coeditor of a number of books in this field including, most recently, *The Handbook of Aging and the Social Sciences*. Professor Shanas has served as vice-chairman of a United Nations Expert Group on Aging, as rapporteur of a United Nations Seminar on Social Research in Aging, as a member of the Executive Committee of the International Association of Gerontology, and as chairman of its Liaison Committee with the United Nations. Professor Shanas was the 1974 president of the American Gerontological Society.

Nada Smolić-Krković, Ph.D., University of Zagreb, is professor of psychology, social work, and gerontology at the University of Zagreb, Yugoslavia. She has made a number of surveys of old people in Croatia and reported on her findings at national and international meetings. Among her recent publications is a handbook on gerontology.

Gordon F. Streib joined the faculty of the University of Florida, Gainesville, in 1975 as graduate research professor. Previously he taught on the faculty of Cornell University. Professor Streib has been a Fulbright professor to Denmark and to Ireland. During 1971–72 he was a visiting fellow at the Committee on Human Development of the University of Chicago. His writings include: *Retirement in American Society: Impact and Process* (coauthored with C. J. Schneider), *The Changing Family: Adaptation and Diversity*, and *Social Structure and the Family* (coedited with Ethel Shanas).

Marvin B. Sussman is professor of sociology and chair in the Department of Medical Social Science and Marital Health at the Bowman Gray School of Medicine. Formerly he held the Selah Chamberlain professorship of sociology at Case Western Reserve University where he was director of the Institute on the Family and the Bureaucratic Society. Professor Sussman has written, edited, or coedited eleven monographs and books and published 50 chapters in books and monographs and over 100 articles in professional journals dealing with the family. His fields of special interest are family theory and research, the sociology of medicine, and the sociology of rehabilitation and human service systems. He is a former president of the

Society for the Study of Social Problems and the Groves Conference on Marriage and the Family and serves as a consultant to a variety of governmental and nongovernmental bodies.

Hannah Weihl is senior lecturer at the Paul Baerwald School of Social Work, Hebrew University, Jerusalem, and research fellow at the Brookdale Institute of Gerontology and Human Development in Jerusalem. She has been engaged in research in aging since 1966 and has published a number of papers in this area in both English and Hebrew. She is a member of the executive committee of the Israeli Society of Gerontology.

Contents

Theoretical Perspectives

Historical/Demographic Analyses

Empirical Studies

Interpretive Analysis

Foreword

In the history of social thought and development of social science we have a very old tradition of typing social entities antithetically. The tradition may be traced back to the philosophical speculation of the classical Greeks and to the epoch of Confucius. Despite the age of the tradition, it still has a marked vitality, and appears to be one of the fundamental approaches to understanding social phenomena. Examples of this tradition are such familiar conceptualizations as Main's status society and contract society, Spencer's militant and industrial forms. Ratzenhofer's conquest state and culture state, Wundt's natural and cultural polarity, Durkheim's mechanical and organic solidarity, Cooley's primary and secondary (implicit) groups, MacIver's communal and associational relations, Zimmerman's localistic and cosmopolitan communities, Odum's folk-state pair, Redfield's folk-urban continuum, Sorokin's familistic versus contractual relations, Becker's sacred and secular relations, as well as such nonpersonalized but common dichotomies as primitive/civilized, complex/simple, literate/nonliterate, developed/underdeveloped, advanced/backward, traditional/modern, and rural/urban.

Obviously these varied polarizations are not interchangeable and do not abstract the same things out of the social world, but they do have something in common. Not only do they frequently represent similar "content," but, in common they exemplify the view that it is necessary to distinguish fundamentally different types of social organizations in order to establish a range within which transitional or intermediate forms can be comprehended. Perhaps more importantly, they set the stage for the study of social forms based upon fundamentally different principles coexisting in symbiotic relationship.

Of all the typifications characteristic of this tradition of thought perhaps the most famous are Gemeinschaft and Gesellschaft. Few concepts have had greater impact upon the development of the social sciences. These fundamental concepts are constructed types which attempt to describe the essence of motivations in human relationships when, on the one hand, natural or spontaneous will has primacy, or, on the other, when rational will has primacy. The creation of the concepts of Gemeinschaft and Gesellschaft resulted from Tönnies's effort to understand the true meaning of both the rational school of natural law and the opposing historical and romantic theories. They permitted a synthesis of two opposing conceptions of social order. Moreover, they enabled social scientists to understand more adequately the essence of Gesellschaft-like logic, upon which classical economics is based, and the standards of efficiency by which such organizations as bureaucracies function, in contrast to the essence of the Gemeinschaft-like motivation in which the relationships are ends in themselves, as in families.

The concepts made it possible to synthesize rationalism and romanticism, idealism and materialism, realism and nominalism. In addition, they made it possible to comprehend the main course of history in terms of structural change from Gemeinschaft to Gesellschaft. Moreover, the concepts made it possible to understand better the functional interpretation of Gemeinschaft and Gesellschaft type relations in concrete social systems. It is this last point that leads us to the substance of this volume on *Family, Bureaucracy, and the Elderly.*

As stated by the editors in a description of this book: "The major theme of this volume is the linkage of aged persons with bureaucratic organizations in complex societies and the role of family networks in such linkages. The problematics of this linkage are how these organizations constrain or support the aged person in developing and using available human services; how family networks operate to assist or hinder the aged family member in developing competence to 'handle' bureaucracies; and how bureaucracies may affect the character and quality of relationships between aged members and their families." This seems very straightforward and makes eminent good sense. So much so that one unfamiliar with the relevant literature might assume that this is research that might have been performed many decades ago and thus would be "traditional." Paradoxically, however, such is not the case despite the fact that the tradition of social thought explicated above literally invites such research. The special history of the development of the social sciences has largely led to the study of bureaucracy, family, and the elderly in separate research traditions, despite the obvious dysfunction of such an approach.

Max Weber must undoubtedly be considered the leading instigator of and contributor to the vast expansion of research on complex organization, specifically bureaucracy, in this century. Weber assumed that all relationships are based upon a continuity of social action. He typed the action context, and then constructed his varied relationship types on the basis of the underlying typical lines of action. The relevant relationship here is the one he typified "in terms of rational orientation to a system of discrete individual ends (*zweckrational*), that is through expectations as to the behavior of objects in the external situation and of other human individuals, making use of these expectations as 'conditions' or 'means' for the successful attainment of the actors' own rationally chosen ends. . . ." The concept of *zweckrational* is essentially expedient rationality and denotes a system of action involving an actor's motives, conditions, means, and ends wherein the actor weighs the possible alternative ends and means available to him in terms of his purposes and selects the course of action most expedient to him. A system of discrete ends exists for the actor, and an orientation toward them involves such considerations as efficiency, cost, undesirable consequences, amount of return, and calculating the results which condition the otherwise unrestrained adaptation of means to the achievement of ends. This formulation (corresponding directly with Tönnies's construct of Gesellschaft) played a dominant role in Weber's overall sociological analysis, which in turn was heavily responsible for the remarkable growth of research on bureaucracy. That research is quite extensive and has become increasingly sophisticated, technically and methodologically, in the past three decades.

The study of the family as a social institution has had a different history. Despite the universality of the family in some form or other, it did not tend to attract theoretical attention to any significant degree except in social anthropology. The sociologists of the early twentieth century tended to view the family in terms of its pathologies or problems. In connection with rapid social change concern was focused on problems of poverty, the disadvantaged lower classes, or backward groups. Attention was directed to the phenomena of divorce, separation, declining birthrates, working mothers, and the "individuation" of family members, with the aspiration of achieving stability or "adjustment." By and large much of the sociological work done on the family up until World War II was amelioratively and "social-problem" oriented. Since then there has been an increased tendency to treat the family within the framework of standard sociological theory. There have been a number of studies which have attempted to treat the family as a social system and which have been concerned with the relationships between the family's structure and function and external systems, and also between the family and the individual. Despite great variation, both between and within cultures, families strongly resemble little communities. Because of its special characteristics, the family is one of the best examples of Gemeinschaft-like groups and as a consequence is difficult to study scientifically. Although still not a particularly well-organized field of special inquiry, there is general agreement that it is of great importance and that significant research strides have been made in recent decades.

The systematic study of older people, in a historical sense, is very modern. Although "age" has been a standard variable throughout the history of the social survey movement, and the demographers have kept us informed about age distribution and structure since census taking started, the study of the elderly has been typically fragmentary and incidental. Social gerontology really started after World War II and received its great push forward in the 1950s, both in the United States and in other developed nations, in the light of practical concerns regarding the rapid increase in the number of aged persons, the problem of their retirement from the labor force, and concern for their support, health, housing, and leisure. In general this was a concern over the plight of many older people and over the impact on society of having an increased proportion of the population in nonproductive and dependent status. Such concerns generated intellectual interest, and a considerable body of knowledge about the social and psychological aspects of aging has been developed in the past two decades.

It has become increasingly clear that the systematic study of bureaucracy, family, and the elderly separately is of fundamental importance in the pursuit of knowledge about society. Each research tradition is intrinsically important because of the phenomena it investigates. The developed nations, and increasingly the developing nations, are characterized by complex organization and the ubiquitous bureaucracy, by the persistence of the family in some form, and by the growth in the absolute number and proportion of the elderly in the population. To return to my earlier remarks about Gemeinschaft and Gesellschaft, we have here a situation that epitomizes the interaction and interpenetration of different social forms in modern society. It is to the great credit of this volume that this phenomenon is recognized explicitly, and viewed in terms of the long-term, overriding importance of the dynamic interrelationship between older people, bureaucracy, and the family as fundamental components of society.

We are all familiar with the fact that in each of the scholarly fields every few years a book or a paper will be published that alters or modifies the paradigm for research. The publications establish a breakthrough or point of departure for a flow of inquiry. In my view this volume is destined for such a role since its substance explicates a plethora of both intellectual and practical problems which can engage the interest of social scientists for many years to come. We can reasonably assume that such effort will benefit our cognitive understanding and policy formation. And we can hope it will also benefit the life situation of older people.

John C. McKinney
Vice-Provost and Dean of the
Graduate School
Duke University

Preface

The original drafts of the chapters in this volume were presented for discussion at a Conference on Older People, Family, and Bureaucracy held at the Quail Roost Conference Center in Rougemont, North Carolina, in May 1973. The conference was funded by a grant to the Gerontological Society by the National Institute of Child Health and Human Development, 1R13HD05959, and by a contribution from Duke University. The general theme of the conference was the linkage of old people and their families to bureaucratic systems. A group of international scholars, each selected for his or her competence and knowledge of social systems, family structure, and aging, was invited to participate in this meeting. Each participant was asked to prepare a paper describing how a selected social system operates vis-à-vis the elderly and extended kin network; how this system influences the quality of family relationships; what criteria are being used to measure quality; and, finally, what current research findings are available and what research is needed to understand the relationships between bureaucratic structure and the quality of family life. With the exception of Dr. Anderson, all of the contributors to this volume attended the conference and exchanged critical comments and ideas each with the other. In addition, Alfred H. Lawton, M.D., the 1973 president of the Gerontological Society, and Tarek Shuman of the United Nations, attended the conference and contributed to the discussion.

Following the meeting, all participants agreed to revise their presentations for publication. Drs. Shanas and Sussman divided the responsibility of working with participants so that the final papers would fully represent the richness of the group discussion.

The success of the conference owes a good deal to the generous contribution of time and hospitality by Betty E. Cogswell of the University of North Carolina and to Kurt W. Back, Ewald W. Busse, M.D., Alan C. Kerckhoff, Juanita M. Kreps, George L. Maddox, and Erdman Palmore of Duke University.

The editors are indebted to Carol Schutz of the Gerontological Society and to Joseph West, grants management specialist of the National Institute of Child Health and Human Development, for their careful surveillance of grant operations, and to Ashbel G. Brice, director of Duke University Press, and Anne Poole, assistant editor, for their patience and overall cooperation in the preparation of this volume. John C. McKinney of Duke University, an insightful critic of sociological thought, has reviewed this volume and commented on its content. His masterful foreword to the analyses presented here serves to place this work in the general stream of sociological inquiry.

The editors hope that the reader will reread this foreword after reviewing the contents of this book.

Ethel Shanas

Marvin B. Sussman

Theoretical Perspectives

1. Family, Bureaucracy, and the Elderly Individual: An Organizational/Linkage Perspective   *Marvin B. Sussman*

Introduction

In complex societies we have long been accustomed to investigating social problems, establishing national priorities, and developing policies and programs largely from an organizational perspective. The usual focus is on relationships between the customer or client and functionaries of bureaucratized institutions and organizations. For instance, in the United States the government has determined that racism, unemployment, poverty, alcoholism, drug addiction, suicide, and human services for the young and elderly are national problems, among many others, and the National Science Foundation through a special program, RANN (Research Applied to National Needs), created in 1971, has been requested to support scientific and technical research with the goal of deriving practical solutions. Heavily emphasized in this program are investigations of institutional responsiveness to such national problems as those listed above.

Research to date puts great reliance on "correcting" the activities of human service systems through appropriate evaluations, including cost/benefit analyses. It is assumed that if institutions and organizations know their clients better and develop more effective programs, then individuals who are the recipients of services will be able to live in greater harmony with their social and physical environment. As the national problem dissipates or at least becomes controllable, a new one tops the priority list.

The image of the omniscient and omnipotent bureaucracy controlling the thoughts and behaviors of its members and the clients it serves is a commonly held notion of the lay person as well as the organizational behavior scientist. It follows that the predominant structural model of the bureaucratic system is superordinate-subordinate. The military is a prototype for the hierarchical ordering of status, power, and position. Such notions as chain of command; obedience and following orders (instructions); and defined and circumscribed authority and responsibility ("the buck stops here") are with various modifications also used in nonmilitary organizations. The human service sector, which is our concern, is no exception. It emulates the military and industrial organizational models, perhaps using a less crass terminology than the military, such as substituting client for boot-soldier or enemy. It will be noted repeatedly in this chapter and elsewhere in this volume that throughout the world the organization is perceived as being superordinate and the individual as subordinate.

The existence and persistence of the modern organization in the foreseeable future suggest that individuals and primary groups such as families, kin networks, or peer groups will have to relate to bureaucracies in some fashion and will need to deal with them competently. Elderly persons must deal with complex bureaucracies in modern societies. Since these individuals are members of primary groups and since most family members, including the elderly, look to their relatives and kin for assistance, it is likely that family and kin networks will play facilitating and mediating roles for the elderly member in dealings with bureaucracies. Consequently the main concern in this chapter is to develop a conceptual framework for explaining and analyzing such relationships.

A fundamental characteristic of all human primary groups is that families, kin networks, peers, and other primary groups are critical interactional systems for the individual. Feelings and responses to authorities of bureaucracies are influenced by these intimate bondings (Katz and Lazarsfeld, 1955; Sherif, 1966; Sussman and Weil, 1960). Except for some total institutions, bureaucratic structures are not dealing with atomistic individuals, although most deal with clients, customers, patients, or citizens in an unidirectional and controlling manner. They are at least constrained in expressing the fullness of their culturally derived or legalized authority, and in very few instances can they rule absolutely even in a paternalistic mode. The potential threat of primary group action outside or within the organization checkmates the use of absolute power. It brings, in varying degrees, to the eyes of the managerial and professional staff the essential and viable properties of primary groups and the need to consider how these interactional systems respond to authority; the group's influence on individual decision making; and the "outer limit" of the reciprocation beyond which bureaucratic–primary group (family) relationships reach an impasse.

In summary, the high level of differentiation of function in industrial society places extraordinary pressure on the nuclear family and collateral members of kinship and social network to capitulate to the normative demands of bureaucratic organizations. The more extensive, permanent, and powerful system (the bureaucracy) may logically be expected to dominate the lesser and weaker one (the family), especially if conditions and situations require role modifications.

Yet some families develop a modus operandi for handling the demands of bureaucratic organizations while maintaining their own internal structure and function, and under certain conditions and situations may surpass the bureaucratic organization in the extent of influence over their members. For example, in modern societies with very complex social security and medical care systems elderly persons tend to be bewildered by the complexity of obtaining assistance to which they are legally entitled. It is in this kind of a situation that the family can have a pervasive influence on its elderly members in showing them how to respond to bureaucratic demands and taking the necessary action to obtain the rights of the elderly member. In some circumstances by acting collectively for noncompliance or in proposing alternative modes of behavior, using techniques similar to those employed by bureaucracies, families can actually influence organizations and institutions to change their policies and practices.

The structural characteristics of these two types of institutions have been cited to lend support to the presumed position of family subordination. The bureaucratic organization is based on an ideology of efficiency and rationality. It functions instrumentally and in a scientific and objective manner to achieve its goal, an orientation that is necessary for the continued survival of complex societies. The family, on the other hand, is an effective structure in which behavior is a response to feelings with little regard for objective analysis. As the social sphere of bureaucratic institutions has extended, their greater power presumably has allowed them to preempt the more important of the adaptive functions once performed by the family. The latter structure has been left with only such tasks as socialization into generalized roles and identities and tension management of family members, chores that more rationally ordered organizational systems cannot perform or find acceptable because these objectives lack specificity.

Family-Organization Conceptual Framework

The essential components of a conceptual framework for providing robust explanations of family-organization relationships are found under the rubric of exchange theory whose elements are accommodation, contest, expertise, compliance, costs, rewards, bargaining, reciprocation, negotiation, distributive justice, power, options, coordination, and linkage (Blau, 1964; Dowd, 1975; Litwak and Meyer, 1965, 1966, 1967; Litwak, 1970; Thibaut and Kelley, 1959; Weber, 1947). A number of these elements will be described with special attention to bureaucratic linkages of the family and its elderly members. A viable explanation of exchange processes is derived from the seminal work of Litwak and his colleagues. The position is essentially structuralist with the assumption that conflict is endemic in mass society and that the stronger (i.e., institutions) control the weaker (individuals and primary groups). Litwak proposes a "balance theory of coordination between bureaucracy and primary groups" and points of departure are from the conceptualizations of Max Weber and Talcott Parsons.

The Weberian position is most extreme in expressing the polar opposites of bureaucracies and families. The normative demands, ideologies, objectives, and practices are so contradictory that both strong institutions (bureaucracies) and families cannot exist in the same society, at least not without extreme conflict (Weber, 1947).

Parsons, while recognizing the inherent conflict between primary groups and bureaucracies because of conflicting norms, goals, and means, feels that both strong family systems and institutions can prosper if they are isolated from one another. Distance is correlated with a successful detente; the greater the gulf the greater the tolerance. The sea of ambiguity between bureaucracy and institutions promotes fear and suspicion but ameliorates the potential for outright conflict (Parsons and Bales, 1955).

The "balance theorist" as exemplified by Litwak assumes an interstitial position, namely being too distant or too close is disruptive of the relationship because of contradictory structures. Coordination between the primary group and bureaucracy is requisite for survival and harmonious relationships and such coordination is effected when groups and institutions are close enough but not too close.

The balance concept of linkage rests on the nature of the task of each bureaucratic and primary group and the presumed competence endemic to each particular structure. The assumption is that primary groups such as families are more competent because they are organized to perform non-uniform tasks while bureaucratic structures are designed to handle uniform ones.

There are three types of tasks which primary groups such as families are more structurally effective in handling than bureaucracies. These are: (1) those which involve the acquisition of general knowledge where family members instruct and communicate with one another in relation to everyday work, values, and competence to relate to and deal with others; (2) those associated with problems and issues bureaucratic experts cannot analyze or solve; and (3) those concerned with idiosyncratic events.

In the first category of tasks there is included looking after one's own or another person's physical needs: those associated with activities of daily living such as eating, dressing, and toileting; and those outside the home such as going to school, shopping, and visiting. Members of the family provide the necessary instruction in these chores, embellished somewhat by such institutions as the school, church, and leisure time agency, largely as a corrective to imperfect socialization by family members.

The tasks of the second category beg for expert advice. They remain in the family because specialists do not have the knowledge or skill to deal with them. Consequently the resolution of issues and problems central to the vital interest of individuals must be self-solutions. These issues and problems include such questions as: What are the best ways to be a parent? What does one have to do in order to attain marital health? What is the best way to help an aged parent who has been independent all his life and now needs assistance? What criteria should one employ in selecting a mate where remarriage is involved? The specialist's contribution is obviously limited because few can command the knowledge required to make an intelligent decision and the variety of options in such problem areas is so staggering that training in their expertness is impossible. Solutions depend largely upon current experience and folk wisdom transmitted intergenerationally in primary or reference groups.

The tasks of the third category include infrequent events for which one cannot justify the expenditure of time, energy, or money in preparing to handle such eventualities. In this group are car accidents, robberies, floods, fires, and earthquakes. Responses to these unique events cannot be predicted or patterned. However, they can be anticipated, and the community can respond appropriately in terms of its survival.

The bureaucratic structure is organized to handle uniform tasks using an ever-developing technology, vast resources, and extension lines of communication, buttressed by the ideology of merit and the model of rationality. It can organize to send persons successfully into outer space, create artificial life-support systems, or incarcerate in elaborate security systems those deemed deviant, and it does this dispassionately and impersonally, and according to rhetoric, with a minimal influence of idiosyncratic factors. In uncertain situations bureaucracies, in contrast to primary groups, have more difficulty in responding quickly. The communication network is extended, with authority and responsibility circumscribed at each hierarchical level. Decisions are likely to be made more slowly and inflexibly than those which occur in families, and more on the bases of policy and precedent than the responses of family members to the particular circumstances of the situation.

The processes used and structural properties possessed by both types of groups are very well suited to the tasks each must perform. A family, by being able to arrive at a decision quickly and flexibly in a nonuniform situation, e.g., rescuing its members from a burning house, is not competent to determine the needed treatment and rehabilitation of an aged member who is experiencing cardiac arrest. The speed and flexibility with which to take action, except to rush the ailing person to a medical facility, is more of a hindrance than a help in this situation. The event which is increasingly becoming uniform requires standardized procedures for diagnosis, prognosis, and treatment and the use of specialists with their technical knowledge and skills.

The theoretical issue centers on how structurally different organizations (families and human service organizations), having identified areas of common concern (in this instance, the ailing aged family member), and having need of one another to reach the objective of this concern, might control their hostilities and accommodate their differences. Coalescing around common concerns and then functioning conjointly to achieve specific objectives is a consequence of the decision that the cost of group differences is less than the rewards of obtaining a goal by cooperative activity. Group differences are shelved or neutralized in the pursuit of a superordinate goal (Sherif et al., 1957).

Given these attributes of bureaucracy and family and that complementarity can and should be developed between them, the effectiveness of any linkage will depend upon the appropriateness of the social distance maintained in relation to the task which brings the bureaucratic organization and family into initial contact. Consequently four dimensions of linkage are considered: bureaucratic initiative, intensity, expertise, and scope. While these attributes are properties of both bureaucracies and primary groups, for reasons of space only the bureaucratic perspective is presented.

Bureaucratic initiative is the amount of initial effort required to establish a meaningful relationship with a primary group. High or low initiative depends on the particular task. High initiative is characterized by direct, face-to-face contact between members of families and bureaucracies; low initiative is exemplified by impersonal modes of communication such as phone calls, bulletin boards, letters, and uses of the mass media.

Intensity refers to the nature and quality of relationships: their extensiveness or briefness, effectiveness or instrumentality. Again the task to be accomplished determines the intensity and the initiating source.

Expertise has already been described. More specifically, it is the application of technical knowledge and complex communications to specific problems. The type of expertise required and its utility depend on the uniformity of the task and the level of influence desired.

Scope is coverage of the bureaucratic-family nexus: the populations that are involved in the interaction where efforts are made to influence one another reciprocally.

Considering these dimensions of linkage, the requisite social distance between primary groups and bureaucracies for effective relationships, and the uniformity/nonuniformity of tasks confronting both groups, two paradigms of bureaucracy- and primary-group-initiated linkage are indicated.

Chart 1. *Basic dimensions of linkage: where bureaucracies seek to influence primary groups*

Task	Bureaucracy too distant	Bureaucracy too close
Task nonuniform, that is, knowledge and resources are products of everyday socialization	(1) *High sender initiative and primary group intensity*: e.g., agency sending indigent people to homes of those needing help such as using local people for homemaker services.	(3) *Passive-low sender initiative with moderate primary group and bureaucratic intensity*: e.g., schools using parent-teacher associations.
Tasks uniform, that is, knowledge and resources are more than that produced by everyday socialization	(2) *High sender initiative and moderate bureaucratic and primary group intensity*: e.g., health agency sending visiting nurse to give home medical care.	(4) *Passive-low sender initiative with bureaucratic intensity*: e.g., schools seeking to convey to parents the ideas of new math through detailed pamphlets or series of formal lectures.

Source: Abbreviated from E. Litwak, D. Hollister, and H. Meyer, "Linkage Theory Between Bureaucracies and Community Primary Groups—Education, Health and Political Action as Empirical Cases in Point" (Paper presented at the Annual Meeting of the American Sociological Association, Montreal, 1974), Appendix. Used by permission.

Chart 2. *Basic dimensions of linkage: where primary groups seek to influence bureaucracies*

Task	Bureaucracies too distant	Bureaucracies too close
Task nonuniform	(1) *High initiative–high primary group intensity and some bureaucratic intensity*: e.g., parents closing down school by picketing and mass protest marches.	(3) *Passive-moderate primary group and bureaucratic intensity*: e.g., single parents contacting Board of Education by telephone, or by semiformal meeting requesting policy change on budget priorities.
Task uniform	(2) *High initiative–high bureaucratic intensity and some primary group intensity*: e.g., use of professional advocates such as lawyers, ombudsman organizations, civil rights commissions empowered to sue for consumer protection.	(4) *Passive-high bureaucratic and low primary group intensity*: e.g., citizen writing letter or sending in organization-supplied forms, or meeting formally asking organizational expert to devise new procedures such as procuring new textbook for schools.

Source: See Chart 1, p. 7.

The assumptions are that if a bureaucracy wishes to change a primary group's task which is nonuniform, it should use a high-intensity linkage involving face-to-face contact. The converse is the case for primary groups such as families who wish to change the task of the bureaucracy in dealing with uniform events. It must develop a linkage which resembles a bureaucratic model, using experts to present "evidence" and employing logical, rational, albeit scientific arguments to contest the technically based decisions of the bureaucracy.

If social distance is so great that coordination around a common goal is impossible or impractical, then the group that wants to reach and engage the other must initiate contact and experiment with the intensity of the contact and communication. The form will depend on the degree of resistance encountered by the initiating group.

The fourth and final assumption espoused by Litwak and his colleagues is that closely linked bureaucracies and primary groups, e.g., the school and the family, should rely heavily on passive linkages lest "familiarity breed contempt." A less proverbial explanation is that teachers, because of their closeness to parents, may lose their objectivity in judging the performance of their pupils, and, on the other hand, because of their overidentification with the school and its norms, may act less as parents to their own offspring and more as judges and evaluators—doing what teachers do.

The balance theory of linkage incorporates several other basic processes. These are accommodation, contest, competence, exchange, and the concept of options. To complete the theoretical analysis, each will be briefiy described.

Accommodation

Accommodation is a particularly viable process through which to view primary group–bureaucratic relations and to analyze the structural basis of the division of labor that exists between family and organization because of the complementarity of objectives and functions of these two social systems. Certain purposes and goals vital to the persistence of the society itself and all of its institutions are shared in common. For example, both family and bureaucracy value the goal of survival and support it with available means and resources. The functions of a family and a bureaucratic organization are complementary in this respect, a complementarity that has been achieved by accommodating behavior on the part of each of the participating structures. This is possible principally because these interaction systems have developed expertise in performing specialized functions and therefore need each other.

Contest

Contest is an ongoing process with accommodation. Organizational experts and family representatives, experts in their own right, are constantly jockeying for positions which aim to reinforce or maintain discreteness in established spheres as a minimal objective and to take over territorial borders as a maximal goal. A give-and-take process is implied in which the hostilities of each party are mitigated and the structures become linked, somewhat loosely. The analogy to contending groups or nations is appropriate; the linkages being described are prototypes of those found in macrosystems.

One important reason for the persistence of the family in modern society is its role in the linkage process; it counteracts domination by bureaucratic organizations through using interstitial groups and socializing its members for competence in linking roles. Consequently, it is appropriate to analyze the sociopsychological bases of linkage for the family.

The linkage phenomenon is based on a number of assumptions. First, it is both a process and a condition interrelating groups, organizations, and individuals. The particular pattern is the linkage condition and how it is formed in the process. A second assumption is that in any linkage, especially between structures, it is possible for one participant to be or become subordinate or superordinate to the other, even after institutionalization of the relationship has occurred. Consequently, in any relationship the family can be in a superordinate position, wielding influence and affecting the policy, structure, and activities of bureaucratic organizations. Or it can be subordinate, accommodating the normative demands of formal structures.

Competence and Exchange

Another assumption is that the family can optimize its possibilities of survival and sustain intact its interactional system and territory if members develop managing, manipulating, and mediating skills in linkage activity. Competence in interpersonal relationships, the use of options, and problem solving are prerequisite and appropriate activities of a family socialization system.[1] Still another assumption is that linkage operates within some system of reciprocity based on bargaining. Specific exchanges are of unequal value, and reciprocals are maintained when each bargaining part receives sufficient payoff to maintain the relationship rather than accept the alternative of breaking off (Schelling, 1956, 1960; Thibaut and Kelley, 1959; Mauss, 1954; Levi-Strauss, 1957).

In reciprocal relationships individuals acting in their own behalf or as representatives of groups or organizations operate within a framework whose elements are investment, profit, cost, and loss. Investments and costs are considered explicitly or implicitly. Choosing an option which will maximize gain at least cost involves some risk. Sustaining losses in interaction is part of the game and is expressed by the phrase, "You win some and you lose some." One may take a loss in hope for a future gain, or anticipated reciprocity. The trick is to maintain a good "win" record in order to sustain interest and participation in the interaction. Unless this occurs, the "stretch line" of the interaction may be reached and the individual or group may opt out of the situation. If this cannot be accomplished because of involuntary relationships such as those between family and school or mental hospital, the responses may be noncompliance, confrontation, withdrawal, or harrassment.

Distributive justice, where one individual (group) receives from another sufficient reward for one's investment, governs most exchanges. Underlying this conceptual element is the pervasive expectation of all incumbents in the interaction that reward for one's investments and costs is to be granted. The source of contention or conflict among participants is over perceived discrepencies between the payoff and the investment. Negotiation and bargaining are continuing processes used to reduce such differences and provide sufficient agreement to sustain the relationship.

Options

The more options an individual or group has the greater are the probabilities of bargaining effectively in exchange networks at reduced risks.

1. Important discussions of competence are found in M. B. Smith, "Competence and Socialization," in *Socialization and Society*, ed. J. A. Clausen (Boston, 1968); R. W. White, "Motivation Reconsidered: The Concept of Competence," *Psychological Review* 66 (Sept. 1959):297–333; N. Foote and L. S. Cottrell, Jr., *Identity and Interpersonal Competence* (Chicago, 1965).

Options are viewed as alternatives or choices and are manifestations of individual or group resources. Options are differentially distributed in a given population according to class, ethnic, caste, racial, socioeconomic, and personality characteristics. Resource options by themselves do not automatically guarantee success in exchanges.

Conceptually one can view options as a sequential process. The process begins with awareness of all possible options; knowledge of routes to their use; selection of one option that will potentially maximize desired outcome; socialization into role behavior requisite for the appropriate utilization of the option; development of appropriate motivation to sustain behavior relevant to the goal of the option; and the actual achievement of the goal of the option.[2]

Bureaucracy–Family Coordination: Processes

The balance theory of coordination between bureaucracies and primary groups such as families establishes the conditions and relationships between relevant variables which influence the potential outcomes of the seeking out and working together of such groups. To reach a desired level of coordination with appropriate distance and intensity involves a set of complicated processes. In the brief description which follows some of the processes are covered from the perspective of family members.

In another paper I developed a theoretical model of family–bureaucratic organization linkage, melding together the objectives and needs of family systems and their members with the notion of life sectors and linkage groups (Sussman, 1972). The basic theme was that the family's objectives and needs are related to internal and external constraints and opportunities and that essential family socialization is to develop a knowledge of options and the skill to utilize them in order to ameliorate and constrain the power of bureaucracies.

Since family members deal with so many specialized organizations and institutions in complex societies, it is appropriate to look at these relationships within such life sectors as government, health, work, community, religion, and leisure. In researching linkage systems, the life sector is a useful concept since it reflects an area of activity occurring, as a rule, within a defined spacial or psychological territory and which can be observed to have a measurable beginning, duration, and end in time.

I would be remiss if I omitted consideration of the role and importance of linkage groups in effecting, mediating, or constraining relationships between primary groups. Five have been identified. These are peer groups,

2. See the "San Juan Document: Cross-National Research Studies on the Family, Theoretical Problems and Approaches," prepared by M. B. Sussman et al. (Jan. 1969). For copies, write to: Institute on the Family and the Bureaucratic Society, Department of Sociology, Case Western Reserve University, Cleveland, Ohio 44106.

kinship networks, special interest groups, voluntary associations, and ombudsman systems. This listing is by no means inclusive but suggestive of a powerful force in all societies for bureaucracies or members of primary groups to use interstitial structures in dealing with one another. The kin network as an important mediating, socializing, and decision-making structure for the elderly member will be discussed in greater detail subsequently. An emergent new linkage form that is growing in importance to primary groups is the advocacy/ombudsman linkage structure. From a historical perspective, the ombudsman is not new but is believed to have been invented in Sweden in the dawn of bureaucratic development to handle the abuses of bureaucracy, take care of grievances, and to keep the bureaucracy "honest." In the modern period variants of true ombudsmanship are emerging. Two such varieties are: (1) families or clients of a human service system such as welfare or health employ a linker to advocate and negotiate in their behalf with the bureaucratic organization; and (2) recipients of government subsidies or allotments may employ a manager to purchase medical and rehabilitation services from health institutions by competitive bidding.

Not all families use linkage groups and some prefer to deal directly with bureaucratic organizations. Among the principal determinants of the use of linkage groups or their circumvention are previous experience and success in direct dealings; the family's history of belonging to representing associations or unions; its intellectual and economic resources; and the desperateness of the situation. Once usefulness and feasibility are established, continued involvement and support of such linking activities depends on the competence of the representative to provide a "payoff." Another consideration is whether such activist behavior will result in reprisals or disturbance to other relationships in various life sectors.

One linkage point where there is an elderly person involved is the family's initial contact with bureaucratic organizations concerned with medical treatment and rehabilitation. The availability of medical care and rehabilitation options depends on the financial position of the family; the knowledge, awareness, and motivation of family members, including the elderly person; and the location of kin, friends, and peer-group members.

The awareness of options is a function of societal constraints and individual competences. The society limits awareness according to the social-class or caste position of the individual. Some options are never made known to the individual, and if they were, the person would be ill equipped to choose or implement a preferred one. Within these limits the member's personal resources, motivation, needs, and objectives are determinants of the type and extensity of the linking role to be performed in behalf of the family. In addition to the information on health care options provided by linkage groups and bureaucratic organizations, kin, peers, friends, and work colleagues may be sources of knowledge. The mass media and educational institutions are other sources of information.

Once an option is chosen and its path or route ascertained, family members or representatives of linkage groups activate linkage roles until the desired outcome is achieved. Here is a strategic point in the linkage sequence. It is necessary to differentiate awareness of options and awareness of routes to option achievement. Option awareness implies knowledge of theoretical possibilities of adequate treatment and rehabilitation for the aged family member while awareness of routes involves a realistic appraisal of available health care facilities given the variety of constraints already enumerated. A decision regarding the selection of one or more options depends initially upon an appraisal of realistic possibilities of achieving the option outcome.

At this stage of the option sequence, the individual selects a particular service. If options for health care are restricted because of discrimination, the individual may seek a special interest group or voluntary association to assist him in increasing the options in this area. In some instances the family may become the target of selection for betterment because a particular community action group feels that increasing options in health care for disabled or elderly family members is in the best interests of the larger society. If one's options in health care are limited, one may join with linking institutions that are part of the marketing system—a credit union, consumers' organization, mutual benefit society, or kinship group that can assist with information, money, and other services connected with the care of the aged member.

Family members serving as representatives for the group take on a linking role at some time during the family life cycle. The motivations, skills, special interests, experience, and training as well as the circumstances, situations, age, and sex of members are among the main factors which determine whether the individual family member takes the initiative in linking.

The assumption of a linking role by a family member has consequences for relationships with bureaucracies and an impact on the internal dynamics of the family system. It suggests that family systems are not completely passive to the needs or demands of bureaucratic organizations. Becoming an effective family representative does provide an opportunity for changing one's status and power position within the family. For example, adolescent children of ghetto families, by taking over major responsibility for the socialization of younger ones, have more to say about what the family will do and how it will spend its money.

Linking is part of the socialization process. The objective is to develop skills and knowledge for dealing with bureaucratic organizations in order to meet family needs and objectives in a particular life sector. Other family members may be taught these skills, or a specialization or expertness may be developed, with each person called upon to provide service in particular circumstances and situations. Family members may use their special knowledge and skill to achieve a positional advantage but in relation to the bureaucracy each one acts in the family's best interest. Other members are sufficiently socialized to function competently in behalf of the family without necessarily jeopardizing the status of the expert in this particular linking role.

Mediation and the Kinship Network: Illustrations

The family from earliest times, at least in the writings of theorists, has been conceptualized as adapting to the demands of a bureaucratic society. Full adult participation in the larger complex and interdependent society often involves geographic or social mobility. Hence the nuclear family of procreation, husband and wife and their issue in neolocal residence, was viewed as best suited for participating in a bureaucratic society. This unit, with the husband as provider and wife as homemaker, tended to be treated as coterminous with the entire institution of the family, at least in the American milieu. Today it is still considered to be a completely integrated unit, surviving because of its superior adaptability (Parsons and Bales, 1955).

While the debate on the universality and functionality of the nuclear family continues unabated, the fact remains that varied family forms exist in all complex societies and among these are flourishing kin family networks, propinquitous and nonpropinquitous, exchanging goods and services and providing on a daily basis or in times of crisis necessary emotional support and economic maintenance (Sussman, 1975). The fact that nuclear families live in separate households does not eliminate the viability and pervasiveness of this network. It vies with other primary and bureaucratic systems for the loyalty of those who are participants and for its ability to provide rewards over costs; real or perceived deficits will determine its function as a relevant complementary social system for family members.

According to a plethora of accounts of middle- and working-class urban families studied during the past thirty years, the primary modalities of the exchange system are visitation, communication, emotional and social support, financial aid, advice, and child care. Such exchanges are not universal or equal and within all networks conflict as well as cooperation exists. Since units have differential resources and the linkages effected are not very different from those already described as existing between bureaucracies and primary groups, as they attempt to meet their own needs and to achieve desired rewards, there is an ongoing struggle among lesser units in each larger system for the achievement of in-group goals. At the point when shared goals cannot be identified, disintegration of the kin network is a likely occurrence.

Cultural factors have proved to be highly influential in assuring family continuity over generational time (Sussman, 1953, 1954). Notable among these are making certain that the socioeconomic cultural background of structures is viewed as inhibiting respective goal achievement. Too great a distance promotes suspicion, anxiety, and uncertainty and extreme closeness produces fear and potential conflict between families and bureaucracies. Thus, reaching a midpoint on a social distance continuum and agreement over the handling of uniform and nonuniform tasks is the balance theorist's solution.

In studies on reading achievement, health practices, and grass roots movements, Litwak and associates substantiated that when organizations are trying to change a primary group in relation to nonuniform tasks they must use linkage processes that have elements of the primary group: face-to-face communication; working in the ecosystem of the primary group; building trust, flexibility, and patterns of behavior not constrained by bureaucratic rules. To modify the technical practices of an organization, the primary group must go beyond presenting the request for desired changes and "make a case," typically using technical experts, gathering demographic and social data and cost/benefit analyses—the linkage resembling the bureaucracy. Senior citizens trying to improve ambulatory care service in a community without producing a break with service providers, which confrontation alone may effect, should link in this formal manner (Litwak, Hollister, and Meyer, 1974).

Two other principles affirmed by Litwak's, Hollister's, and Meyer's research are concerned with initiative in communication and interaction in relation to the distance between the family and organization. Where the social distance is great, high initiative is required by one group trying to reach the other. Where groups are close and complementary, little or no initiative is required. In the former instance the more stimuli a sender presents the more likely will receivers respond. In the latter case each structure has specified complementary tasks, e.g., uniform or nonuniform, and too much participation with one another may reduce the contribution of each structure's unique purpose and function (Litwak, Hollister, and Meyer, 1974).

This theoretical explanation and pioneering research provides a reasonable macroexplanation and some guidelines for structuring family-organizational relationships. Litwak and associates recognize the need for further microlevel research on internal family and organizational dynamics and how these may affect the motivation and pattern of linkage; the location of balance points in any linkage system because of asymmetry, a consequence of where the linkage was initiated; and required resources to effect reasonable parity linkages—issues that have already been presented in this chapter.

Conclusions

In this discussion I have used exchange theory in considering primary group–bureaucratic linkage. The focus is on the family unit or its network

marriage mates of the younger generation are similar to the older
determining the type of courtship and wedding ceremony that preced
formation of a family unit; influencing the type of child-rearing philosc
and practice; and developing a help pattern between parents and t
newly married children. Residential propinquity as it is utilized by the fai
to forge closer links or, alternatively, to lessen tensions, has also b
found to be a factor which influences family continuity.

One principal function of the kin network is to assist its member famil
to adapt to as well as to influence organizational policy and practices. E
counters with bureaucratic organizations in different life sectors are
reciprocal learning experience for all participants, clients, patients, cu
tomers, and functionaries. There is a learning of new roles as well as ne
knowledge. The former task is usually achieved in the family and kin nei
work setting, and although the latter takes place in the institution in questio1
the family often exercises influence over its performance. The responsive
bureaucracy recognizes the social and economic characteristics of the
families it serves, their patterns of socialization, and their home environ-
mental conditions and adapts its practices to these conditions as well as to
the needs and demands expressed by its clients (Sussman, 1968a, 1968b).

All families and networks are not equally prepared to perform such
mediating and socialization functions for their members and the relevant
variables are location and activity in the kin network, life-cycle stage, and
experience with organizations. If the family member has the "credentials,"
the network can become an opportunity structure with optimal conditions
and resources to adjust to the priorities of the bureaucratic society while
simultaneously achieving individual and nuclear family goals.

Many lower-class families consider that the intrinsic advantages of
familism take precedence over those of increased mobility. This may be a
cause or a condition of little security in the larger social sphere, one which
may encourage dependence on kin for economic services as well as for
emotional support (Sussman, 1968a, 1970). Such integration within a viable
kin network is not necessarily coincident with family-unit effectiveness in
coping with the larger society.

In review, in this analysis of family–bureaucratic organization linkage
using exchange theory I have described the rationale, objectives, and
process of such linkage without discussing the problematics. The essential
questions are: Is it possible to have coordination rather than conflict between
primary groups and bureaucratic organizations? Can a parity model "take
over" from the current superordinate-subordinate one? Litwak and his
associates have examined this issue and proposed a "balance theory of
coordination" to explain the possibilities of having vital primary groups and
bureaucratic organizations in the same society even though their structures
and functions are contradictory (Litwak, Hollister, and Meyer, 1974). It will
be recalled that social distance or intimacy between these two types of

as a mediating system for elderly persons in the latter's efforts to obtain responsible services from human service organizations, and to obtain and exercise new options for retirement roles and careers.[3] A linkage process model was presented and the balance theory of coordination suggested by Litwak and associates provides the rationale and optional conditions for linkage.

A remaining task is to apply a component of exchange theory to one of the problems of the elderly. How can one provide a creative noninstitutionalized home environment for elderly persons with reciprocal benefits to them and families who are providers? The family network is one of the remaining primary social systems that has been utilized in the past for the care of its members but with different bases for such care. Since we live in highly differentiated societies in which specialization has occurred and with phenomenal growth of human service systems concerned with providing various kinds of educational, welfare, housing, social, recreational, income maintenance, and other forms of supports and services, one would expect a considerable reduction of feelings of filial responsibility. In fact, the whole program of society-wide transfers, where those in the productive years between the ages of twenty-five and fifty-five work for the support of the very young and old, mitigates against any efforts to induce family members to assume caretaking responsibilities of the elderly on the bases of family loyalty and identification. Moreover, the stress upon achievement, success, and mobility indicates that a variety of incentives that could be considered components of an overall incentive system must be employed so that families can see the advantages of assuming these caretaking roles.

Consequently an "experiment" to investigate the potential role of the kin family network in the care and, if necessary, rehabilitation of its elderly members has been proposed. This is a critical issue throughout the world since current support for the extensive development of health care systems is problematical, given most government administration postures on expenditures for such services, the absorptive capacity of the society where there is a continuous imbalance and conflict over the need and demand for services, and the capability of the society to support them. With the further expectation that there will be insufficient monies and trained workers to meet the increasing demands for quality health care, rehabilitation, and other human services, an investigation has been proposed of the circumstances and conditions under which members of a family network (not necessarily immediate family members but such relatives as cousin, grandchild, niece or nephew) would care for the aged and the receptivity of those in need of long-term attention to have a unit of the family network provide this service.

The research concentrates on economic and human service incentives,

3. For an analysis of possible retirement careers and roles, see M. B. Sussman, "An Analytic Model for the Sociological Study of Retirement," in *Retirement,* ed. F. M. Carp (New York, 1972), pp. 29–74.

i.e., remuneration, which make possible a family care milieu without diminishing the resources of the caretaking unit and which will enable the elderly person to maintain and increase his (her) self-esteem and sustain other rehabilitation gains. This study "randomizes" feelings of filial responsibility held by the kin family member for the elderly relative. Proposed incentives include cash payment; low-cost loans or subsidies to remodel or expand current living space in order to accommodate the aged member; use of the elderly person's resources; rent subsidies; tax write-offs or deductions; and special social and medical services such as patient-, baby- or house-sitting, transportation and shopping assistance, home medical and nursing care, vestibule training in care of the patient and similar supports.[4]

Family caretaking of its aged members is not intended as a replacement for existing institutionalized care systems, especially those which provide terminal care and care for exacerbating medical conditions. It is complementary to formally organized ones and can only be successful if it can develop appropriate linkages with professionals and obtain their support, instruction, and interest in a family-oriented care system. The objective is to provide an environment for family members and the aged relative that is denuded of stresses of an economic and service burden of caring for an elderly person; maximizes the use of available options and through pooled resources may increase the available number; and encourages a parity socialization relationship which provides reciprocal rewards for the disabled and nondisabled.

The research is being conducted in the United States in Cleveland, Ohio. It involves interviews with family members of 452 households randomly selected from census tracts stratified according to race and working-class status (blue- or white-collar), and with 100 aged persons in various living arrangements. The one-hour questionnaire, using fixed- and free-form questions and abbreviated case studies, taps the central theoretical issues discussed above. Under what conditions and circumstances would families of kin networks at different stages of the life cycle be willing to provide a home for one of their elderly members? In turn, what would be the acceptable conditions for the elderly to consider such a prospect?

A preliminary analysis of some questionnaire items from 100 of the 282 interview schedules was completed in the fall of 1975.[5] Given the small number of cases, the findings should be considered tentative. Fifty-seven percent indicated a willingness to share a household with an older relative regardless of the offering of incentives; 32 percent would not; 8 percent were not sure; and no information was obtained from 3 percent of the re-

4. M. B. Sussman, "Family Networks and Care of the Aged," research project underway (1974–76) in the Institute on the Family and the Bureaucratic Society, Department of Sociology, Case Western Reserve University, Cleveland, Ohio 44106.
5. Edward Prager of the Institute research staff prepared this preliminary analysis.

spondents to this question. There were no significant differences in proffering a home to an elderly member according to race or working status.

Respondents who were in the twenty-to-twenty-nine age bracket expressed a greater willingness than those in all other age groups to share their households with an older relative. This difference may be due to the need and perception by this age group of potential reciprocal relationships with the older person. The elderly individual can help in household chores and in the parenting, caretaking, and socialization of younger children.

The first choice of an economic incentive is a monthly cash allowance; for services and home-centered medical care it is readily available, especially when needed for the elderly member. Both these incentives are highly correlated.[6]

These preliminary findings may be confirming the obvious. If the current rate of invitations received by the elderly member to join a unit of the family network persists, then the economic and service inducements being offered can "lock" in this expressed attitude and provide pragmatic and contractual bases for its effectualization.

Research along this line, beginning with a primary socialization group, the family network, may move the aged care system back to the household, neighborhood, and community. If it stands the test of cost/benefit analyses and is attractive and comfortable because of reciprocal rewards, then we will have an optional caretaking system that may be more in consonance with the wishes of both the elderly and members of family networks, a system that is a practical alternative to institutionalization.

References

Blau, P. M. *Exchange and Power in Social Life.* New York, 1964.
Dowd, J. J. "Aging as Exchange: A Preface to Theory." *Journal of Gerontology* 30 (1975): 584–94.
Katz, E., and P. Lazarsfeld. *Personal Influence.* Glencoe, Ill., 1955.
Levi-Strauss, C. "The Principle of Reciprocity." In *Sociological Theory,* ed. L. A. Coser and B. Rosenberg. New York, 1957. Pp. 204–94.
Litwak, E. *Towards the Multifactor Theory and Practice of Linkages Between Formal Organizations.* Final Report, Grant No. CRD-425-cl-9, U.S. Department of Health, Education and Welfare. Washington, D.C., June 1970.
———, D. Hollister, and H. Meyer. "Linkage Theory Between Bureaucracies and Community Primary Groups – Education, Health and Political Action as Empirical Cases in Point." Paper presented at the Annual Meeting of the American Sociological Association, Montreal, 1974.
———, and H. J. Meyer. "Administration Styles and Community Linkages of Public Schools." In *Schools in a Changing Society,* ed. A. J. Reiss, Jr. New York, 1965. Pp. 49–97.

6. Other economic incentives are tax deductions, low-cost loans, food stamps, and rentals on property-tax allowance. Service incentives other than medical care are visitant programs, social centers for elderly persons, information center services, home aide services, and "meals on wheels."

———. "A Balance Theory of Coordination Between Bureaucratic Organizations and Community Primary Groups." *Administrative Science Quarterly* 11 (June 1966):31–58.

———. "The School and the Family: Linking Organizations and External Primary Groups." In *The Uses of Sociology*, ed. P. Lazarsfeld, W. Sewell, and H. Wilensky. New York, 1967. Pp. 522–43.

Mauss, M. *The Gift, Forms and Functions of Exchange in Archaic Societies*, trans. I. Gunnison. London, 1954.

Parsons, T., and R. F. Bales. *Family, Socialization, and Interaction Process*. Glencoe, Ill., 1955.

Schelling, T. "An Essay on Bargaining." *American Economic Review* 46 (June 1956): 281–306.

———. *The Strategy of Conflict*. Cambridge, Mass., 1960.

Sherif, M. *In Common Predicament*. Boston, 1966.

———, et al. *Intergroup Conflict and Cooperation: The Robbers' Cave Experiment*. Norman, Okla., 1957.

Sussman, M. B. "Adaptive, Directive and Integrative Behavior of Today's Family." *Family Process* 7 (Sept. 1968a):239–50.

———. "Family Continuity: Selective Factors Which Affect Relationships Between Families at Generational Levels." *Marriage and Family Living* 16 (May 1954):112–20.

———. "Family, Kinship and Bureaucracy." In *The Human Meaning of Social Change*, ed. A. Campbell and P. E. Converse. New York, 1972.

———. "The Family in the 1960's: Facts, Fictions, Problems, Prospects, and Institutional Linkages." In *The Bond of Matrimony*, ed. W. Bassett. South Bend, Ind., 1968b. Pp. 223–46.

———. "The Four F's of Variant Family Forms and Marriage Styles." *The Family Coordinator* 24 (Oct. 1975):563–76.

———. "The Help Pattern in the Middle-Class Family." *American Sociological Review* 18 (Feb. 1953):22–28.

———. "The Urban Kin Network in the Formulation of Family Theory." In *Families in East and West: Socialization Processes and Kinship Ties*, ed. R. Hill and R. König. Paris, 1970.

———, and W. B. Weil. "An Experimental Study of the Effects of Group Interaction Upon the Behavior of Diabetic Children." *International Journal of Social Psychiatry* 6 (1960): 120–25.

Thibaut, J. W., and H. H. Kelley. *The Social Psychology of Groups*. New York, 1959. See esp. chap. 3.

Weber, M. *The Theory of Social and Economic Organization*. New York, 1947.

2. Intergenerational Transfers and the Bureaucracy
Juanita M. Kreps

A decade ago a small group of scholars met at Duke University to consider some aspects of the changing reciprocal relations among members of families living in industrialized countries. Within that context, one analysis underscored the major economic characteristic of such current reciprocity: the reliance of both retirees and youth on the middle generation of workers for current output, the allocation of this output being made via a transfer of money claims between whole generations rather than between members of the same family. Governmental arrangements for retirement benefits, financed by payroll taxes on those at work, now largely replace intrafamily support; each generation of workers is taxed, presumably in order to provide for its own future retirement. But in reality annual tax receipts are used to pay benefits to current retirees.[1] Hence, as Kenneth Boulding notes, "The support which the middle-aged give to the young can be regarded as the first part of a deferred exchange, which will be consummated when those who are now young become middle-aged and support those who are now middle-aged who will then be old. Similarly, the support which the middle-aged give to the old can be regarded as the consummation of a bargain entered into a generation ago."[2]

In turning now to a consideration of the linkages of old people with their children and with the bureaucratic organizations—an inquiry designed to help describe the quality of life of the aged—we come up against the question of how old people cope with the bureaucracy in all its complexities. Do the elderly's own children and grandchildren provide the means of entry into the social order and a buffer against the pressures of bureaucracy? Or have these functions, too, become a part of the formal organization, so that information and advice are now provided primarily by professionals in the health and welfare fields?

Further questions, partly economic in content, are raised. As the bulk of the aged person's money income comes to be guaranteed through governmental transfers and private pension arrangements, does he not shift his financial reliance away from his children, depending instead on his past earnings record and the actions of Congress? Moreover, if independent retirement incomes enable the elderly to maintain their own homes, often quite distant from the location of their children, will these living arrange-

1. J. M. Kreps, "The Economics of Intergenerational Relationships," in *Social Structure and the Family: Generational Relations*, ed. E. Shanas and G. F. Streib (Englewood Cliffs, N.J., 1965), pp. 276–88.
2. K. E. Boulding, "Reflections on Poverty," in *The Social Welfare Forum* (New York, 1961), pp. 45–58.

ments not reduce further the family linkages, while making dependence on the bureaucracy ever more pronounced?[3]

One possible effect of the aged's decreased financial reliance on their own children would be a change in the quality of the intergenerational relationship, from one of dependency to one based on mutual interests, affection, and psychological support. To the extent that aged parents cease to be an economic burden to their children, vying for the family's limited resources, frictions within the family should be greatly reduced. In the same manner financial provision for young adults not yet in the work force (through scholarships, stipends, training allowances, etc.) which enables youth to live on their own funds, apart from their parents, minimizes intrafamily conflict.

The freedom from the burden of providing economic support directly to one's aged parents is of course counterbalanced by the necessity of paying taxes out of which the economic support is funded. Thus the middle generation's escape from financial responsibility for the aged (and the aged's escape from dependence on their children) is illusory. But the illusion is important nonetheless—perhaps more important than the reality. For the payment of taxes is compulsory and the receipt of benefits is virtually universal. As a result the aged's income is guaranteed, being dissociated from any caprice of their own children. The independent source of income allows the aged to live separately and make their own decisions for longer than would be the case if economic resources were shared within a family unit. It allows the middle generation greater independence of action as well. By insuring that elderly parents have incomes regardless of any uncertainties that befall their children, Social Security transfers permit the middle generation greater freedom and control over their own financial decisions. Again the parallel between the middle-aged and youth may be appropriate: each generation would increase its range of independent decisions if transfers of income to youth were intergenerational rather than intrafamily.

There can be little doubt that the growing economic independence of the three generations, each from the other, affects the nature of the interrelationship between the children, parents, and grandparents of a particular family. One of the major bases of both cooperation and conflict is being removed. But when it is no longer necessary for grandparents, parents, and children to join forces and work through the process of allocating family resources, will a joining of forces actually occur? Except for periods of psychological stress, illness, and the like, will there be a sufficient mutuality

3. See M. B. Sussman, "Relationships of Adult Children with Their Parents in the United States," in *Social Structure and the Family: Generational Relations*, ed. E. Shanas and G. F. Streib (Englewood Cliffs, N.J., 1965), pp. 62–92. More recently Dr. R. A. Ravich of the Cornell Medical School was quoted in the press as saying that "Institutions exist to destroy the family. . . . The more the family goes downhill, the more the power of the institutions increase."

of interest to hold the three groups together on a continuous basis?[4] Even if the elderly's children provide a buffer against the pressures of the bureaucracy, these linkages may well be intermittent, occurring primarily in times of crises.

Any trade-off between increased financial independence and a geographical (and perhaps psychological) estrangement of the elderly from their children can be appraised only if the terms of the trade-off can be defined. Research would reveal the extent of the aged's reliance on their children for entry into the social order; similarly a review of the data will indicate the components of the aged's income and the extent to which they are financially independent of their children. Leaving to other chapters in this volume the first set of questions, the discussion immediately following focuses on the second issue, i.e., that of the elderly's income sources. After the financial picture is drawn, attention is given first to the manner in which the allocative mechanism, in concert with the process of economic growth, produces significant intergenerational income differentials; and second, to the possible conflict between generations (as distinct from differences of view between the aged and their own children) arising from the allocation process.

The Changing Composition of the Elderly's Income

The shift from intrafamily to intergenerational support can be demonstrated by the growth in the proportion of the aged's income provided by Social Security and other income-maintenance benefits. This increasing component of income in the form of benefits reflects both the maturing of the nation's social security system and the secular decline in the labor force activity of older men. To illustrate the latter: from a labor force rate of about two in three older men at the turn of the century, the proportion had dropped to one in three by 1960, and has since fallen to one in four.

In aggregate terms the elderly's earnings of $7–8 billion at midcentury was several times the size of their total benefits. By 1958 total income going to the population aged sixty-five and over had risen substantially and about two-fifths of the total came from Social Security benefits. Even with the addition of other public transfers of income, earnings were higher than benefits during most of the decade. By 1960, however, when the aged's aggregate income had reached $33 billion, the ratio of earnings to benefits had reached one to one.

4. For a discussion of the interrelationships of the generations, particularly the degree of communication and frequency of contact of the elderly with their children, see the works by E. Shanas, notably *Family Relationships of Older People*, Health Information Foundation Research Series 20 (New York, 1971); and the research reports from a cross-national study of elderly people conducted in Britain, the United States, and Denmark by E. Shanas, P. Townsend, D. Wedderburn, H. Friis, P. Milhøj, and J. Stehouwer, *Old People in Three Industrial Societies* (New York, 1968).

During the past decade the composition of income has mirrored even stronger trends toward transfers, with less than one-third of the total coming from earnings by the end of the 1960s. Social Security payments constituted over 30 percent, with railroad retirement and government pensions adding 6 percent, public assistance 5 percent, and veterans' benefits 4 percent. Thus, more than 45 percent of the aggregate income of the elderly came from public transfers in a year when only about one-fifth of all old people were working. The addition of private pensions swells the income from transfers to about half the total amount received.

Social Security coverage, along with public benefits provided for civil servants and railroad employees, is now virtually complete, and recent increases in the size of benefits will have the effect of making this source of income an even more significant portion of the elderly's aggregate income. The decline in labor force activity of men over sixty is expected to continue with further erosion of earnings. Even now, the elderly's wages are those received by persons in their late sixties; most older people have no earnings, but must rely almost exclusively on Social Security benefits and on Supplemental Security Income administered by the Social Security Administration.

Total money incomes going to the aged are relatively low, despite Social Security's coverage. Of the more than 21 million aged Americans representing approximately 10 percent of the 1972 population, 4.3 million were classified as poor by current standards. This means that almost 20 percent of the poor were aged. There is also a substantial amount of hidden poverty among the elderly. More than 2 million old people live with their families—families whose incomes are above the poverty level. Adding these to those officially classified as poor, the number of aged poor rose to 6.3 million, which represented almost one-third of all people age sixty-five or older in 1972.[5] The median family income of the aged is much lower than that of younger families; indeed, the aged's family income was less than two-thirds that of the national average. For whites of all ages in 1974 median family income was $13,356; for those over sixty-five the median was only $7,519. For blacks of all ages, the median was $7,808, while that of the black elderly was $4,909.[6]

Monthly Social Security benefits and the number of people covered under Old Age, Survivors and Disability Insurance have risen substantially during the past two decades. Currently about 17 million men and women aged sixty-two and over receive monthly OASDI payments. Average monthly benefits paid to retired workers in September 1975 were $226 to male and $131 to female beneficiaries, many of whom had taken retirement prior to age sixty-five.[7] Wives and husbands of retired workers, most aged

5. U.S. Senate Special Committee on Aging, Information for Initial Hearings, "Future Directions in Social Security," mimeographed (January 15, 22, 23, 1973).

6. U.S. Bureau of the Census, Current Population Reports, Series P-23, No. 59, May 1976.

7. Social Security Bulletin, Annual Statistical Supplement, 1975.

sixty-two and over, received $105 a month on the average,[8] and widows and widowers, $192.[9]

Improvements in the level of benefits have been accompanied by increases in payroll taxes on workers, the benefits being financed from these receipts. The most recent rise in Social Security taxes again drew attention to the volume of transfers to retirees from workers, particularly low-income workers, who are taxed a higher proportion of their earnings than are those workers who earn higher salaries. The regressive nature of payroll taxes, a source of constant criticism from students of public finance, led to a recent tax revision that mitigated the initial impact on low-income workers.

Allocative Mechanism and Intergenerational Differences in Income

Recent legislation has provided for substantial increases in average Social Security benefits, has federalized old-age assistance, and has tied Social Security payments to the cost of living—all of which will tend to reduce intergenerational differences in income levels. But the basic distributive scheme will nevertheless continue to favor those currently at work over those currently retired, at least as long as economic growth continues.

Economic growth is made possible from an increase in the quantity or an improvement in the quality of resources, and from the development of better combinations of resources in the production process. Thus higher real income may result from improved technology, a better educated or more skilled labor force, or heavier investments in capital equipment. When such forces raise the level of output, year after year, consumption levels can be raised for the society as a whole. But the fruits of growth are not conferred evenly over the population; the impact of growth on income and consumption levels may, in fact, accentuate intergenerational differences in economic levels.

A systematic tendency for incomes of the retired to lag behind those of employed persons was demonstrated earlier in a model developed by Blackburn,[10] in which he shows that the relation between the level of consumption of retirees and that of workers depends, *ceteris paribus*, on the rate of growth. Specifically Blackburn assumed an average age of labor force entry of twenty, retirement at sixty, and death at age eighty. On the average, then, people work forty years and spend twenty in retirement. Assuming further a 5 percent rate of interest, and supposing that the worker throughout his

8. Ibid.

9. Ibid.

10. J. M. Kreps and J. O. Blackburn, "The Impact of Economic Growth on Retirement Incomes," Hearings Before the Special Committee on Aging (Washington, D.C., 1967), pp. 58–64.

labor force years saved that fraction of earnings necessary to provide a retirement consumption level equal to the level *of that year*, he notes that:

1. Consumption at the beginning of the retirement period, as a proportion of average consumption of workers, would be 100 percent only if the growth rate were zero.
2. If the income growth rate were 1 percent, the worker would enter retirement on 77 percent of the average workers' consumption level; if the growth rate were 2 percent, on 60 percent of workers' consumption; if 3 percent, 48, and if 4 percent, 35 percent of workers' consumption.
3. Since workers' incomes would continue to rise in accordance with economic growth, the divergence of incomes would continue during the twenty-year retirement span. Half way through the retirement period, for example, the retiree would have a consumption level equal to 45 percent of an average worker's level if the growth rate is 2 percent, and 36 percent if growth is 3 percent. (pp. 59–60)

The significance of this tendency of earnings to reflect current growth, while retirement benefits (public and in most cases private) are based on some portion of the earnings of an earlier, less productive era, has been obscured by the debate over tying benefits to the cost of living. Throughout recent discussions of the inflationary spiral and its impact on the purchasing power of the fixed-income aged, the growth question was ignored. From congressional hearings one might easily conclude that once benefits were adjusted automatically to price increases, erosion of the financial position of the elderly would cease. Yet the relative deterioration in retirement income occurs even when cost-of-living adjustments are made. In brief, the faster the pace of technology and the higher the rate of economic growth, the greater the disparity between earnings and retirement benefits, under present allocation arrangements.

The manner in which savings are accumulated (privately, or through tax deductions) does not affect the process of widening generational differences in income, although the form of investing the savings will of course affect the return received. To the extent that savings are invested in equities which keep pace with economic growth, some of the difference in current and past earnings could be offset. But since the gap results from the fact that succeeding generations enjoy progressively higher earnings, whereas the retiree's savings have been derived from lower incomes, the consumption levels of retirees are bound to be lower than wages unless a bureaucratic reallocation of aggregate income occurs.

The relative deterioration in the incomes of retirees, occasioned by growth in earnings and perpetuated by the distributive arrangements, could be at least partially offset under a different allocation scheme. If a share in growth were imputed to retirees through some strategy such as the social credit plan introduced by Spengler,[11] the erosion of standards during the retirement period could be prevented. However, such action appears unlikely and in any event would not take account of the gradual rise in earnings during work life. Because of the rise in consumption levels through the middle years, peak incomes are generally received near the end of work life; the drop that accompanies retirement is a sharp one, although the level to which income falls may be comparable to an earlier one in the life cycle.

Since our system of economic incentives is couched in terms of wage increases based on the rise in productivity, it is difficult to imagine any leveling of earnings during the work life. On the contrary, wage differentials may be increasing. Recent study indicates a slow but persistent increase in the concentration of earnings during the 1958–70 period,[12] which may be in part a reflection of a greater range between wages earned early and those earned late in work life. As a long-run problem, intergenerational differences in income may become more acute, giving rise to age-related distributional questions to which the society has not given serious attention. Resolution of differences in these views will be found in the political arena, however, rather than within families.

Sources of Intergenerational Conflict

The reduction of labor force participation of elderly men and, in particular, the downward drift in the retirement age of males lengthens the retirement period during which support is drawn from past earnings. As the numbers of retirees grow relative to the size of the working population, and as school age is extended to a later age, the dependency relationships are affected even though, as Philip Hauser points out, the dependency ratio itself is expected to drop by 1980, rise by 1990, and drop again by 2000.[13] Although the heavy influx of women into the labor force during the twentieth century has offset the decline in work activity of younger and older men, the concentration of work in the middle years has nevertheless sharpened the economic distinctions between generations. Youth now has an extended period of schooling, the cost of which is increasingly the responsibility of the whole society, and retirees' incomes, as we have seen, are largely independent of family connection. During this century about five years of nonworking time have been added at the beginning and another five years at the end of work.

11. J. J. Spengler and J. M. Kreps, "Equity and Social Credit for the Retired," in *Employment, Income and Retirement Problems of the Aged,* ed. J. M. Kreps (Durham, N.C., 1962), pp. 198–231.

12. See P. Henle, "Exploring the Distribution of Earned Income," *Monthly Labor Review* 95 (1972):16–27.

13. Philip Hauser, "Extension of Life—Demographic Considerations," mimeographed (Paper delivered at the 25th Annual Conference on Aging, Ann Arbor, Mich., 1972).

When the support patterns for these longer periods are clearly identified as flows of income between generations, some basis for conflict between generations emerges, replacing perhaps an earlier intrafamily conflict over the allocation of the family's resources. The probability of intergenerational debate concerning how the nation's output will be distributed is heightened when the allocative mechanism tends to award current income to current participants in the economic process, and when this process is well understood by members of the three generations.

It is not surprising, therefore, to see references in the popular press to the burdensome load of Social Security taxes on the workers. Setting the economic well-being of the younger family against that of the old person, it is easy to show that the drain of tax dollars in the latter's direction is a source of a genuine hardship, particularly on the low-income worker. One article, devoted to the cut in take-home pay resulting from 1973's increase in the payroll tax rates and base, publicized some interesting projections. Assuming that wages continue to rise and Social Security benefits rise sufficiently to cover an estimated 2.75 percent a year cost-of-living increase, the maximum monthly benefit for a worker retiring at sixty-five in 2011 would be $1,819. Adding 50 percent for a dependent wife, the couple's monthly benefit would be $2,729, or an annual Social Security income of nearly $33,000.[14] From the viewpoint of the worker paying taxes, the need for supporting old people in such supposed affluence would surely be questioned.

A review of the tax rates and wage bases indicates that the amount paid by low-wage workers has become quite a significant proportion of earnings. From the time of the passage of the legislation in 1935, when the tax was 1 percent on employer and employee for earnings up to $3,000, the tax has risen to its present level of 5.85 percent on each, on all wages up to $15,300. Total taxes collected from an individual worker earning as much as the taxable base have thus grown from $346 in 1965 to $1,790 in 1976.

The worker whose income falls at $15,300 or below has been taxed on all his earnings, whereas the wage earner who is paid $30,600 is taxed on only half of his. The percentage of income paid in Social Security tax has been higher, the lower the income. Taking into further account the proposition generally held by economists that the worker actually bears the cost of the tax on the employer as well as the one levied directly on him, his total liability is now 11.7 percent of all wages up to the taxable base.

As mentioned earlier in this chapter, the regressivity of the payroll tax has brought sharp criticisms, even from proponents of higher Social Security benefits.[15] Proposals have been made for shifting the cost altogether

14. *U.S. News and World Report*, December 18, 1972, pp. 39–43.
15. See J. A. Brittain, *The Payroll Tax for Social Security* (Washington, D.C., 1972); J. A. Pechman, H. J. Aaron, and M. K. Taussig, *Social Security: Perspectives for Reform* (Washington, D.C., 1968).

to general revenues; for shifting a portion of the costs, perhaps one-third, to general revenue funding; and for exempting low-income families (those on income at or below the poverty threshold, at least) from the payroll tax, just as they are exempt from the federal income tax. Counter-arguments have held that the regressive impact of the tax is largely mitigated by a progressive benefit return;[16] hence, on balance, the system is acceptable. Under the tax reduction act of 1975 families with children were given an income credit that had the effect of eliminating their OASDI tax when wages were under $4,000 per year. Between $4,000 and $8,000 the tax is progressive, between $8,000 and $15,000, proportional, and over $15,300, regressive.

The fact that the size of the benefit is subject to change by congressional action is nevertheless recognized. Older people correctly perceive that insofar as their economic status is dependent on their Social Security benefits, that status is in the hands of the bureaucracy. Political pressure thus becomes the medium through which one improves his retirement benefit, *once he is in retirement,* just as political pressure is the means by which he holds payroll taxes in check *while he is in the work force.* The interesting question arises: How much conflict of interest over income allocations do the two generations perceive? If the conflict appears to be significant, what impact does it have on each generation's view of the other, and more importantly, on each one's view of those family members who are in the other generations?

How Much Conflict?

On this century's changing pattern of intergenerational support, a simplistic appraisal might conclude that the bureaucracy has assumed the family's earlier function of allocating scarce resources among the generations and with this preempting of the distributive role the voting booth has replaced the family budget conference. Given the depersonalization of this allocative process, moreover, each generation can now be expected to vote for its own interests, despite the recognition that its higher incomes would be gained, temporarily, at least, at the expense of the economic welfare of the other generations, which contain members of the same family.

Institutionalization of income allocation between generations has indeed occurred, with the incomes of retirees (and even those of young adults) being more and more often determined politically. And there is some evidence of generational solidarity on issues such as tying Social Security benefits to the cost of living and, more recently, complaints against the rise

16. R. J. Myers, "Employee Social Insurance Contributions and Regressive Taxation," *Journal of Risk and Insurance* 34 (1967):611–15.

in payroll taxes. At the local level some of the rising sentiment against bond issues and property-tax revaluation has been attributed to the fact that older property owners have articulated their own interest. But these examples hardly make a generational war.

Stronger action by the elderly might be voiced, perhaps, if they thought their political action would be effective. For it seems unlikely that today's aged would interpret their position of, say, being against property taxes as being against the young or their middle-aged parents. Certainly there is no evidence that in their plea for stabilizing the value of retirement benefits the elderly have felt any conflict of interest with the middle-aged taxpayer. The Congress was under attack for letting living costs rise and erode benefits; but the trade-off of income for the aged versus income of the worker went unacknowledged.

The mystique of retirement benefits – the notion that the retiree has paid for them while working, and the money has been held in trust, drawing interest – bolsters the belief that the amount paid out is no drain on current workers, who are merely building up their own dollar accounts. Even the coupling of a rise in benefits with a rise in payroll taxes can be explained by the need for today's worker to put in more dollars for his own future retirement, rather than a need to increase revenues for the current generation of retirees when benefits are raised. Until the retiree has a clearer understanding of Social Security financing, intergenerational conflict will be happily minimized. It may well be that the explanations economists think necessary are in fact unwise.

Among people now at work the view that retirement benefits will accrue because one pays Social Security taxes during his working years (rather than because the money paid is in any way earmarked for his individual account) is widely shared. Thus, a clear understanding of benefits as a transfer of money claims does not negate one's feeling of entitlement. In the future the issue in any intergenerational difference of view on transfers will not be the right to a benefit in old age but the amount of that benefit. In the resolution of that question the generations must confront the allocative issue. Since total money income cannot exceed the aggregate volume of goods and services produced (without inflationary pressure), an increase in the claims of one generation means a decrease in the claims of another. Debate over one recent 20 percent increase in Social Security benefits, accompanied by an increase in payroll taxes, is illustrative.

Yet even when the financing of public transfers to the elderly is clearly understood, some of the ambivalence remains. Those paying higher taxes are in a sense insuring that their own benefits will be higher; benefits have never been reduced, and tomorrow's retirees assume that gradual improvement will continue. Moreover, workers with aged parents are unlikely to protest an increase in payroll taxes when, at the same time, they see their parents' incomes increase.

Rather than a hardening of generational lines on the income issue, debate is more likely to continue on the issue of the extremely low incomes of persons of all ages. Within this group the elderly have a disproportionately heavy representation, as earlier discussion indicated. Insofar as the public attends to the income dilemma of the poor in general, the solutions will not be divisive of the generations. On the contrary, children and aged widows below the poverty line would receive the same attention. Moreover, particular legislative actions (notably HR 1 as it finally passed) often separate out certain age groups for income supplements, leaving other equally poor persons without relief. The failure of the Ninety-third Congress to legislate federal standards for all welfare recipients was perhaps not surprising, given our history of state control and state financing. What was surprising was the enactment of federal standards for the elderly. We have yet to see whether this action on behalf of the aged, but not for children, will produce complaints that one generation is gaining over another.[17]

Alternatives to Conflict

As Professor Sussman has indicated,[18] the functions of the family and bureaucracies often overlap, resulting in competition over roles. He further points out that "the family can optimize its possibilities of survival and sustain intact its interactional system and territory if members develop managing, manipulating, and mediating skills in linkage activity."[19]

Along with the expansion in bureaucratic roles that has preempted many of the functions formerly performed within families, is there evidence that the somewhat disenfranchised family is indeed helping the individual to adapt to the bureaucracy or influencing the larger society on behalf of the individual? As it has yielded to the bureaucracy the role of allocating family income between generations, has the family assumed the role of mediating between bureaucratic structures and individual need?

Such a mediating role is clearly needed, particularly in the case of the elderly person. His reduced physical mobility means increased dependency on others for transportation to the location of the services, even when the services are provided at public expense. The even more complicated process of proving his eligibility for services (or cash payments for Supplemental

17. Earlier, a secretary of Health, Education and Welfare commented on the fact that larger governmental expenditures were being made for the elderly than for children. He included Social Security benefits in the total amount going to old people and was immediately under attack for doing so. But the significant point raised by his comment lay in the allusion to intergenerational differences in public benefits and in his obvious concern to balance the needs of the young against those of the old.

18. M. B. Sussman, "Family, Bureaucracy, and the Elderly Individual: An Organizational/ Linkage Perspective," chap. 1 in this volume.

19. Ibid.

Security Income, for example) taxes the patience of the most persistent and knowledgeable citizen. Misinformation, fear of governmental reprisal, pride in the ability to handle one's own affairs all militate against the older person's taking full advantage of mandated services.

Children or other relatives of the elderly could play a major role in bringing the parent and the bureaucracy together and in interpreting for the aged person the range of options available to him. Since it is clearly to the advantage of the middle-aged as well as their parents to utilize all the services that are provided at public (that is, largely the middle-aged's) expense, the children's investment of time and effort in making the necessary arrangements for their parents is well spent. To the extent that the family's role of direct support is replaced by the responsibility for seeing that the support is in fact forthcoming and that it is adequate, the family role continues to be important, though markedly different from the one assumed earlier.

The role of watch-dog of the bureaucracy has a certain popular appeal at present. Concern with major problem areas — racism, poverty, inflation — is fed to an ever-increasing pitch by the media. But equal attention to the fine details of legislation which govern the income and services of particular groups of people is not readily apparent. For while it is easy to be righteously indignant about issues such as Watergate, it is difficult to interpret the terms of welfare legislation, and far more difficult to see that unsatisfactory legislation is rewritten.

There are some optimistic signs, however. It is increasingly clear that blacks are now demanding a more careful consideration of their income needs in old age; that working women are far more sensitive to Social Security coverage than nonworking wives; that recent retirees are better educated and more attuned to bureaucratic systems than the very old. Specific incidents reveal the attention paid to policing the law. One research firm, concerned with the extent to which mandated services failed to reach eligible clients, proposed that the government be held responsible for delivering the services it owed to the citizens in the same way that citizens are held responsible for paying taxes owed the government. Needless to say, spokesmen for governmental agencies were appalled at such a prospect.

Yet such a calling of the bureaucracy to account is quite likely when strong advocates are involved, and the resulting impact can be quite marked. The consumer movement in this country now has power to influence not only the government but private industry as well. The civil rights movement had unprecedented influence. The women's movement has brought a raft of new governmental and industrial policies.

In examining the family's role in reshaping the bureaucracy (as opposed to redefining its own role to accommodate to the increased power of the bureaucracy), the questions need to be sharply focused. To what extent is the family attempting to bend other institutions to serve its needs? What would be the evidence? Since the family's action is by definition a single attempt at a local level, the impact of such action does not attract attention in the manner of a group movement. The voting behavior of family members of certain ages would reveal their views toward institutions and policies; older people's vote against bond issues for school construction are a case in point. But there the vote is along generational rather than family lines.

Survey might reveal the degree to which the family is a force which countervails the power of the larger institutions in the economic sphere. If the adults in the family usually agree on important issues, such as the relative levels of living appropriate for the older and the middle generations, one might conclude that family pressure on the bureaucracy would reflect this preference. In such a case, intergenerational conflict on economic issues would be minimal and the bureaucracy would simply provide the mechanism through which aggregate allocations were made.

Some Questions

In the United States, where Social Security is newer than in many Western European countries, the maturing of the system is only now occurring. With that maturation economic support during old age has come to be financed largely through transfers of money claims from those currently at work and paying payroll taxes to those now retired. These public transfers are supplemented by savings and private pension claims which, although substantial for higher-income workers, constitute a minimal portion of the retirement income of the low and middle-income wage earner; and by the needs-based Supplemental Security Income, available when incomes are extremely low. These forms of income maintenance in old age have largely replaced intrafamily support in which the wage earners provided income for their own aged parents and have enabled most older people, having their own financial resources, to live apart from their children and grandchildren.

The question posed here—whether, given this bureaucratization of economic support, the elderly nevertheless rely on their children and other relatives to provide entry to the social system and to act as a buffer against the bureaucracy—is of course not an economic question. However, the extent of the aged's reliance on their own children (as opposed to the bureaucratic arrangement) can be researched once again, taking into account the most recent changes in institutional setting.

An important question is posed by changes in the economic framework. Have the shifts to intergenerational (as opposed to intrafamily) support resulted in conflicts of interest that set one generation against another? The tentative answer is no, in part because the allocation process has been poorly understood; the payment of taxes is thought to give one his own future claims to benefits. To the Congress it is clearly necessary to balance the needs of the generations in the overall allocation of money claims. Although there has been little evidence that this balancing has led to conflict between the generations, there is a growing tendency to make the choices explicit: emphasis on priority setting may well generate strong differences in viewpoints.

The fact that the elderly do not perceive their interests as being inimical to those of the middle-aged and the young could change in time, particularly if the gap between earnings late in work life and retirement income grows. A sharp decline in income with the cessation of work could well evoke protest; hence the persistent tendency for earnings to grow and for retirement incomes to lag behind—tendencies inherent in the process of growth and the way its fruits are allocated—may bring into focus an intergenerational point of conflict which has not yet been emphasized, except by economists.

A second question has to do with the impact of this shift in income sources on intergenerational family ties. Does the removal of the income-allocation issue from the family lessen conflict and thus improve family relations? Or by eliminating one of the needs for persons of different ages to rely directly on one another, does the bureaucratization of financial support remove an important link between the aged and their children and grandchildren?

The new role that needs to be assumed, given the bureaucratization of income support, is that of supervising and holding accountable the larger institutions. If the family is able to intervene on behalf of its older members, interpreting governmental rules and even protesting the rules when necessary, the rights of the aged and the viability of the family are assured. The allocation of retirement income along generational lines has the advantage of allowing older people and the middle-aged greater independence of decision making and more freedom of action than could ensue in an intrafamily setting. Family linkages with the bureaucracy would seem essential, however, if the aged are to have full access to the range of services and income supports that are now promised them.

Historical/Demographic Analyses

3. The Impact on the Family Relationships of the Elderly of Changes Since Victorian Times in Governmental Income-Maintenance Provision   *Michael Anderson*

Over the past 150 years, in Britain as in all other so-called advanced societies, there has been a transformation in income-maintenance provision for those who fall into situations where they are unable, temporarily or permanently, to support themselves. Central to this transformation has been the emergence of the principle that individuals, because they are citizens of a society, should have, as a right, access to a standard of living which, while not luxurious, will at least allow them to participate as full members of their society on terms not markedly disadvantaged compared with the mass of their fellow men. In most countries, moreover, the legal duty to provide, administer, and finance this respectable minimum has come to rest basically on the individual on the one hand and the central government on the other (though additionally for some contingencies on employers, spouses, and the parents of minor children); in Britain, where this trend has gone further than in most other societies, since 1948 no liability for support has been imposed on children, relatives, neighbors, or the local community.[1]

In the case of Britain this transformation has involved a number of changes of principle. Under the Poor Laws, which effectively governed state-provided income maintenance in Britain from the late sixteenth until the mid-twentieth century, hard-line administrators continually stressed that the right to relief was based not on poverty but destitution, and that the aim was to provide only the mere minimum necessary to prevent death from starvation, curable sickness, or exposure to the natural elements.[2] Particu-

---

1. For historical surveys of the development of publicly provided income maintenance provision in Britain see, e.g., J. D. Marshall, *The Old Poor Law 1795–1834* (London, 1968); M. E. Rose, *The Relief of Poverty 1834–1914* (London, 1972); B. B. Gilbert, *The Evolution of National Insurance in Great Britain* (London, 1966); S. Webb and B. Webb, *English Poor Law History*, Part 2, Vol. I (London, 1929); *R. C. On The Poor Laws; Report*, PP.1909 XXXVII (esp. chap. 7 of the Minority Report).

2. The English Poor Law was, until 1834, administered locally by parochial officers and was financed by an assessment on property known as a "rate." In the early 1830s a commission of enquiry into the working of the "Old Poor Law" was set up and so-called "Assistant Commissioners" toured the country collecting evidence. In the subsequent reorganization ("the New Poor Law") parishes were grouped into "Unions," each of which was administered by an elected "Board of Guardians" who were, however, subjected to a central control which increased steadily over the period under review. Finance continued to be by rates but a greater emphasis was placed on "Indoor Relief" (which required the recipient to live in a local workhouse), and "Outdoor Relief" paid to recipients living in the community was to some extent discouraged. The Scottish Poor Law remained parochially organized although greater central control was introduced from the 1840s onwards. In Scotland, to secure poor relief, in addition to destitution, it was necessary to demonstrate "debility," an inability to work on medical grounds; by the early twentieth century, however, this had frequently become a formality (*R. C. On The Poor Laws: Report on Scotland*, PP.1909 XXXVIII, 78–80).

larly after the reorganization of the Poor Law provision in 1834, this first principle was reinforced by a second, often known as the principle of less eligibility, which insisted that no pauper should be better off in receipt of poor relief than he would have been in the absence of the contingency which made it necessary for him to apply for assistance.

It follows from these ideas that a right to assistance could only exist for those who had fallen into a specific contingency which made them unable, at the moment of application, to keep themselves and their dependents out of destitution. Moreover, strictly speaking, no relief could be given which simply raised the destitute above destitution unless it also imposed upon them some associated deprivation which was not suffered by those who by their own efforts were just above the margin of self-support.

Clearly, under these rules, no one with resources of his own which could be mobilized for his maintenance, could have an entitlement to relief. This idea was, however, extended to include ineligibility on the grounds that specified close relatives had resources which could be employed for one's maintenance. Under the famous Statute of Elizabeth of 1601, "The father and grandfather, and the mother and grandmother, and the children of every poor, old, blind, lame and impotent person, or other poor person not able to work, being of a sufficient ability, shall at their own charges, relieve and maintain every such poor person in that manner, and according to that rate as by the justices . . . shall be assessed." In Scotland, but not in England, married daughters and grandchildren were also liable and so, under some circumstances, were some collaterals.[3] Moreover, even where no legal liability was enforced, the principles meant that the level of relief was typically set so low that some supplementation from other sources would usually be required if extreme hardship were to be avoided.[4]

The transformation from locally administered, partial, and means-tested income maintenance based on these principles of a citizenship-based welfare state has involved frequent piecemeal tinkering with the existing system and the occasional more fundamental reform of the basis on which a particular contingency is handled. The result of all these changes is that the prime

3. PP.1909 XXXVIII, 215.
4. The local administration of poor relief permitted very wide variations both within a Poor Law Union and between unions. However, evidence on the general inadequacy of poor relief for independent subsistence is widespread throughout the nineteenth century; for example, the Clerk to the Caernarvon Poor Law Guardians estimated subsistence at 3/9d. without rent and coal and 5/3d. with (and compare Rowntree's estimate of 3/-d. for food and 2/6d. for household sundries [B. S. Rowntree, *Poverty: A Study of Town Life*, London, 1901]). In Caernarvon the relief paid was 1/6d. - 4/-d. (*R. C. On the Aged Poor, Mins. of Ev.* PP.1895 XIV, 374–5). This was probably a typical normal range of relief in England and Wales (and cf. PP.1895 XIV passim). Its inadequacy was condemned in the Report in these words: "It is rare to find a union in which it is not the exception to give sums which would suffice alone to provide even the barest necessities of life" (PP.1895 XIV xx. Cf. also *Report from S. C. on Cottage Homes Bill*, PP.1899 IX vii).

responsibility for income maintenance in Britain today rests firmly on a centrally controlled, bureaucratically organized social security system. The general question to which this chapter is addressed is what effect do changes of this kind have on those social institutions which have supposedly more traditionally fulfilled these functions? In particular, what is their effect on the family, and specifically on the relations between the aged and their kin? In the present context I focus particularly, as a kind of test case, on the effect on the family relations of the aged of the introduction of old-age pensions in 1909.

The typical Victorian answer would have been relatively simple and can be summed up in the words of the Poor Law Commission of 1834, which were also cited favorably by its successors of 1909:[5]

> The duty of supporting parents and children in old age or infirmity is so strongly enforced by our natural feelings, that it is often well performed, even among savages, and almost always so in a nation deserving the name of civilised. We believe that England is the only European country in which it is neglected. . . . If the deficiencies of parental and filial affection are to be supplied by the parish, and the natural motives to the exercise of those virtues are thus to be withdrawn, it may be proper to endeavour to replace them, however imperfectly, by artificial stimulant and to make laws, distress warrants, or imprisonment act as substitutes for gratitude and love.

The striking thing about this and many other similar statements is the assumptions that lack of assistance to parents is due to a lack of "natural feelings," "gratitude, and love" and that, in the main, Poor Law provision is simply replacing provision which family members should, and in most cases could, otherwise be making for their kin. Indeed some saw the effects as even more insidious for, as one Assistant Commissioner argued in 1834, "social ties . . . [are] now in the course of rapid extinction by the Poor Laws. It is to be feared, indeed, that feelings and motives, are gradually becoming lost to the labouring orders."[6] The corollary of these ideas is clear. If one introduces a policy of scanty allowances and rigorous administration of poor relief, "it is a means of encouraging thrift and family affection."[7]

If these views were correct, the consequence of the relatively liberal policies of today should presumably be a serious weakening of all relationships between parents and children. In fact, it has been clearly demonstrated

5. PP.1909 XXXVII, 551 citing *Report from Commissioners for enquiring into the administration and practical operation of the Poor Laws*, PP.1834 XXVII, 249.

6. *Commission for enquiring into . . . Poor Laws; Reports of Assistant Commissioners*, PP.1834 XXVIII, 258A.

7. PP.1895 XIV, 80.

in many studies[8] that children and other relatives are still today engaged in a wide range of functionally important relationships with old people, and one important study[9] has concluded that welfare services do not, in the main, "conflict with the interests of the family as a social institution, because either they tend to reach people who lack a family or whose family resources are slender, or they provide specialised services the family is not equipped or qualified to undertake."

Until now, however, no scholars seem to have tried to use historical data to assess in detail the consequences for family relationships of changing social security provision and to assess the validity of the Victorians' views. It is the aim of this paper to make a first attempt at this task, though clearly this is difficult, given the scanty and inevitably biased nature of surviving historical data and the nature of the problem at hand.

One important preliminary matter merits some discussion, and this is changes which have occurred over the past 150 years in the nature of old age itself. Two conflicting trends seem to be apparent. On the one hand, as is well known, the expectation of life of the aged has been markedly increasing, and one might then imagine that today the old are at any given age far fitter and healthier than they were 150 years ago. The expectation of life of persons of sixty-five fell slightly for both sexes during the nineteenth century but in this century has risen by nearly two years for men and nearly five years for women. Perhaps more significantly, the probability of a person of twenty surviving to reach sixty-five has risen from under half in the nineteenth and early twentieth centuries to 0.72 for men and 0.84 for women.[10] Since these changes have been contemporaneous with a marked fall over the same period in family size, the consequence has been that the aged as a proportion of the population have increased from under 5 percent of the population in 1851 to 12 percent in 1961. One other effect of these changes is that old people today who have children have on the average fewer surviving than ever before, and this in turn means that fewer will have the daughters who have been shown in some recent studies to be so important in the family relations of old people.[11] Somewhat paradoxically, however, high rates of marriage and decreasing child mortality make it likely that overall more old people have some children than was the case in the nine-

8. E.g., E. Shanas, P. Townsend, D. Wedderburn, H. Friis, P. Milhøj, and J. Stehouwer, *Old People in Three Industrial Societies* (London, 1968); P. Townsend, *The Family Life of Old People* (London, 1957); also, more generally, the studies cited by L. E. Troll, "The Family of Later Life, A Decade Review," *Journal of Marriage and the Family* 33 (1971):263–90.

9. Shanas et al., *Old People*, p. 129.

10. *Supplement to the 65th Annual Report of the Registrar General of Births, Deaths and Marriages in England and Wales*, PP.1905 XVIII, xlviii–li; *Registrar General's Statistical Review*, 1970, 9.

11. Cf. the studies referred to under note 8, passim, particularly, C. Rosser and C. C. Harris, *The Family and Social Change* (London, 1965), chaps. 5 and 8.

teenth century.[12] The decline in mortality also means that larger proportions of over sixty-fives of both sexes have currently surviving spouses.[13]

Turning to health, the situation is a little more complex because it is clear that both one's own perception of bodily health and the social implications of any given level of health are highly related to expectations and to the health of one's reference group. Nevertheless, even in rural areas, at the turn of the century only half of the persons aged sixty-five to sixty-nine were rated by their local clergyman as in "good health" on a four-point scale. For the over eighties the figure was only 28 percent. In a 1962 survey, by self-rating on a three-point scale, the comparative figures were 58 percent and 55 percent, with 71 percent and 27 percent being adjudged to have no major incapacity for self-care.[14]

In terms then of health and life expectation, aging occurred earlier in the nineteenth and early twentieth centuries than it does today. It is perhaps significant that most Boards of Guardians in the nineteenth century seem automatically to have treated people of sixty and over as aged and infirm. In the 1875 and 1887 Friendly Society Acts old age was defined as any aged over fifty.[15] However, for those not totally incapacitated, wider occupational roles remained open in the nineteenth century than is the case today. Traditionally, and especially in rural areas, disengagement from employment could be gradual. As they grew older men worked more slowly and perhaps at lighter work, and their pay was reduced in proportion. Even when unable to do a full day's work, through a wide range of casual employment, the old of both sexes were able to earn a few shillings a week to support themselves or supplement other income. The trend towards universalistic employment standards, the increasing bureaucratization of employing organizations, the introduction of ever more sophisticated technology, and the decline in domestic industry all tended to disrupt this gradual transition from a work role to that of "retired."[16] The insistence of trade unions on standard mini-

12. In 1962 76 percent of old people interviewed in their homes had at least one surviving child (Shanas et al., *Old People*, p. 139). My calculations suggest that in Preston in 1851 about 67 percent of old people were in this position. Given the high urban mortality rates, rather larger proportions of old people elsewhere were probably in this position (M. Anderson, *Family Structure in Nineteenth Century Lancashire* [Cambridge, 1971], p. 140).

13. In England and Wales in 1851, 62 percent of men aged sixty-five to seventy-four and 45 percent of men aged seventy-five and over, and 40 percent of women aged sixty-five to seventy-four and 18 percent of women aged seventy-five and over had surviving spouses (from *Census of Great Britain 1851*, Population Tables II, Vol. I, pp. 1852–3 LXXXVIII, Part I, ccc–cccxliv). In 1966 the proportions were 79 percent, 56 percent, 45 percent and 19 percent respectively (from General Register Office, *Sample Census 1966*, England and Wales, Housing Tables, Part I, Table 27).

14. The earlier data are from a survey on pauperism and the aged conducted at Charles Booth's instigation in a sample of English villages (C. Booth, *The Aged Poor in England and Wales* [London, 1894], p. 355). The later data are from Shanas et al., *Old People*, pp. 36 and 53. In both surveys men tended to be healthier than women.

15. PP.1909 XXXVII, 899n.

16. Booth noted that this trend was already occurring in the last half of the nineteenth century: "Life runs more intensely than it did, and the old tend to be thrown out. Not only

mum wages and the introduction of compulsory compensation schemes for industrial injuries have also been suggested as factors tending to make employers more unwilling to employ older workers.[17] Even in rural areas employment opportunities for the old declined as wages for the able-bodied rose.[18] Even casual work repairing the roads, traditionally old men's work, disappeared when the new county councils took over responsibility for road maintenance.[19]

An important point, therefore, to be borne in mind when one considers changes in the family relationships of the aged since Victorian times is that today old people of, say, seventy differ in important respects from people of the same age even sixty years ago. Relative to the rest of the population there are more of them, they are slightly more likely to have spouses alive, they will live longer and be healthier, but be less able, regardless of their own wishes, to continue to support themselves in the same way as the rest of the population, that is, through employment.

However, the shifts referred to in the last paragraph in the availability of employment for the aged, while important, are only some of a number of factors which have drastically changed the ability of old people to keep themselves free of destitution. By far the most significant changes have, of course, been due to changes in statutorily provided incomes.

Although there was some variation both regionally and over time in prepension Poor Law policy, in most areas there were two ways in which destitute old people could obtain relief.[20] Throughout the period official policy was to pay relief, fixed at below-subsistence rates,[21] to old people in their homes as long as they were deemed respectable and were willing to live outside the workhouse on the pittance which was paid. Those who were

---

on the whole does work go faster, and require more perfect nerve, but it changes its character more frequently, and new men, younger men, are needed to take hold of the new machines or new methods employed. The community gains by this, but the old suffer. They suffer beyond any measure of actual incapacity, for the fact that a man is old is often in itself enough to debar him from obtaining work" (PP.1895 XIV, 579).

17. PP.1909 XXXVII, 175; PP.1895 XIV, 797, 909, 930.

18. Booth, *The Aged Poor*, p. 426.

19. PP.1895 XIV, 311.

20. Poor Law policy was to a considerable extent at the whim of both local administrators and of the inspectors of the central administration. There was thus considerable local variation. Policy almost everywhere was hardened after the Act of 1834, hardened again in the 1870s and 1880s and then softened somewhat from the 1890s onwards. (See esp. here Webb and Webb, *English Poor Law History*.)

21. For the inadequacy of rates of payment see note 4 above. In Scotland down to 1845 and to some extent throughout the century, Indoor Relief was rare and Outdoor Relief usually only a tiny pittance, quite inadequate even for subsistence, and it is clear that the friendless, destitute aged in Scotland frequently died of slow starvation. In Wick outrelief rates in the 1840s ranged from 1d. to 5d. per week (*Report of Commissioners enquiring into the administration and operation of the Poor Laws in Scotland*, PP. 1844 XX, 41) and even in Edinburgh only 9d. or 10d. was paid (ibid., 71). Rates and criteria for relief varied widely in different parts of the country. A minimum subsistence income at this time was probably at least 3/-d. Begging by those on poor relief was, in consequence, widespread, at least in the towns.

denied outrelief (and in a few areas very little outrelief was paid) were forced to enter the workhouse. After 1834 workhouses in general were made deliberately and deterrently unattractive with rigidly enforced discipline and a basic and monotonous diet so as to test, as rigorously as possible, the destitution of those who might otherwise be able to work.[22] This policy inevitably had deleterious effects on the aged.[23] Clearly, many old people, however deserving, suffered severe social and emotional deprivations and these were made worse by the fact that workhouses were often also effectively the local lunatic asylum, as well as the main source of hospital provision.

Faced with a situation where 30 percent of seventy-year-olds were on poor relief, where increasing numbers were being forced into workhouses, and where many hard-working and honest citizens were quite clearly unable, because of low wages and large families, to make any adequate provision for their old age, public and parliamentary opinion began from the mid-1880s to move in favor of some kind of pension for the "deserving" aged poor. In 1908[24] came the final success of legislation to award Exchequer-financed noncontributory old-age pensions to all resident British nationals aged seventy and over who met certain criteria and could thus be officially considered "deserving." The pension was still set at below subsistence level and was means tested, but although help in cash or kind (including lodgings) received from relatives was counted as income, for most purposes this act abolished the obligation on relatives to provide basic support for their poor dependents since few relatives gave support worth anything like the maximum income allowed. In spite of the low level of pension, within four years Poor Law outrelief fell by 95 percent and three-quarters of all the destitute aged were relieved of the stigma of pauperism.[25] Subsequent modifications have both humanized means-tested assistance and gradually extended old-age pensions, based them on a contributory principle, and reduced the qualifying age.[26]

22. The 1834 commission and the subsequent act were almost entirely concerned with the able-bodied poor and with attempts to remove the various forms of supplementation of wages by the local Poor Law authorities. The problems of other Poor Law recipients (who actually made up the majority of paupers) were almost entirely ignored. See, e.g., Marshall, *The Old Poor Law.*

23. One extreme example is the fact that until 1847 it was quite normal (up to 1842 compulsory) for aged married couples to be separated in different parts of the workhouse (PP.1895 XIV xxii, and passim; PP.1899 IX, 19–20). *One Witness to the Select Committee on the Aged Pensioners Bill* (PP.1903 V) notes that "no-one will go in if they can possibly avoid it; in fact they almost prefer, I should say, to starve outside" (65) and, referring to Newington workhouse, that "it is infinitely worse than in the Russian prisons" (67).

24. The act came into force in 1909 for most old people, and in 1910 for those who had received poor relief in the previous year.

25. An excellent summary of the 1908 Act and its history can be found in D. Collins, "The Introduction of Old-Age Pensions in Britain," *Historical Journal* 7 (1965):246–59.

26. It is interesting to note, however, that in spite of several attempts to raise the rate of pensions to a subsistence level comparable with the standards of living of the rest of the popula-

A survey conducted at Charles Booth's instigation in the 1890s, although confined to villages, enables us to make some interesting comparisons with the sources of income of the aged in 1962.[27] In Booth's survey 22 percent of the population received Poor Relief (the national figure was about 30 percent), 46 percent had income from earnings, 18 percent received charity, 25 percent help from relatives and 35 percent had income from private "means." In the 1962 survey 27 percent received public assistance. Only 20 percent had income from employment and only 12 percent from "other" sources including charity and kin (though kin assistance here excluded help in kind which was included in Booth's survey). The "means" category has no direct parallel but probably between 30 percent and 50 percent of old people in 1962 would have been so classed by Booth's investigators. The big difference in the situation in the 1890s and that in 1962, however, is that in 1962 81 percent of the aged had a state pension.

The Function of Kinship

This brings us to the core of the problem at hand: How have the functions of kinship and the quality of kinship relationships changed for the aged since Victorian times and, in particular, how have they changed in that section of the population for whom state-provided social security has clearly had most impact, the poorer sections of the community?

We have seen in an earlier section that many middle-class Victorians frequently argued that family relationships were in danger of being undermined by liberal Poor Law provision.[28] Unfortunately, however, no one throughout the period seems to have attempted a systematic survey of family relationships in an attempt to investigate this charge. Moreover, it is clear on close reading that the Victorian viewpoint is a rather superficial one in that it tends to treat family relationships holistically, and to extrapolate from lack of regular support in money terms not merely to other kinds of tangible assistance to relatives but also to affection and purely social support. It was able to do this because it equated what was seen as the "natural duty" of supporting parents (based at least in part on ideas of "natural justice" in that it repaid parents for the children's support when

tion, some form of means-tested supplementation has remained an essential feature of British social security provision until the present day and, if one compares the situation in 1962 with the situation of 1906 one finds that a larger proportion of women of sixty-five and over, and about the same proportion of old men, were in 1962 in receipt of state-provided, means-tested, public assistance. From PP. 1909 XXXVII, 37 and PP.1909 XXXVIII, 24; Shanas et al., *Old People*, p. 356. Subsequent attempts to increase take-up by eligible old people have considerably increased the number of old people on the successor of poor relief, supplementary pensions.

27. Booth, *The Aged Poor*; Shanas et al., *Old People*, chap. 12.

28. The extent to which this view was a propaganda ideology or was actually believed by any middle-class Victorians is unclear. Indeed, the whole topic of the ideologies used to justify welfare assistance to the aged is clearly one for further research.

young)[29] with the "natural duty" to be affectionate to them. The fact that most middle-class adults were presumably affectionate children, though few perhaps needed to contribute substantially to their parents' support, seems to have been almost universally overlooked.

Modern sociological work on parent-child relationships has been more discriminating, and in a recent review Troll[30] has isolated a number of discrete elements of kinship relationships including residence patterns, frequency and type of interaction, economic interdependence and mutual aid, and the strength of affective bonds. In the rest of this paper I shall similarly attempt to differentiate elements of parent-child relationships, and review evidence on each in turn. I shall begin by looking at the institutionalized population.

If major changes occurred in the willingness or ability of individuals to help aged relatives, one might expect this to be reflected in changes in the proportion of old people living in institutions since, given the choice, in general even today and certainly in the nineteenth century most old people would consider an institution an undesirable place to live out their old age. Some data are available on changes in the institutional population over time.

In 1851 3.2 percent of the population of sixty-five and over were living in workhouses, hospitals, and asylums for the mentally ill and mentally subnormal.[31] From that date until the introduction of old-age pensions in 1909 this figure rose spectacularly. By 1891 the figure had reached 5.1 percent even if non–Poor Law hospitals are excluded, and 4.3 percent of old people were living in workhouses.[32] By 1906 the figure for Poor Law institutions alone had shot up to almost 6 percent.[33] In the four years following the introduction of the old-age pension, the number of old people living in Poor Law institutions fell by 20 percent[34] and by 1931 (excluding rate-aided [assistance] patients in mental hospitals) it was down to 2.2 percent,[35] though this figure is almost certainly artificially low as a result of changes in administrative procedure and changes in presentation of statistics. The figures for the 1966 census show 1.9 percent of old people living in homes for the aged and disabled, 1.7 percent in hospitals, and 0.9 percent in psychiatric institutions, an overall figure of 4.4 percent.[36]

Superficially, then, it would seem that a side effect of the late-nineteenth-century policy of tightening up the offer of outrelief to the aged, with the express effect of "encouraging to some extent thrift and family affection"[37]

29. PP.1895 XIV xliii.
30. Troll, "The Family of Later Life."
31. From PP.1852–3 LXXXVIII Part I, ccc–cccxliv.
32. From *Census of England and Wales*, 1891.
33. From PP.1909, XXXVII, 37; PP.1909, XXXVIII, 24.
34. *Old Age Pensioners and Aged Paupers* (PP.1913 LV, 8–9).
35. *Persons in receipt of Poor Relief, England and Wales* (PP.1930–1 XXV, 23).
36. *Sample Census 1966 England and Wales*. Housing Tables, Part I, Table 27.
37. PP.1895 XIV, 80; cf. ibid. 117. –

was actually greatly to increase the workhouse population and remove absolutely from the old any possibility of maintaining affective or small-scale help relationships with relatives. The implementation of a policy based on the popular notion that "the refusal of outdoor relief tends to make the friends and relations of the poor more willing to assist than they would be if outdoor relief were freely given" and that "if they think that the alternative to their assistance will be that their friends will enter the workhouse they are more likely to assist"[38] seems at the very least to have been ineffective and indeed actually to have been counterproductive. It is, in fact, clear that one effect of this policy was to force into the workhouse many old people who were unable to support themselves and who had no kin able or willing to do so.[39] Moreover, the number of such people increased during the nineteenth century as a result of the changes in employment opportunities referred to above. However, in many areas the strong moralistic strain in Victorian Poor Law policy,[40] involving as it did discrimination against the "undeserving" poor, had the further effect of taking some old people away from relatives who, though willing to help them, were not, in the words of one observer, "quite satisfactory"[41] to the authorities, and of putting these old people into the workhouse, since this was the only way in which they would be granted relief.[42]

So it is clear that the introduction of a pension as a right allowed some old people to leave the workhouse who were kept there previously as a result of administrative decisions. Does this then mean that there are now more old people in institutions as a result of decisions by their relatives to keep them there? This interpretation does not wholly stand up if one makes a more detailed study of the institutional population at different points in time, for the striking thing is its constancy of composition.

An important finding of research into the status of the institutionalized aged today has been that, despite popular opinion, they are not in general people rejected by their relatives. Townsend, for example, has shown that the institutionalized aged are heavily biased towards the never-married, the widowed, the childless, and those with few other relatives.[43] The data that are available on the prepension period suggest very similar patterns by age, marital status, and family structure. Age, with its associated infirmities and fall in income, was clearly an important factor, though, since the nineteenth-century institutionalization rates tended to be higher for the sixty-five

38. PP.1895 XIV, 222.
39. PP.1895 XIV xix, 815, 910, and passim.
40. The evolution of this policy is well described in PP.1909 XXXVII.
41. PP.1903 V, 64.
42. Ibid.
43. P. Townsend, "The Effects of Family Structure on the Likelihood of Admission to an Institution in Old Age," in *Social Structure and the Family,* ed. E. Shanas and G. F. Streib (Englewood Cliffs, N.J., 1965); P. Townsend, *The Last Refuge* (London, 1962), chaps. 3 and 11.

to seventy-four age groups (particularly for men) and lower for the seventy-five and over group (particularly for women), the overall effect of age seems to have been smaller.[44] Data on marital status were never systematically collected but one observer supports the view that the unmarried and the widowed were the most likely to be institutionalized in old age,[45] and a survey conducted by Booth in 1891 gives figures on the inmates of the Poplar workhouse which, when related to the total aged population, show clearly that the currently married were much less likely to be workhouse inmates even in an area in which outrelief had been almost wholly abolished.[46]

Firmer information is available on the kinship structure of the workhouse population as a result of inquiries conducted by Edith Sellers in the early 1900s in an attempt to ascertain the possible effect of the introduction of pensions on the workhouse population.[47] She describes researches into the situation in at least twelve workhouses, some in London and some in rural areas, and estimated that out of just over 2900 inmates about 45 percent were so infirm that they needed constant nursing, while another 14 percent also required considerable nursing care. The former group she adjudged unable to leave the workhouses, while none of the latter group, even if they had relatives, could persuade a relative to care for them if they brought a pension of 5/- with them. Of the rest 37 percent reported having not one single living relative while another 30 percent had only a distant relative or had "lost sight of their relatives," usually through migration. Thus, out of the entire population of these workhouses, only about 16 percent had any relatives with whom they might even hypothetically have lived.

Thus the general impression to be gathered from these data is that both in the prepension and postpension period the majority of the institutionalized population are not living in the community either because they need intensive medical attention or because they have no relatives to help them. Clearly, then, in the past, the overall numerical significance of those compelled to stay in institutions because of administrative decisions was rela-

44. For example, in 1851 for men the institutionalized figures were 3.6 percent for the sixty-five to seventy-four age group and 5.0 percent for the seventy-five and over age group. For women they were 2.2 percent and 3.5 percent respectively. In 1961 the figures were respectively 2.6 percent, 6.9 percent, 2.5 percent, and 8.8 percent. For sources see notes 31–36 above.

45. PP.1895 XV, 900.

46. C. Booth, "Enumeration and Classification of Paupers, and State Pensions for the Aged," *Journal of the Royal Statistical Society* 55 (1891):606.

47. E. Sellers, "Old Age Pensions and the 'Belongingless' Poor. A Workhouse Census," *Contemporary Review* 93 (1908):147–57; cf. the impressions of a Buckinghamshire agricultural labourer in PP.1895 XV, 784; similar data were gathered from a number of Scottish poorhouses by the 1903 Committee on the Aged Pensioners Bill (PP.1903 XV, 134–37). In the Dundee poorhouse, out of 322 aged inmates, 30 percent were in the hospital and 45 percent had no relations. In the Govan workhouse, of 296 aged inmates, 24 percent needed hospital treatment and a further 31 percent had no relatives, while in the Glasgow poorhouse, out of 965 inmates, 45 percent were adjudged mentally or physically unfit to leave, and a further 27 percent had no kin available for living with.

tively small. Equally clearly, not many of those in workhouses had relatives who might have cared for them even by middle-class Victorian standards. But an interesting fact is that if one compares the situation seventy years ago with that today probably about the same proportion of old people who had children alive actually lived in institutions even though they were relatively healthy, and this in spite of the unpleasant living conditions offered by the workhouses.[48] If we turn attention to residence patterns in the wider community some plausible interpretations of this finding seem possible.

Unfortunately the quantitative data on residence patterns for the pre-pension period are at present patchy. So far only part of the necessary data for a comparison of residence patterns in 1851 with those of the present day have been gathered, but some interesting points have already emerged.[49]

In Britain today it is clear that most old people either live with relatives or live so near to them that contact can take place on a day-to-day or week-to-week basis. In 1962, for example, only 22 percent of old people lived alone and 33 percent lived only with a spouse.[50]

However, in all communities so far studied the nineteenth-century figures are even lower. For 1851 preliminary analysis of data for the northern half of Scotland suggests that about 11 percent of the aged population lived alone and 16 percent with no one but a spouse. In these data little difference seems to appear between urban and rural areas. In the English cotton-manufacturing town of Preston, however, only 6 percent of the aged lived alone and only 13 percent with only a spouse (though there is some evidence to suggest [and this will be discussed below] that the Lancashire cotton towns may have had particularly strong parent-child relationships).[51] For rural England little data are available but in a peasant farming and handloom weaving area of rural Lancashire I have found only 3 percent living alone and 21 percent with a spouse.

If one controls for marital status, the differences become even more marked. Taking first the married, in Scotland in 1966 about 77 percent of

48. In 1906 about 6 percent of old people were in Poor Law institutions (PP.1909 XXXVII, 37; PP.1909 XXXVIII, 24) and it is reasonable to assume that about 50 percent of these were effectively hospitalized (PP.1903 V, 131–37, Sellers 1908) so that about 3 percent were in the equivalent of present-day old people's residential homes. If Sellers's figures are generalizable then 37 percent of these would have had no living relatives and 30 percent would have had only a distant relative or have lost sight of any relatives. Thus about 1 percent of all old people were institutional inmates even though they had contact with some fairly close relatives. An unknown proportion of the remaining institutional population would have had at least one child but have lost contact with that child. Today about 1.7 percent of old people are in residential homes and of these about one-half have a living child (Townsend, "Effects of Family Structure") so that rather under 1 percent of old people are in institutions even though they have a child.

49. The relevant data are being collected in the National Sample from the 1851 Census of Great Britain, based in the Department of Sociology at the University of Edinburgh under the direction of the author and supported by the Social Science Research Council.

50. Shanas et al., *Old People*, chap. 7.

51. Anderson, *Family Structure*, chaps. 5 and 10.

married old people lived only with their spouse.[52] This compares with 40 percent in the northern part of Scotland in 1851, 37 percent in Preston, and 38 percent in the environs of Preston. Among those not currently married 43 percent in Scotland lived alone in 1966, the same figure as found for the whole of Britain by the 1962 survey. In 1851 in the area of Scotland so far surveyed, the figure was 24 percent, while in Preston it was only 10 percent and in rural Lancashire only 6 percent.

Superficially this might suggest a major fall in family cohesion over the past 115 years. The pension may have allowed old people to move out of institutions. But was its only effect to compel old people to live and die alone in squalid little homes? A number of factors force one to search for other interpretations. First, if, instead of taking the proportion of old people living alone, one takes the proportion of nonmarried old people not living with any relatives, a rather different picture emerges; this figure is 49 percent today and varies in the nineteenth-century communities between 22 percent (in Preston) and 41 percent (in Scotland).[53] Clearly in the nineteenth century there were pressures not to live alone on old people who could not find a relative to live with. Most of these old people were classified in the census as lodgers or were technically household heads but had usually just one lodger living with them. In Preston no fewer than 17 percent of the nonmarried over sixty-fives (for men the figure was 21 percent) were living in the subordinate status of lodger, a status which today is very uncommon among the elderly.

Just what these pressures for coresidence were is more difficult to assess but they were almost certainly financial. Particularly for those living on poor relief or at a level approaching it, rent would make up a very significant element in any budget. Cottage rents in Lancashire started at a level only marginally below normal outrelief rates[54] while even the cost of a bed in the family bedroom would have absorbed over a third of a normal outrelief payment.[55] Since Poor Law outrelief at this time seldom exceeded the cost of a minimum subsistence budget excluding rent,[56] some economy on rent was clearly required of many of the poorer sections of the community. Similar factors operated to encourage the married to share with others. One Leicester framework knitter noted in 1845 that he went to live with his wife's parents because they could not afford 2s.6d. a week for a house[57] and there are other similar references for Lancashire.[58]

52. *Sample Census 1966, Scotland*, Household Composition Tables, Table 37.

53. Data are from ibid. and from enumeration book samples.

54. *Morning Chronicle Supplement*, December 24, 1849.

55. *Fifth Report of the Medical Officer to the Privy Council* (PP.1863 XXV) 312, 136–37, 339; Manchester Statistical Society, *Enquiry into the Educational and Other Conditions of a District of Deansgate, Manchester*, (Manchester, 1864), p. 12.

56. Anderson, *Family Structure*, pp. 31, 201.

57. PP.1845 XV, 283.

58. Anderson, *Family Structure*, p. 220, n. 24.

So one factor which probably underlies this change in residence pattern between 1851 and today is that adequate pensions have made it possible for the old to live alone. It is also clear that the Poor Law authorities put more direct pressure on both the widowed and the aged to share accommodation (particularly with kin), and many Guardians almost automatically took those unable to do so into workhouses.[59] Even where direct pressure was not used, it was often stated that low outrelief was justified because it would encourage children and other kin to care for relatives.[60]

However, there are also a number of reasons why declines in kinship-based coresidence do not necessarily indicate true changes in family relationships. Recent data on how often people today see relatives show contact to be very frequent for most old people. In the 1962 survey 53 percent had seen a child within the previous forty-eight hours and 66 percent within the previous week. If the 24 percent who are childless are excluded, 86 percent had seen a child in the previous week and only 6 percent had not seen a child in the previous month. Of those who had not seen a child during the previous week (including the childless), half had seen some other relative. In all, therefore, only 17 percent of all old people had seen no relative during the previous week, and almost half of these claimed to have no relatives at all.[61]

In the prepension period evidence on contact is much less easy to assess. However, in a period before mass literacy and modern techniques of communication and in a situation of very high population turnover within towns as well as of mass migration, it was much easier for families to become split up more or less accidentally, and it seems certain that some old people, particularly those left behind in villages by their migrant children, did lose sight of their children forever.[62] Moreover, some people claimed that it was in the interests of children to disappear, because they thus avoided the need to pay poor relief.[63] This is interesting as yet another example of ways in which the prepension social security system, with its policy of assessment of relatives, may actually have had consequences counterproductive to the aims of maintaining family cohesion which its official ideology claimed to support.

Another important factor is that data on coresidence, taken alone, are not necessarily a good indicator of harmonious family relationships. Young and Willmott have written of Bethnal Green in the 1950s: "The couples who choose to live with parents are the exception. Most people do not

59. E.g., PP.1844 XX, 23; PP.1895 XIV passim.
60. PP.1844 XX, 29; PP.1895 XIV, 222 and passim.
61. Shanas et al., *Old People,* chap. 6.
62. *R. C. On The Poor Laws: Enquiry in certain unions into cases of refusal of out relief,* PP.1910 LII, 9–10; Booth, *Aged Poor,* from Pontefract; Sellers, "Old Age Pensions," pp. 148–49.
63. *R. C. On The Poor Laws: Effect of Outdoor Relief on Wages and Conditions of Employment,* PP.1909 XLIII, 339.

want to live with them, they want to live near them;"[64] and this conclusion helps to explain the apparent paradox that one of the most closely knit urban communities yet described by sociologists has one of the highest figures yet reported for old people living alone, with over a quarter of its aged in this situation.

It is clear that this view that sharing was not necessarily desirable was also common in the nineteenth century and that it was frequently held by both parents and children. Thus the high rates of coresidence, typically compelled, I have suggested, by poverty and sometimes directly by the Guardians in many cases obviously involved considerable tensions.

One respondent to Booth's 1890s survey noted: "Children living near sometimes offer a widowed parent a home, but old people as a rule are averse to living with their children and it seldom answers";[65] in Hartimere it was noted that children did offer a home to their parents but "their presence is seldom welcome," and in Birmingham it was observed that "the numerous applications for almshouses would make it appear that the arrangement is not always acceptable, either to parents or children." It is clear, moreover, that it was not just interpersonal incompatibility which was at work here though many references to this occur[66] and in some of these cases, the old people "are of intemperate habits and their families pay to get them kept in the poorhouse."[67] In Scotland, and this seems also to have been relevant elsewhere,[68] the small size of the children's homes, the overcrowding, and the wish to have a greater amount of amenity and privacy were specifically noted.[69]

The most important problem, however, seems to have been the feeling of dependence which living together with children imposed on the old people. It is now a well-established principle of the sociology of kinship that relationships of mutual interdependence are those most likely to be maintained on a harmonious basis and that this will be particularly true if the interdependence is on a day-to-day rather than a long-term basis.[70] This stress on short-term mutual interdependence, I have argued elsewhere, is likely to be particularly important in populations living at the subsistence line because unless resources are used in the optimum pattern of social relationships, actual starvation is likely to ensue.[71] It is perhaps not surprising then that

64. M. Young and P. Willmott, *Family and Kinship in East London* (London, 1957), p. 20; cf. also Townsend, *The Family Life of Old People*, pp. 25–26.

65. Booth, *Aged Poor*, on St. Columb Major.

66. E.g., *Reports to the Committee of the Liverpool Domestic Missionary Society*, 1860, p. 15; *Correspondence and report relevant to the case of Duke William Beale*, PP.1849 XLVII; PP.1895 XIV, 44–5, 123; PP.1903 V, 134; Booth, *Aged Poor*, on Hertford.

67. PP.1903 V, 134; cf. PP.1849 XLVII.

68. Cf. Anderson, *Family Structure*, pp. 49–51.

69. PP.1895 XIV 498; cf. also Sellers, "Old Age Pensions," pp. 148–49.

70. I have summarized and attempted to formalize this general perspective in Anderson, *Family Structure*, esp. chaps. 2 and 12. For specific reference to the importance of interdependence in harmonious relationships between old people and relatives today, see, e.g., Townsend, *The Family Life of Old People*, chap. 5.

71. Anderson, *Family Structure*, chaps. 2 and 11.

there is a great deal of evidence which suggests that old people who were able to make some contribution to the family with whom they lived were most likely to be welcomed, while those who imposed a particular strain on the family were most likely to be rejected. The clearest example of this can also be used to explain the high levels of residence of aged parents with children in Preston and probably in the other Lancashire cotton towns. Writing about Stockport in 1842, a Poor Law assistant commissioner said:

> Even the aged members of a manufacturing community have a different social position from that of the same class of persons in many parts of England. . . . Many . . . , especially aged females, afford a service very appropriate to their condition, and of not inconsiderable value, by keeping house and taking care of the youngest children, while the working part of the family are absent at their work. . . . With such assistance in the care of her household, during her absence at the factory, many an industrious married woman is enabled to add 8s., 10s., or 12s. weekly to the income brought in by her husband and the elder of her children. It is not uncommon for aged females to become domesticated for the purpose of affording service of this nature in the families of those who have no elderly relatives to support.[72]

There are many similar cases of children somewhat willingly giving a home to relatives who were able to give help of this kind.[73]

Another important positive incentive, and one particularly significant in the present context, was the ability to bring cash resources into the house. The most interesting comment of all perhaps is that of a ninety-year-old married man who lived with one of his children, when asked for his reactions to the introduction of the pension in 1909. Before the pension, he said, "Often 'ave we thought as 'ow it would be a-best for us to go, and sometimes a-most 'ave prayed to be took: for we was only a burden to our children as ke'p us. . . . But now we wants to go on livin' forever, 'cos we gives 'em the ten shillin' a week, and it pays 'em to 'ave us along with 'em."[74] The vice-chairman of the Manchester Board of Guardians, referring to his own private fund for giving pensions to old people, referred to the case of "a woman whom we had been helping for some time. I gave her help, although I heard she had two sons living in the town who were doing nothing for her at all. She was living with an unmarried daughter and I gave her 4s. a week. When it became known that she was getting this 4s. then there was a competition between the two sons as to who should get the old lady into one of their

72. *Report by the Assistant Poor Law Commissioners sent to enquire into the state of the population of Stockport,* PP.1842 XXXV, 7.
73. E.g., *Morning Chronicle Supplement,* January 1, 1850; *First Report of the Commissioners on the Employment of Children in Factories,* PP.1833 XX D2, 3; E. Waugh, *Factory Folk during the Cotton Famine* (Manchester, 1862), p. 85; PP.1895 XIV, 168; Booth, *Aged Poor,* on Ormskirk and Whitehaven.
74. H. Avonson, "Liberalism in the Village," *Nation,* May 18, 1912.

houses, because she was getting something."[75] A Birmingham artisan engineer claimed: "If it were possible for the Poor Law system to be more liberal in granting a little more Outdoor Relief, then I am certain the great bulk of the working classes would hail with pleasure the opportunity of their aged parents living with them rather than having to go into the house";[76] and a Birmingham carpenter said: "I believe that many aged women would be able to find a home among their friends if they had some little income that would relieve their friends from the burden of their keep."[77] These assertions also received more tangible support from the experience of 5/- pensions paid from colliery disaster funds which, it was reported, even induced nonrelatives to care for aged widows.[78]

Those who had no such contribution available clearly found this a topic for concern. An old woman in Huddersfield who lived, together with her husband, with her married daughter, told the *Morning Chronicle* investigator that her husband "was wearing himself away fretting at the idea of being a burden upon the husband of his daughter."[79] Another observer commented that "so far from feeling pauperised the aged mother (who received a regular payment from the Guardians) enjoys a sense of security and independence, and is glad to know that she is relieving a good son of part of the burden of supporting her."[80]

At the other extreme, where old people introduced a special disadvantage into the household, it is clear that help, if given at all, was given unwillingly. It was observed by one Manchester witness that an old man was less popular as a sharing relative than an old woman:

> He is more in the way, he expects not only a larger portion of the food, but to share in the better portions. He does not fit into the household of a working family as an old woman does, and is not so useful in domestic matters. His welcome is colder, and he desires to get out of the way, and goes to the workhouse. A decent old woman will cling to a house where she may be regarded as the drudge rather than as the grandmother or the aunt, and she will wedge in both day and night without encroaching much on the means of the family.[81]

75. PP.1895 XIV, 265.
76. PP.1895 XV, 795.
77. PP.1895 XV, 912; and cf. Booth, *Aged Poor*, on Partington and Bradford. Small savings (Booth, ibid., on Bradford) or a cottage and garden (Booth, ibid., on Tarvin) also seem to have fulfilled a similar function.
78. PP.1903 V, 51.
79. *Morning Chronicle*, December 3, 1849.
80. PP.1909 XLIII, 187.
81. PP.1909 XXXVII, 908–09; and cf. Booth, *Aged Poor,* on Mansfield and Whitehaven and pp. 425–26. While in a peasant society old men can continue to help around the farm, and anyway are in a position of some power over their children through their ability to control inheritance, in a community based on wage labor employment they have neither control nor a useful function in the house. Old women's power may, by contrast, actually increase in urban industrial areas, since the functions that they perform may be relatively more important to their children.

Where a household-means test was imposed, a great reluctance to take in relatives, particularly by married daughters, who were not legally liable for support, was often noticed since "the effect of this policy is to prevent persons offering lodging and personal attendance to aged relations, unless they can also find them food and clothing without stinting their own families."[82] Finally, at least one case was noted where nonrelatives refused to take in an old lady because: "They would not always have the relieving officer poking and prying into their affairs."[83]

It seems likely then that the pension was important in reducing tensions of coresidence by reducing in most cases this feeling of obligation and dependence. Certainly present-day studies point usually to the mutual interdependence of sharing kin and only usually describe tensions of this kind in cases where the old person introduces special disadvantages into the household. Sharing today can more often be voluntary.[84] However, it is clear that adverse reactions to this lack of interdependence were not just confined to help in the form of coresidence. From Wycombe, Booth received the reply: "Parents are unwilling to ask help from children and expect very little";[85] while a Norfolk trade-union leader reported that not only did children dislike being forced totally to care for their parents but the old women did not like it either; "they do not like to feel dependent fully on their sons."[86] Later Booth described the case of an old lady whose sons supported her. They made no objection but: "She felt that her sons offered to keep the house going for her, to pay the rent of their home . . . and she felt that she did not like being dependent on them altogether. That was her idea."[87] Where relief was actually compelled by the Guardians the tensions were even more severe. From Chipping Sodbury, Booth received the reply that the "aged prefer a pittance from the parish (reported as their due) to compulsory maintenance by children; compulsion makes such aid very bitter."[88] From Cambridgeshire it was reported that Poor Law officials "agree that such collecting causes much friction among the families concerned. Children round on their parents for informing the officers of their whereabouts, or parents round on the officers for pressing the children, contending that they have a right to relief in old age."[89] It is clear, then, that the obligation to assist was often a source of tension between parents and children throughout the nineteenth century. The "quality" of relationships were thus clearly worsened in these cases.

82. PP.1909 XXXVII, 936; cf. similar cases in Norwich and Ipswich where children left home and lived by themselves saying, "Why should we stay at home and never have a penny to ourselves?" (PP.1909 XLIII, 63).

83. PP.1909, XXXVI, 936.

84. Townsend, *The Family Life of Old People*, chap. 3; J. Tunstall, *Old and Alone* (London, 1966), chap. 2.

85. Booth, *Aged Poor.*

86. PP.1895 XV, 363.

87. PP.1895 XV, 364.

88. Booth, *Aged Poor.*

89. PP.1909 XLI, 338.

However, tensions were also caused between an old person's children by the obligation to assist. In a heterogeneous society where old people could seldom sanction deviant children, and in a situation where no scales for child assistance were officially adopted until 1940, it is not surprising that children frequently were unable to agree over assistance to aged parents. It was reported from a number of areas that children solved this problem by putting parents onto poor relief in order to make the Guardians lay down a fair division of responsibility.[90] The parents were in consequence technically made paupers with all the disabilities that this implied, while they were nevertheless fully supported by their children. The inevitably arbitrary nature of assessment which resulted from the near impossibility of making adequate investigation of each case[91] only made things worse.[92] When the authorities reacted by assuming that old people had some help from relatives or friends, as they often did when faced with an impossible task, the inevitable consequence was suffering for some old people, increased tensions, and great efforts on all sides to conceal resources and aid.[93] In terms of regular cash support, there is, moreover, no doubt that on the part of the children there was widespread resistance to supporting their parents, although smaller contributions on an occasional basis were common. Less than 20 percent of the extra–Metropolitan Unions to which Booth wrote in the early 1890s asking, among other things, about how well relatives supported the aged, gave replies which, when I attempted to classify them, could be categorized as "well"; and many of these were qualified and most involved only partial support.[94] About 20 percent gave replies which could only be classified as "badly" and in these areas there are frequent references to the need felt by Guardians to use compulsion.[95] Interestingly, areas with large numbers of old people on poor relief were not much less likely to give "bad" replies than areas with few on poor relief.

Some of the more immediate reactions by children to supporting parents clearly shocked contemporaries: "They, instead of desiring a lengthened existence to their parents, almost, in some instances, wish that their existence were terminated."[96] The East Anglia Assistant Commissioner in 1834 was clearly shocked when: "In the account book of an adjoining parish,

90. PP.1895 XIV, 165–6. An interesting question which seems to have been little explored is the ways in which in different societies children allocate among themselves responsibility for the care of aged relatives and the principles on which these allocations are based.

91. PP.1895 XIV, xxi, 332; PP.1834 XXVIII, 543A, and passim; PP.1870 XI, 289.

92. PP.1895, xxi–xxii, 779; PP.1909 XXXVII, 554.

93. See, e.g., PP.1895 XIV, xx; PP.1834 XVIII, 338A; PP.1909 XXXVII, 522, 747–8.

94. E.g., from Sheffield: "Children are not on the whole slow to recognise filial obligations, there is much natural affection and manly independence. Near relatives show a fair amount of kindness." Or from Bellingham: "Children and relatives help to a large extent, the kindly feeling being increased by frequent intermarriage."

95. E.g., from Berwick: "Children help to a very limited extent. If a son crosses into Scotland, guardians cannot compel him to assist his parents." Or from Teesdale: "Children do not as a rule help; they themselves marry improvidently. Neighbourly help among the poor is a common and pleasant feature."

96. PP.1895 XIV, 248.

I saw the following entry 'To —————— for nursing her mother during her illness.'"[97] In 1909 in Faversham it was reported that "some inmates of the
workhouse go and live with their children in the summer, either doing a
little field work, or looking after grandchildren, while the wife goes out to
the fields." However, in the winter the old people were sent back to the
workhouse.[98] In one town it was reported that men earning 40s. and 50s.
per week threatened to turn their mothers-in-law out into the streets if the
poor relief were withdrawn.[99]

How can we understand these attitudes? Many contemporaries blamed
this kind of behavior very firmly on weak Poor Law administration. Octavia
Hill, for example, believed that strictness had an immediate effect. "Directly
you begin to feel the people making efforts for themselves and for one another, directly you remove the extraneous grants, you find the relatives
coming forward."[100] Taking this as their creed, some unions more or less
completely abolished outrelief even for the aged, supplementing self-help
by the aged with carefully discriminating charity aimed at encouraging the
"deserving" and condemning the so-called "undeserving" to the workhouse.
One advocate of this view, aiming, be it noted, at "the permanent benefit
of the working class" and "to restore relationships to the condition which
God intended for them," argued: "If relations do not contribute voluntarily
we think the parents ought to suffer, and we offer the house, and, if the house
is accepted then, and not till then, do we put the law into force."[101] In some
areas relief was simply refused to those believed to have relatives able to
assist them, and in some cases this went beyond the legally required children
to relations who it was argued were "morally liable" to maintain the poor
old person in question.[102]

As might be expected, when a serious investigation was at last made into
the policy of these "strict" areas, major suffering was revealed.[103] It is clear,
in retrospect, that some of the old people concerned had no relatives to help
them, and most had none who on any reasonable grounds could have given
more than casual assistance. As the special commissioner reported, "In no
case was the support by relatives increased through the refusal of outrelief.
In practically all the cases they were so poor themselves that they were not
in a position to give systematic assistance. If such additional help had been
given, it would have been at the cost of the physical efficiency of the younger
generation."[104] Working-class resistance to supporting parents on a regular,
total-support, week-by-week basis was clearly based on their own abject

97. PP.1834 XXVII, 230A.
98. PP.1909 XLIII, 159.
99. PP.1909 XXXVII, 72.
100. PP.1895 XIV, 53.
101. PP.1895 XIV, 227–29.
102. PP.1895 XIV, 347, 244; PP.1909 XXXVII, 910.
103. *R. C. On The Poor Laws: Enquiry in certain unions into cases of refusal of out relief,*
PP.1910 LII.
104. Ibid., p. 60.

poverty, resulting from low wages. All investigations of social conditions in the nineteenth century have shown a life cycle of poverty with below-subsistence destitution in childhood, in the period after marriage when children had been born but none were working, and again in old age.[105] Even in Preston with its well-paid cotton workers and ready employment for wives and children, over half of all families for whom I could make an income estimate, were in primary poverty at the middle point in their life cycle.[106] In the low-pay-wage labor/agriculture areas of eastern England where rural pauperism reached its peak levels, and in London with its mass of casual employment, most married children were themselves technically starving without the need to contribute to parental support as well, though contributions of 1s. a week were nevertheless sometimes exacted from them.[107] The basic problem, of course, as one contemporary wrote, was "that the children's own families are costing most, just at the time of (greatest parental) need."[108]

However, a further objection was also beginning to be raised among the poor by the 1890s, and this was based on ideas of citizenship. It came to be believed that the contribution of a citizen during his working life, in whatever task, entitled him to some kind of pension in old age. This philosophy was clearly rejected by the dominant groups within the middle class but in many areas the idea became current that a certain amount of outrelief was more or less a right. Under these circumstances resistance among relatives of the poor was further increased,[109] particularly since often the only consequence of assistance by kin was a saving on the rates of the full amount of the assistance.[110]

Under these circumstances it is hardly surprising that resistance was strong, hardly surprising that every effort was made to conceal income from the Guardians, hardly surprising in the words of an old agricultural laborer that "it causes a good deal of ill feeling among their wives and that, and causes things very unpleasant,"[111] and hardly surprising in view of the ideas on interdependence discussed above, that old people "would sooner struggle on in poverty and distress than apply there and have it demanded from their children."[112] In Scotland, where destitution was worst and allowances lowest the minister of the High Church in Edinburgh remarked that respect for parents and "a disposition to aid them as far as they possibly can is con-

105. Rowntree, *Poverty*; also J. O. Foster, *Capitalism and Class Consciousness in Earlier Nineteenth Century Oldham* (Ph.D. dissertation, University of Cambridge, 1967), pp. 334–42.

106. Anderson, *Family Structure*, p. 31.

107. There are widespread references to poverty inhibiting aid to parents. Cf. Booth, *Aged Poor*, passim; PP.1895, XIV, 244ff, 344ff, 362, 431, 439, 483; PP.1895, XV, 819, 859; and the data for Lancashire in Anderson, *Family Structure*, chap. 11.

108. Booth, *Aged Poor*, from Warwick.

109. PP.1909 XXXVII, 551; PP.1909 XLIII, 187, 189.

110. PP.1895 XV, 926; PP.1834 XXVII, 396A.

111. PP.1895 XV, 793.

112. PP.1895 XV, 864.

siderably broken down by destitution" and that far from destitution inducing affection "it renders them callous and reckless even in regard to themselves, personally" — if any help was given it certainly "cannot be permanent"[113] — while the minister of St. John's stated that the low rate of allowances, far from promoting kindly feelings among relations "tends to destroy their habits, and to extinguish the very feeling of human nature."[114]

The evidence therefore would seem to suggest that, far from maintaining good relationships with children, strict Poor Law administration tended to undermine them by forcing a one-sided obligation from which the givers received little return, on those who were often already below the subsistence level. It also led to a wide range of subterfuges being adopted by children to reduce their liability, some of which further inhibited parent-child relationships. It is interesting that a number of Booth's respondents noted that in part of their areas where wages were higher and employment conditions better, more help was given.[115] Also interesting is the observation by one clearly sensitive observer, commenting on an area where poor relief was generously given, to the effect that a "weak sense of responsibility exists side by side with much natural affection and concern for each other's health and well being between parents and children among farm labourers." Both parents and children resist children's contributions but "all this does not imply want of affection but rather the existence of an institution — outrelief — to whose privileges the poor think they have a claim, and to the acknowledgement of which they have become accustomed."[116]

Conclusion

In the light of the above discussion, the argument that the introduction of state-provided income-maintenance provision undermines family relationships seems extremely oversimplistic. It is based on a false historical premise, on a partial and oversimple definition of what a "strong" family relationship consists of, and on a lack of understanding of the basis of harmonious kinship interaction.

It is quite clear that even when the law required contributions and made strong attempts to exact them, it only succeeded very partially in doing so. In part, this was for ideological reasons, as a citizenship idea that a contribution to society through a working life gave one a right to a reasonably comfortable old age became more firmly established. But above all the enforcement of support from kin failed for other reasons. First, it seems difficult or impossible to enforce kinship contribution in a society where some

---

113. PP.1844 XX, 48.
114. PP.1844 XX, 89, cf. 65.
115. Booth, *Aged Poor*, from Cheadle, Ashby-de-la-Zouch and Cardiff.
116. PP.1909 XLIII, 189; cf. PP.1895 XIV, 248.

individuals can reasonably claim either their absolute incomes are too low to make contributions possible, or that they have other and more pressing obligations. In the nineteenth century the other obligations of the young married man with children were clearly overwhelming, but the fact that poverty can only be defined as a relative and not an absolute concept makes this argument equally applicable in all societies. If it had been possible to distinguish certain groups who could clearly be exempted on grounds of income and other obligations, a workable policy could perhaps have been established; the extreme heterogeneity of the population, however, precluded such a solution. Given that children were at different points in the life cycle with a different number of dependents, how did one determine a fair cutoff point and a fair sliding scale of contributions? Given that family incomes might well vary according to the earnings of wives and children, a problem arose in determining which income (family head's income or family's income) should be taken into account and in this context there were clear implications for the motivations of supplementary earners to seek employment. Different seasonal and life cycle patterns of income and differences in rents and other costs of living all made the task of prescribing scales that much more difficult; even more of a problem was the fact that some people were able to make contributions in kind from their own garden plots to their relatives but such contributions were normally excluded by the Guardians on the perfectly reasonable bureaucratic excuse that they were impossible to monitor or estimate in value. Yet a further problem was the constant clash of principle between encouraging self-help in the younger generation through contributions to friendly societies, sick clubs, and savings, and taking income from this generation to support their parents, thus threatening to perpetuate a cycle of poverty. All these problems may be clearer to us today but they are no nearer a solution.

Furthermore, it is quite clear that the forcing of contributions from relatives only strengthens family relationships if one accepts that the only indication of family strength is in terms of economic assistance. In practice, as we have seen, tensions were frequently increased both by the need to contribute and by the pressures applied by the authorities, so that, while the economic functions of kinship rose in importance, affective functions frequently declined. This problem, once again, does not seem to be confined to the nineteenth century. Exactly similar conflicts appear frequently to occur in the British university student-grants system where all but the poorest parents are supposed to make some contribution towards their children's support.

Finally, the underlying model of kinship behavior implied by the Victorian analysis seems misguided. I have argued that kinship relationships are likely to be strongest in situations of interdependence rather than of one-sided dependency. Thus, a comparison even with the present day suggests that, by making possible a relationship more approaching equality, and one where mutual interdependence of assistance can occur, the development of state-provided income maintenance in old age has markedly decreased the tensions and conflicts in family relationships and has made functional relationships in many areas more, not less, possible. While income is a scarce resource for most families, with great competition for its expenditure, the remaining needs of the aged tend to demand time and affection and for most women, and at least until recently, these have not been particularly scarce. Thus it seems that once the tension-inducing cash-support functions have been removed, the family is able to complement the state's provision of income-maintenance services with better provision of affective and idiosyncratic functions of a kind difficult to bureaucratize and not involving demands on scarce familial resources. In consequence, over time, a major improvement in the "quality" of relationships has become possible.

4. Bureaucratization of Old Age: Determinants of the Process, Possible Safeguards, and Reorientation *Paul Paillat*

Individual aging is an unavoidable phenomenon built into every type of living organism, but the aging of population is a new development — new because it was neither perceptible nor recognized before the twentieth century. The aging of population was first experienced in France, which as early as the latter half of the nineteenth century reached a rate of aging recorded in other countries some fifty years later. This phenomenon, the aging of populations, started and developed so insidiously that some time elapsed before demographers were able to understand its underlying causes and to measure its implications accurately. It should be stressed that only a proper demographic analysis makes it possible to avoid errors of judgment which result from common-sense analyses. Demographic analysis is a positive counterpart to constraints imposed by any statistical approach.

Roles may shift from families to the whole community under many influences, but no reversal of these steps is possible within the contemporary age structure of aging populations. For instance, how would it be possible to entrust families with responsibilities for the elderly when there are no families at all or when existing families no longer have the same patterns? Who, for example, will take care of aged childless couples, a frequent case in France since the decline of fertility and the death of sons in wars? In rural areas what kind of social system will substitute for the former family network broken by the out-migration of younger generations? Who is going to face the increasing number of aged people in a poor state of health, the so-called "surviving invalids"? One may wonder whether the pendulum has swung too far from the equilibrium point; thus it might be good to allow for a new role to be given to families (if any) in the implementation of social policy. As a consequence of an aging population there is a disturbing change which is worth a thorough analysis. This change is, and will be, a major social issue: no country will escape it, but for the time being it is more significant in industrialized countries with low fertility. However, due attention should also be paid to the expected quickening rate of aging in the less developed countries of today.

In developed nations the numerical importance of the aged population is increasing, but contrarily — and in sort of a counteraction to this trend — its economic and social importance is dwindling. The measures which have been taken under the double pressures of individual needs and social progress have resulted in the adoption of a variety of regulations and the creation of hundreds of organizations for their implementation. No old person, with the very limited exception of those in the most-favored social strata, can expect during the final stage of his life to be allocated some financial resources without a previous membership in one or more pension funds, without fulfilling various conditions (e.g., age, seniority, length of membership, amount of past dues, and so on) which require blanks to be filled and records to be completed. After due acknowledgment of his pension rights, the retiree confronted with a number of difficulties of various types, which often increase with his age, will be more and more referred to social services related to different organizations, i.e., municipalities, pension funds, mutual societies and associations. To the extent that employees of these organizations are guided by routine regulations, the old person will soon find himself in the grip of the bureaucracy or, put another way, he will be dependent on an external structure, the operation and rationale of which he does not know or understand.

What factors have transformed the situation of yesterday into the situation of today? What kind of short-term palliatives are possible? More ambitiously, what kind of long-term reorientations are possible? These are the issues to be discussed in this chapter.

Factors Involved in the Past Evolution and in the Situation of Today

Demographic, economic, social, and technical factors which have affected the situation of old people will be discussed in order. Of course, these factors are not independent; this plan of analysis is only adopted for the sake of clarity.

Demographic Factors

Comments here will be limited to the populations of industrialized countries, particularly the Western countries. However, many of the mechanisms described in this paper operate also within the developing countries.

First, we should remember that any deep and sustained decrease in the birth rate leads automatically to the aging of the concerned population, i.e., to an increase in its proportion of aged, whatever may be the medical progress during the same period. In order to give some idea of the magnitude of the elderly population, it should be noted that the percentage of people aged sixty-five years and over (this age group will be used as a reference unless otherwise specified) in Europe today is between 8 and 13 or 14 percent instead of the 3 or 4 percent of nineteenth-century Europe. Because France was the first country in which the birth rate was voluntarily reduced, it was also the first country in which the aged reached 8 percent of the total population. This occurred at the very beginning of the twentieth century.

Table 1. *Number of survivors, by age for each ten thousand persons reaching sixty years: France, 1933–38 and 1966–67*

Age	Male survivors		Female survivors	
	1933–38	1966–67	1933–38	1966–67
60	10,000	10,000	10,000	10,000
65	8,420	8,769	8,970	9,453
70	6,535	7,187	7,555	8,614
75	4,435	5,363	5,700	7,320
80	2,403	3,420	5,063	5,486
85	925	1,652	1,669	3,272

Source: P. Paillat, *Sociologie de la vieillesse* (Paris: Presses Universitaires de France, 1971).

It is because the United Kingdom, Germany, Belgium, and Austria have embarked on the same path of limited fertility, beginning later but with an accelerated trend, that their degree of aging is now the same as that in France. The proportion of aged will be even higher in these four countries in the future because they did not increase and maintain a relatively high birth rate after World War II, a phenomenon which slackened the aging process in France.

Second, longevity did not increase at the same pace for both men and women; thus in the old-age group women constitute the large majority (and would have been a majority in France even if past wars had not thinned out the concerned male generations). Moreover, most of these aged women are widows, i.e., the least protected individuals in our society and the more prone to being isolated. In France the average female life length is seven years longer than that of the male, not the four-year, so-called "normal" gap due to differences in ways of life and biophysiological factors. This gap in length of life between females and males has tended to widen recently, particularly because the male death rate has stopped decreasing. It should be underlined that the expectation of life at sixty or sixty-five has increased less than is commonly believed and that this increase is by no means the cause of aging. In the present field of concern, however, it plays a role by increasing the number of elderly and very old as well as the average number of years of retirement.

Progress in achieving longer life recorded by medicine and its allies (such as biochemistry) is likely to produce generation after generation of "survivors" (see Table 1), a large number of whom are often completely dependent. Living a long time is not necessarily associated with being in good health.

Some comments may be added relative to the above observations. First, the sex ratio (i.e., the number of men per one hundred women) after age sixty-five is in most cases much less than a hundred, a statistical way of saying that the aged population is mostly female (see Table 2).

Table 2. *Ratio of men per one hundred women aged sixty-five years and over in selected countries*

Country	Ratio	Country	Ratio
Austria	60	Netherlands	76
France	62	Poland	64
Israel	90	United States	72
Japan	78	Yugoslavia	73

Source: P. Paillat and C. Wibaux, *Les citadins âgés* (Paris: Presses Universitaires de France, 1969).

Further, this ratio is associated with high percentages of aged widows. For instance, of one hundred women aged sixty-five years and over fifty-three are widows in France, sixty-six in Japan.

Third, due to limited fertility, family size is now smaller. Contemporary elderly people have fewer brothers and sisters than their own parents and forefathers. Thus, through the combined effects of fertility and mortality, many old people now have no siblings. (See Table 3.)

Along with this smaller number of siblings old people also have a limited number of surviving children. It should be emphasized that a restricted number of surviving children is the single most significant indicator of the former process of aging as well as of its consequences for aged people. The French case offers a good demonstration of interrelationships between demographic factors in the aging process. (See Table 4.)

Among the aged particular attention should be paid to the female heads of households. In France these are mainly widows (or divorcees) and single women, but thousands of wives live with a physically or mentally incapacitated husband who cannot take up the role of household head. World War I, the demographic consequences of which are obvious, increased somewhat the proportions of single women but mostly the proportions of widows. In

Table 3. *Number of surviving brothers and sisters of city dwellers aged sixty-five and over (percentages): France, 1964*

Number of surviving brothers and sisters	Men	Women
0	34.4	39.3
1	28.1	29.8
2	18.9	14.4
3 or more	16.5	15.4
No reply	2.1	1.1

Source: J. Maslowski and P. Paillat, *Les ruraux âgés non agricoles* (Paris: Presses Universitaires de France, 1973).

Table 4. *Surviving children of aged city-dwellers, farm people, and rural nonfarm people (percentages): France, 1964, 1967, and 1968**

Surviving children	Men			Women		
	City	Farm	Rural non-farm	City	Farm	Rural non-farm
None	25	17	27	33	16	28
1	30	22	29	30	24	28
2	22	23	20	18	25	20
3 or more	22	38	24	17	35	25

Source: Maslowski and Paillat, *Les ruraux âgés non agricoles*, p. 45.
* Among those with no children, 80 percent or more never had a child. The figures include replies from never-married people.

the older French population, women, irrespective of their wishes, were granted a higher probability of becoming a household head for three reasons: (1) demography (differences in length of life), (2) history (male war casualties), (3) sociology (a lesser degree of sharing of households under the same roof, which labels women living alone as heads of households and artificially increases their number). Table 5 shows the number of French women who are household heads. Two of every five households with a female head has a head aged sixty-five years and over. Out of 1.8 million households with female heads aged sixty-five years and over, 1.4 million are one-person households, a figure which may be compared with the 316 thousand men in similar positions. In the female population, then, the variable "isolation" plays an outstanding role.

Keeping in mind the percentages of childless old people and taking into account the adult children who are themselves heads of family, it becomes obvious that the family network, which offered help and assistance during many centuries, does not—or cannot—play its role as completely and efficiently as before. It is significant that, thanks to the network mechanism,

Table 5. *Aged female heads of households (in thousands): France 1968*

Age group	Total all female heads	Living alone		
		Total	Unmarried	Married
Total, all 65 years and over	1,784.2	1,428.3	1,322.0	26.3
65–74	960.1	793.9	694.9	19.0
75+	824.1	634.4	627.1	7.3

Source: Institut National de la Statistique et des Etudes Economiques, Recensement de 1968 "Ménages-familles." Unpublished census tabulation sheets.

Table 6. *Population structures of selected countries*

Age	Austria 1970	U.S. 1970	France 1968	Israel 1968	Nether-lands 1970	Poland 1970	Yugo-slavia 1969	Japan 1970
Percentage of population aged 65 years +	14.2	9.8	13.4	6.2	10.3	8.5	7.6	7.1
Aged as propor-tion of adults (20–64 years)	25.8	18.8	24.6	12.9	19.2	15.5	13.8	11.8

Source: *United Nations Demographic Yearbook 1972* (New York: United Nations, 1973).

the USSR in its early years was not compelled to add old-age pensions to its list of top social priorities but was later able to propose a system of pensions which was possible as a result of the young age structure of the population (8 percent persons aged sixty-five and over).

As an example, Table 6 gives the ratio of the aged people to adults aged twenty to sixty-four years in the countries represented among the contributors to this volume and in Japan. Compared with "young" nations such as Japan (temporarily), Israel, and Yugoslavia, Austria and France are facing problems of quite a different magnitude,. while the United States and the Netherlands are in a middle position.

In the case of France a century ago, the ratio of those sixty-five and over to those twenty to sixty-four was half that of 1968. Furthermore, the higher birth rates between 1946 and 1964 will have no major effect on these increasing ratios although in 1985, when the aged will include the survivors of the so-called "hollow generation" born between 1915 and 1919, there will be a temporary drop in the ratio of the aged to other adults. (See Table 7.)

In summary, in every developed country the ratio of the aged to the adult population aged twenty to sixty-four is increasing and these changes

Table 7. *Aged as a proportion of adults aged twenty to sixty-four: France, 1861–1995*

Year	Ratio	Ratio Each Year (1861 as base)
1861	11.7	100
1901	14.8	126
1954	19.9	170
1968	24.6	210
1975	25.0	213
1985	22.0	188
1995	24.4	209

Source: Maslowski and Paillat, *Les ruraux âgés non agricoles.*

in the ratio of aged to younger adults have resulted in the solidarity between generations passing from the family network to society as a whole.

Economic Factors

Economic factors such as growth in national income and structural changes in manpower have also affected older people.

On the one hand, a considerably larger national income (gross and per capita) provides an industrialized country and its inhabitants with many more resources from which, theoretically, it should be easier to meet the needs of older people. It will be seen later on, however, that this advantage has not been as great as may have been expected.

On the other hand, the economic progress which has occurred was the result of deep structural changes in the productive sectors and of new working methods. The primary sector (farming, forestry, and fishing) is diminishing; and in highly industrialized countries such as the United States or the United Kingdom it includes less than 10 percent of the total working population. As a corollary, the working farm population in France is composed of fewer members of the farm family, and the other two sectors now employ more salaried workers. This twofold trend puts the currently aged generation at a disadvantage. In an average farming family daily life implies job-sharing and multiple roles. Economic activities are an essential part of family and home lives. Theoretically, in this flexible scheme the less physically able old people should have a better position and treatment because they may work on a part-time basis or only during the peak season, or they may abstain from very hard jobs but remain active members of the family unit. These elderly feel that they are still useful; they belong in the daily picture, including participation in the work place, even if they play a lesser role than before.[1] Mechanized agriculture, however, is changing this picture.

In the salaried groups, whether farm or town, working places and homes are separated. In the metropolis the distances are so great that commuting is more tiring than working. Above all, management is now the business of a third party, i.e., the employer himself or his attorney with whom the prospective retiree has to deal directly. In large companies bureaucracy hides behind impersonal behavior. The bureaucrat likes to refer to bylaws and regulations. The push for improved productivity, a "must" for economic progress, puts more and more pressure upon men and women who may no longer be at the peak of their physical faculties. This drive for productivity

---

1. Since people tend to live longer, the son working for his father has to wait longer before becoming the boss. If his patience is worn out, if eventually his own wife can no longer tolerate being her mother-in-law's servant, they leave the farm. As a result, the father is left without help and has to work as long as his physical condition allows it. Should we overlook the case of the aged farmers who do not know who is going to take over the farm after their retirement or death? In some parts of France they represent 30 to 50 percent of the total farm group.

too often leads to firing the worker or to reducing his salary, and both factors will yield bitter interest in old age, either directly by reducing pension levels or less directly by premature wearing out of the individual and his resulting proneness to psychological self-retirement as he sees himself "excluded" from progress.

Along with economic progress one observes a decrease if not the disappearance of the consumption of one's own production which provides a sort of vital minimum to aged rural people still able to work. For instance, the aged eats his own corn, his eggs, and his produce. Aged city dwellers of today are more dependent but, as rightly indicated by Marvin B. Sussman, the individual near retirement "is expected to become consumer-oriented, even though he may not have the means to consume extensively."[2] Perhaps more emphasis should be given to Sussman's statement: there is simultaneously on the part of society an external pressure on the old person towards a consumer's status exclusive of any other, and a resistance to providing appropriate means to these consumers. Does one need to add that the permanent solicitation towards potential buyers develops a feeling of frustration in those who are unable to respond positively? Of course, the elderly are not the only social group that feels this way but they have less hope and fewer ways to overcome it than others.

Social Factors

Along with changes in the trend of fertility the geographic distribution of the French population has changed. It is rapidly becoming more urbanized. Living in an urban environment does not fit very well with keeping together large families in which several generations coexist. Not only are the dwellings too small but the occupants—mostly renters—cannot readily add rooms as is possible in a rural setting.

In spite of the urbanization process, it has been possible, as Townsend's survey in London has shown,[3] for a family to maintain a sufficiently close network which permits frequent contacts, but this surviving way of life is threatened by the construction of large dwelling blocks in the suburbs in which the young couples find accommodation far from the heart of the city where their parents live. The contacts between these couples and their parents will become less frequent, and their own young children will be raised in an artificial world limited to two generations—their own and that of their parents. Yet demographic trends register an increasing number of four-generation and even five-generation families.[4] To whom should aged

---

2. M. B. Sussman, "An Analytic Model for the Sociological Study of Retirement," in *Retirement*, ed. F. M. Carp (New York, 1972), p. 53.

3. P. Townsend, *The Family Life of Old People* (London, 1957).

4. It is relevant to point out that the case of retirees who themselves have a surviving parent (usually the mother) will be less and less an exception.

Table 8. *Proportion of elderly people with no children living in the neighborhood: France, 1964, 1967, and 1968**

	Men	Women	Total
City Dwellers	42	41	41
Farmers	28	29	29
Non-Farm Rural	28	29	68

Source: Maslowski and Paillat, *Les ruraux âgés non agricoles.*
* Including childless old people.

city-dwellers, whose children (if any) do not live in the neighborhood, turn when they are confronted with problems? The figures in Table 8 show that such cases are not exceptional.

In the farm population where larger family size seems to imply a better outlook for the aged, it should be mentioned that paradoxically parental fertility is such a strong factor in migration that a couple with many children may find themselves even more isolated in old age than couples with far fewer children.

Fortunately, all social trends are not so gloomy. Under the pressure of workers who want to draw some benefits from economic progress in which they have been so much involved, various measures have been adopted, first in a scattered fashion, then more generally, in order to reduce such risks as sickness, unemployment, and the problems of old age. Lacking a family network, an income great enough to permit savings, or protection of savings against inflation or erratic moves of economic cycles, the elderly, far from having time for relaxation and freedom, often lived in the darkest misery. The frequency of such dramatic situations could no longer be tolerated without protest when a country's resources increased so much that it was obvious to every member of the working class. Social relief was only a temporary answer to such claims; further steps were needed. With the exception of army and navy pensions, it was not until the twentieth century that vocational or regional pension funds were founded and expanded in terms of the number of people covered and the level of allocations and pensions. This was an earlier stage of pension coverage than the various national pension schemes covering everybody (Scandinavia, Eastern European socialist countries), a stage still very far away for many industrialized countries, including the United States. The trend toward national pensions seems inevitable. This point will be discussed more fully later on.

As a counterpart, however, the social mechanisms safeguarding the aged have become more and more the province of persons unknown to the elderly. In low-income groups saving was equal to privation, to a limitation of current consumption, a process very different from saving from an excess income. Instead of saving voluntarily and recognizing this as a sacrifice, operating schemes, whether they are based on law or on collective bargaining, directly take from the employer's payrolls the sums corresponding to pension contributions. Who nowadays knows with certainty his gross salary? It is likely that the workers themselves overlook completely the amount of money deducted from their gross salaries. The funds gathered through this channel are distributed to retirees. Technically speaking, this financial mechanism, the distributive system, has nothing to do with a private, "personal" saving. It is a contribution to the running of social institutions. It is also the origin of conflicts between generations when there are increasing numbers of older people in proportion to those in the work force. The first group feels that they have a "right" to their pension since they have "paid for it," but the second group realizes that such pensions paid to the retired are in fact paid from the earnings of the workers. It will be some time before we see the disappearance of misunderstandings which have arisen in the transitional phase during which insurance and security concepts are confused. Furthermore, for the retiree, receiving a check or money order on a regular basis does not have the same meaning as drawing an equivalent amount regularly from one's bank account. Eventually a positive value will be given to the pension check, but this is not yet the case for those who are very old now.

Because people live longer, the "survival" of property-holders delays the time for inheritance. The younger generation must build up its own estate. This is an additional factor in pushing adult children to search for jobs and life independent from their aging parents.

In order to cope with the extraordinary variety of social needs of the present elderly new vocations have appeared as substitutes for religious orders or charity institutions which did similar tasks in the past. Social workers act as intermediaries between the elderly and the bureaucratic structure. Within the social services a new person operates, the expert in social regulations, who is a sort of by-product of the increasing complexity of the given area. Unfortunately a good knowledge of texts and rules is not tantamount to a good knowledge of men. Social trends then appear to be developing in two directions. On the one hand is the decline of the traditional family support system in all its ramifications. On the other is the development of social structural supports with an accompanying bureaucratic structure focused on meeting the needs of the elderly.

Technical Factors

Changes in technology affect older people in many ways. From the whole arsenal of technology two examples will be drawn: medical technique and information science.

The press reports — supported by some drum-rolling — technical prowess in medicine such as heart grafts, artificial kidneys, or outstanding prosthesis, but very seldom do the newsmen point out that such developments are only possible with a very sophisticated and expensive infrastructure. In order to make them available to the largest possible number of patients, more sophisticated equipment than that of the general practitioner, of a neighborhood clinic, or even of a neighborhood hospital, is needed. Therefore a hospital bureaucracy now confronts the old person. As an example, an elderly patient has a long wait before he is given a bed and attention, a distressing contrast with his former reassuring environment — his home — from where he has just arrived. Even being transferred to a hospital is likely to be stressful for the elderly patient, especially when the conditions for admittance are not familiar to the specific psychology of old patrons. On a more modest level, the value of preventive regular health check-ups is emphasized. In order for these to be conducted on a large scale they also need a proper infrastructure, files, and records. One would like to be convinced that the medical bureaucracy is closer to an old individual than is the administrative one. Free medical care for the elderly cannot meet the needs of old people, however, unless one takes into account the fact that patients are also human beings.

One may be surprised to have information science mentioned here as having an impact on the elderly, but new developments concentrate account-handling services for the sake of efficiency. Such a concentration may provide more rapid data processing, but it also has its negative aspects. Pension fund headquarters are further and further away from retirees who indeed feel as though they were standing at the foot of a new Great Wall of China, more and more difficult to pass through or to overcome. The retirees see less and less how they can penetrate these strongholds. The retiree has become a serial number, which reinforces his inner conviction that he is no longer a subject but an object.

Thus technology, whether in the field of medicine or in the field of information sciences, results in the depreciation of the sense of self-worth of older people.

Possible Palliatives and Reorientations

One should avoid pessimism, however, and look for the means to efface slightly or completely the major drawbacks mentioned earlier. The same order will be followed to make references easier, but the possible steps and measures outlined should be seen as parts of a whole. In other words, these measures should be the components of a global policy in favor of the aged, either on the short-term or long-term basis.

Demographic Action

It would be quite unrealistic to argue in favor of demographic structures similar to that of the past: to double the current birth rate with the present low death rate would produce rates of increase in the industrial countries of the same magnitude as those of underdeveloped countries. However, it is not impossible to slacken the aging process by a better matching of the levels of birth rate and death rate, in other words to work to obtain a "stable population" (unvarying age structure), but many decades would be necessary to obtain a "stationary population" (stable with zero growth). Conversely, trying to slow down the birth rate too abruptly would accelerate the aging process before proper preparation has been made to ensure a decent position for the elderly.

Devoting more efforts to reducing the excess male mortality would tend to limit the risk of widowhood. It would be rewarding to pay more attention to specific mortality risks for men from childhood on.

Any demographic changes designed to ameliorate the situation of the elderly, as should be obvious, call for sustained activity in the long run.

Economic Action

Only an overall increase in the national income can permit a more equitable income distribution, but if such an increase is a necessary condition for income redistribution it is not a sufficient condition. Every increase does not cover the same content and one may regret that indices in this field have a very limited value. Frankly speaking, to produce more of anything at whatever cost may be implied for the following generations is not a proper solution. A serious reappraisal of the concept of growth is wanted, with due attention to the widening gap with the underdeveloped countries.

Within industrialized countries new types of production processes or interindustrial relationships require attention. Instead of lowering the retirement age, it would be much better to improve the conditions of work, to add flexibility to timetables and jobs, and to prevent physical or nervous exhaustion. Of course, from the employer's point of view, it is much easier to offer early retirement to worn-out workers than to change completely the conditions prevailing in workshops, but the goal should be to avoid exhaustion caused by work and working conditions and not to eliminate those affected by it. Pending mechanization or automation, strenuous jobs in foundries or card-punching workshops, to give examples, should be taken only for a limited period of time, after which workers should be transferred to less tiring jobs without loss of pay. What is the use of retirement at fifty years of age if the retiree has no strength to enjoy his new freedom? Gerontology may help one to rediscover the unity of life and to avoid solutions aimed at isolated phases: whatever the point of view, the quality of life in retirement depends on each preceding step. Of course, such changes in industrial organization involve large sums of money, especially in undertakings where there are many strenuous jobs, but this handicap may be overcome if all industries share in the process. Gerontologists are ready to join forces with those who fight for more healthy and less stressful working environments. To sum up, efforts must be made to make work less painful for the worker, if not more attractive.

Unless decent resources can be provided, it is unrealistic to propose any specific social move. This point has been vigorously stressed during the preparation of the French VIth Plan, but the corresponding bill will be expensive for the country even if it simply raises the old-age social minimum allowance to 80 percent of the minimum salary. Such a plan would be better accepted if the supplementary levy necessary for payments comes from increases in the gross national product which allocate state resources to the aged, thus avoiding increases in the level of taxation on workers' incomes.

Social Action

Action in the social field lends itself easily to short-term reforms but the social area also provides an opportunity for long-term reorientations.

First, it is necessary to eliminate from the laws and regulations now in force anything which obliges the future retiree or the already retired person to act as a suppliant who has to provide evidence to support his claims. For example, current social allowances granted under a means-test are an already obsolete stage of social progress. It is degrading for anyone to have to prove that his financial resources do not reach a statutory ceiling. The conditions adopted in some Scandinavian countries in regard to national pensions demonstrate the possibility of eliminating such processes. Such a move falls within the responsibilities of legislators. It is a political move, closely related to the status which other adults are ready to give to the elderly.

Second, on a less ambitious level, technical management and social action should be separated. In the area of social action retirees should be given a larger role: they might fulfill various tasks and duties currently entrusted to adult volunteers or employees. The same line of thought could be followed in scrutinizing the operation of cultural or other services oriented towards old people, including broadcast and television stations.

The personal delivery of a letter or a daily paper is more than a postal duty when the addressee is an old and isolated person. Under these circumstances, to cancel the home delivery of mail by the post-office carrier is proof that the public authorities overlook the social role of this employee, especially if he is born in the neighborhood and if he works on a regular basis. In a French rural community the township's clerk who, on a part-time basis, gives a hand to the mayor and who is usually chosen from the more educated men or women of the village (e.g., the local school teacher) in fact plays an important role not only because he takes care of filling out administrative blanks, but also because he acts as a link between the inhabitants, the mayor, the tax, and social institutions. As a middleman he often becomes a confidant, a good side of his function, and sometimes a one-sided or indiscreet man, a bad side. Nevertheless whatever his faults there is no one like the township's clerk in huge dwelling developments or in city blocks.

Generally speaking the implementation of any regulation dealing with an aged individual should be governed by a simple rule: priority is to be given to the interest of the aged person. For example, retirees should not be the victims of delays in administrative operations. For a monthly pension remittance to be late may be tragic for the retiree who feels he is being drowned in an ocean of pending records.[5] Incidentally, the conditions associated with the payment of the first monthly remittance after retirement from work should be given a good deal more attention since they play a significant role in the retiree's attitude. It is suggested that a provisional pension be granted until the final amount of the pension is computed. This proposal stems from the observation that in France the new retiree has to wait six months on the average before receiving his first check and this delay is deemed an improvement! Relationships of aged people with bureaucrats are likely to be better if the aged are not plagued by anxiety or distress.

A good mark of concern for the aged could be the improvement of reception halls and hours of operation. This would help any citizen but it is especially relevant in the case of the aged, who are easily intimidated or bewildered. A better environment has a good influence, however, only when the staff is properly trained. In this field advice from gerontologists can be invaluable. It is imperative to provide any staff in contact with old people, whatever the rank and skill, with proper psychological training. Many recently hospitalized aged people would not become permanently bed-ridden if they were made to feel welcome in the hospital and if they were always considered as "urgent cases" and treated accordingly. Bureaucratization is an obstacle to humane relationships in a collective environment where the responsibilities of everyone seem so obscure, so diluted, that the family, despite its efforts, is hardly able to cooperate efficiently. Who has thoroughly investigated the relationships between medical doctors and nurses and families of hospitalized patients, especially in the case of old people with a limited capacity for movement? Does not bureaucratization tend to brush aside any third party's intervention? At a more modest level the absence of training of home-helpers may be the origin of failures which

5. It was necessary to wait until an old lady committed suicide near Paris before the concerned institution realized how scandalous were delays of payment imposed by the difficult adoption of a new system of record processing!

limit the success of a policy, the aim of which is to keep old people living at home as long as possible. Training programs should also include the staffs of institutions where a good number of elderly live permanently. A first move in the right direction would be to raise the standards and the wages of such employees.

Proper information before retirement could help to lessen the retiree's dependency vis-à-vis the bureaucracy. Unfortunately, one cannot entertain too much hope regarding the success of such efforts, since it is difficult in a society with a high degree of vocational mobility to limit, on the one hand, the complexity of social regulations and, on the other hand, the extreme variety of individual cases.

Technical Action

The prevention of physical and psychiatric illness, as well as social and cultural integration, should be supported by every available technical device. The telephone is sometimes the only link between an aged person and other people, the only way also for other people to keep in touch with the old person without intruding into his privacy. Through the telephone much administrative information can be obtained without useless motion. In the case of scattered populations the radio may substitute for the telephone. All of these techniques should be used to help integrate the aged.

In spite of their uneven or ill-assorted character, all actions here proposed have a common goal, safeguarding the independence of the self. Only an independent person is able to entertain proper relationships with the bureaucracy and when necessary to oppose it. Such independence in the aged is threatened from everywhere, either unobtrusively or openly. Therefore one ought to put the issue at a higher level and frankly state that a new type of civilization is a primary condition for offering a decent status to the elderly. Before this achievement, however, it is obligatory to devise and keep up to date the list of measures, limited though they be, whose adoption would prove a collective will to improve the living conditions of our predecessors.

5. Aging, Bureaucracy, and the Family
Nada Smolić-Krković

Bureaucracy and the Social System in Yugoslavia

Bureaucracy is endemic to complex societies. As Max Weber pointed out, the overall rationalization and bureaucratization of social life is unavoidable in industrialized and highly differentiated countries regardless of political ideology. While bureaucracy is a fact of life in socialist as well as in nonsocialist societies, the development of social structures such as the worker organization in Yugoslavia has the prospect of humanizing the relationship between those who run the organization and consumers. Such worker organizations can effectively diffuse the power normally held by the administrators of the traditional bureaucratic structure. The model of organization tends towards parity relationships and in doing so reduces the controlling influence of the central administration and makes the bureaucracy more people-oriented. The success of worker organizations and self-government is still developing. Before this is discussed further it is necessary to present a brief description of Yugoslavian social structure and self-government.[1,2,3,4]

The social system in Yugoslavia is a self-government system.[5] A self-government socialist society can be described as one which is directed and whose development is determined by a group of associated producers. Self-government in Yugoslavia implies a political system in which the producers, that is, workers, gradually take over the management of all social labor, especially including the management and disposition of the products of work.[6]

During the first years of socialism in Yugoslavia, its social development was especially responsive to a number of special circumstances out of which varied social phenomena, bureaucracy among them, arose and developed. Social development in Yugoslavia is characterized by changes in the mode of production, in the social and political structures, in the form of social consciousness, and in the way in which international and political connections are formed. Early development in that country was especially difficult due to the insufficient material bases for such changes.

1. L. A. Coser and B. Rosenberg, *Sociological Theory—A Book of Readings* (New York, 1964), pp. 463–517.
2. M. Weber, "Der Sozialismus," in *Gesammelte Aufsätze zur Soziologie und Sozialpolitik* (Tübingen, 1924), pp. 492–518, esp. p. 508.
3. M. Djurić, *Sociologija Maxa Webera* (Zagreb, 1964), pp. 168–69.
4. V. Ćetković, *Savremena birokracija* (Beograd, 1971), p. 28.
5. E. Pusić, *Problemi upravljanja* (Zagreb, 1971), pp. 100–107.
6. S. Šuvar, *Samoupravljanje i druge alternative, političke teme* (Zagreb, 1972), pp. 32, 42, 44, 58.

Immediately after the Socialist Revolution (1941–45), a powerful administrative-centralistic government was formed. With the increasing complexity of the state apparatus bureaucracy became increasingly centralized. In time such bureaucracy became both self-serving and a complex social-political power. The centralization of social-economic relations made it possible for bureaucrats to gain the highest positions in the state and the economy. In this gradual restructuring of power, the administrative-centralistic organization was transformed into a system in which bureaucracy played an increasingly important part.

Beginning in 1950 a change in the nature of social development took place in Yugoslavia. This was marked by the introduction of "workers and social self-government." Instead of a centralized state apparatus, stress was put on the decisive role of each producer, the working man himself. True self-government only occurs when all the important decisions are made by the social group itself, that is, by the workers themselves, while the professional management is restricted to problems of administration. Because group decision making also characterizes good management, such management also acquires some of the attributes of the self-government system. The transformation of the state system from a centralistic one to one of self-government was designed, among other things, to prevent the further spreading and strengthening of the process of bureaucratization.

One may have assumed that the acknowledgment and recognition of certain weaknesses in the centralist system, together with the new conditions of self-government, would bring about the disappearance of bureaucracy and bureaucratic tendencies. This did not happen. The discrepancy between theory and practice and the controversy which accompanied social development show that the goal of self-government, however desirable, is not easy to achieve. Although in theory bureaucracy and self-government contradict each other, in practice they often coexist. Even now the new social relations arising from self-government have not completely eliminated bureaucracy, which still continues to deform and impede progressive development. The paradoxical nature of the existing situation may be seen in certain services such as social insurance, health insurance, banks, communal organizations, and others, which, according to their content and mode of operation, are part of the self-government system but which still continue to show the characteristics of the bureaucratic system.

Demographic Data on the Age Structure

The population of Yugoslavia has undergone recent marked changes in its age structure owing to demographic, economic, social, and other factors. Yugoslavia as a united national entity is a new country, dating from the end of World War I. Its population, which had lived through World War I,

Table 1. *Age structure of the Yugoslav population*

Census Years	Population (1,000's)	Percentage in Each Age Group		
		0–19	20–59	60+
1921	11,985	45.5	45.8	8.7
1931	13,934	43.9	47.9	8.2
1948	15,772	43.4	47.9	8.7
1953	16,937	40.8	50.3	8.9
1961	18,549	38.5	51.5	10.0

Source: D. Breznik, *Population Trends, Structure, and Projections* (Belgrade: Federal Employment Bureau, 1963).

experienced the devastation of World War II. As the available population trend data reaching back forty years show, one can say that the structure of the Yugoslav population has been changing during that period both under the influence of all the usual factors governing the course of age-structure formation, that is, natality, mortality, migrational trends, and also under the direct influence of the two vast and difficult world wars (Statisticki godišnjak Jugoslavije, Beograd, 1972). (See Table 1.)

According to the 1961 census, 25.6 percent of persons aged sixty-five and over in Yugoslavia lived in urban settlements and 74.4 percent in rural settlements. These proportions are changing, but most of the elderly in Yugoslavia still belong to the peasant population.[7] It should be pointed out that it is only recently that investigations stimulated by the work of Ethel Shanas[8] have helped us obtain an insight into the structure and problems of the aged in Yugoslavia.[9,10]

The Aged Between Family and Society

Family life in Yugoslavia was traditionally patriarchal.[11] All family members lived in the same household, with the role of every member being known, and the position of each member being determined by his age, his work, and his family relationship.[12] Over the entire Slavic south a coopera-

7. Y. Nedeljković, *Old People in Yugoslavia* (Beograd, 1971), p. 15.
8. E. Shanas, P. Townsend, D. Wedderburn, H. Friis, P. Milhøj, and J. Stehouwer, *Old People in Three Industrial Societies* (New York, 1968).
9. N. Smolić-Krkovic, D. Milinković, and A. Visinski, *Social Protection and Needs of Aged People in the Rural Areas of SRCroatia* (Zagreb, 1971).
10. M. Živković, *Socijalna i fizička sredina starih 1 judi u lokalnoj zajednici* (Beograd, 1972).
11. A family is a body of people bound by a legal or illegal marriage, birth, or adoption.
12. Family members are the married couple, their children and adopted children and their spouses, grandchildren and their spouses, great-grandchildren and their spouses, etc. Note: If the parents are dead, married children may separate as individual families though they continue to live together. Therefore, if they break off as separate households they are considered as separate families.

tive family system existed for centuries in which the aged had a much higher status than they had in other parts of the country. Further, in those areas where such family communes may have long since disappeared, the relations of family members were tinged with a traditional assignment of roles. This general closeness of the family even today has not weakened much. In such a family the older man satisfies all of his needs inside the family and he is taken care of by the family until the end of his life.[13] The most familiar form of the patriarchal family in Yugoslavia is the so-called *porodična zadruga* ("big house").[14] A *zadruga*, the oldest form of patriarchal family, consists of several families living together. The absolute number is not known today because the zadruga is not a statistical unit in the census. However, it can be deduced that it still exists in various forms, especially in the underdeveloped regions of the country. The fact that families are reported consisting of eleven or more members shows that the porodična zadruga has not entirely vanished. It is certain, though, that the number rapidly diminished after the Second World War. Most of these families of eleven or more members are in Kosovo (15 percent), Macedonia, Montenegro, parts of Serbia, Bosnia, and Hercegovina and in Lika in Croatia.

The porodična zadruga rests on certain democratic principles. The power of the head of the family is not as pronounced as it may be within other forms of the patriarchal family. The owner of the family possessions is the family itself and not certain of the family members. Sons become equal to their father and the other mature members of the zadruga when they reach maturity. Female children and female family members in general are in an inferior position to males. The zadruga is run by a leader who is elected, and who may be removed by the other members. The leader does not necessarily have to be the oldest member of the zadruga. The death of the leader, even if he should happen to be the oldest of the family, does not automatically cause the separation of the family.

The porodična zadruga is found only in rural areas. The smaller family in rural areas is also patriarchal in its structure because of its close connection with private agricultural holdings. However, there are certain special characteristics of this type of family, reflecting the degree of general economic development of the region of Yugoslavia in which it may be found, as well as geographical, historical, and social factors, and the strength of tradition and various local customs. The traditional relations and customs of this type of rural family are preserved most strongly in those republics where the development of industrial and urban relations has been slower, and especially in those areas which are still untouched by the decisive influence of urbanization (Kosovo and Metohija, Sandžak, Lika, parts of Montenegro, Macedonia, Bosnia, and Hercegovina and parts of Serbia).

13. V. St. Erlich, *Jugoslavenska porodica u transformaciji* (Zagreb, 1971).
14. M. Mladenović, *Uvod u sociologiju porodice* (Beograd, 1969), p. 261.

Surveys show an increasing transition of rural, farming-type households into industrial worker households. Apparently, it is the poorer farm families rather than the richer ones who are more likely to become industrial workers. Thus earnings due to work outside of the family household are becoming the principal source of income for an increasing number of rural households. In 1961 the income from work outside the farm household was 49 percent of the total income of agricultural households in Yugoslavia.

The mixed family (the mixed household) represents a specific transitional form of the patriarchal family. The rural population among the mixed families can be divided into three types: (1) peasants who remain on the farms and slowly but steadily, by participation in cooperative farming communities, approach the socialistic forms of labor in agriculture; (2) peasants who migrate to the cities to become industrial workers, leaving behind their families in the villages; and (3) persons who work in industry but who still live in the rural villages, the so-called mixed type of family household. According to the 1961 census, the number of such mixed families of all three kinds was 1,009,405, or 21.7 percent of all Yugoslav families.[15]

While these are the three main categories of so-called mixed families, there are variations among each category. It frequently happens that the husband goes to the city first, and the wife, children, parents, and the other relatives join him later. Cases of family dissolution because of the husband's working in the city are not uncommon. Because of the difficulties in obtaining living space in the city, however, most of the new industrial workers continue to live in the village. Research done in the Republic of Croatia[16] shows that the agricultural members of the mixed type of household derive many benefits from those of their members who are employed in nonagricultural activities. For example, a comparison of the family budgets of the average worker, farmer, and "mixed" families show the mixed family with the highest cash income. However, along with this relatively good economic situation, a number of new problems arise in the mixed family. The data also show that there is a marked increase in the number of women and aged persons totally involved in agricultural work. A major problem, then, for these families is how to farm the land and maintain an agricultural household when the male members of the family are industrial workers. This problem brings forth many confrontations within the family.

It should be pointed out that industry and the development of the socialistic system in the villages not only influence the economic relations in agricultural families but also affect the forming of villages, the location and building of houses, amenities within the house, dressing and food habits, and the budgets of the family and its spending patterns. The psychology of the peasant is especially affected by industrialization. More and more he

15. Ibid, pp. 263, 274.
16. Smolić-Krković, Milinković, and Visinski, *Social Protection.*

wants the advantages of urban living. But the opposite also holds: the peasant's mentality leaves a profound mark on the surroundings he acquires as a new industrial worker. This happens especially during accelerated industrialization, when the transition from peasant to industrial worker is rapid and when a city suddenly must absorb a large number of peasants. This phenomenon affects the productivity of work, social life, ways of leisure, even art and music.

There are other transitional forms of the patriarchal family in Yugoslavia as, for example, the family of the independent skilled artisan such as the shoe repair man, or the families of the members of free occupations such as lawyers.

But, more and more, the nature of family ties in Yugoslavia is changed today from what it once has been, primarily because of the overall increase in the migration of young people from the villages to the cities, as well as the migration from Yugoslavia to other countries, and also because of the declining birth rate and the smaller proportion of children. The aged are left alone, without the necessary help they once might have received from their children, while the extended family (brothers, sisters, other kin) cannot help—its members need help themselves because of their equally advanced age.

Despite these demographic and societal changes, nearly 70 percent of old persons in Yugoslavia with children live in the same household with one of their children. A considerably higher percentage of old persons in Yugoslavia than in Great Britain, Denmark, or the United States live with their sons and daughters. The high degree of help that old persons report receiving from their children (as well as from sons-in-law and daughters-in-law) is largely a consequence of these conditions. Seventy-five percent of old persons in Yugoslavia are still living in villages, where family relations, as has been pointed out, are still predominantly patriarchal. Only 36 percent of those in villages live alone or only with a spouse. On the other hand, 62 percent of old people in towns live either completely alone or with their spouses only.[17] The data show that the single most important factor in the lives of old people, both in rural and urban areas, is whether or not they have children. Children are the chief support of the elderly in every way. The most unfavorable conditions of life are those of elderly bachelors and childless widowers.[18,19,20]

The organized system of government and its related bureaucratic mechanism is the same among the Yugoslav republics. Nevertheless differences exist among old people in regard to their usage and manipulation of the bureaucracy, depending on the old person's level of income, his education, whether or not he is literate, and other factors. Old people, with better

17. Nedeljković, *Old People*, p. 64.
18. Ibid, p. 75.
19. Smolić-Krković, Milinković, and Visinski, *Social Protection*, pp. 77, 89.
20. Živković, *Socijalna i fizička sredina*, pp. 13–15.

education and income, have more options in their style of life. They can live on their own or in the family of their children, or go to a home for the aged if they so prefer.

The rapid economic and social development which occurred in postwar Yugoslavia was accompanied by a great amount of strain. The development of the country saw a rise in the standard of living, so that the parental generation (it is they who are "elderly" now) could give their children better schooling and a higher standard of life—automobiles, houses, apartments, clothing. But the generation of "children," today's "dual-worker family," tries even harder than their parents did to raise their standard of living. Both husband and wife work and earn income. One consequence of this is that they have no "time" available that they might use for the fulfilling of the needs of either their own children or the older members of the family.

The needs of family members developed more rapidly than did the identification of these needs by society. The problems of an aging population therefore have just recently emerged as a phenomenon society should "do something about."

In Yugoslavia, as the needs of the elderly impinge on the bureaucratic mechanisms of society, a variety of laws have been enacted which affect the elderly. These are:

1. The law governing the relationship between parents and children (Art. 32, et al. Basic Law on Parents-Children Relationship, of December 1, 1947, Official Gazette SFRY, No. 104/1947; and Law on Changes and Amendments of the said Law of March 1, 1965, Official Gazette SFRY No. 10/65).
2. The law on pension and invalid insurance (social-security law). (The law on pension and invalid insurance, Narodne Novine, No. br.55/ 1972—30.XII.1972).
3. The law on the social welfare protection of the elderly. This law is not the same for all of Yugoslavia. Every republic has its own legislation.
4. The Constitution (Narodne Novine SFRJ and SRH, 1963).

The basic law on the relationship between parents and children enacted in 1947 states: "Children are obliged to take care of their parents in the case of illness, weakness, and advanced age if they are unable to work and without income or property they can live on if the children are in a position to do so."[21] According to this law, if the children have income, the community will not pay for the living expenses of an old person in a home for the aged. Instead, it will share the cost at a level determined by the children's resources. Paragraph 196 of this law speaks of the duties of parents towards children and says that parents are subject to criminal law if they do not care

21. Under Article 32 of the cited law, mutual rights and obligations to support exist between married or unmarried parents and their children, between adopted and the adoptee, while in all other cases they exist only between matrimonial relatives, i.e., in the direct ascending and descending lines between grandparents and grandchildren, and laterally between siblings.

for their children. But this law does not regulate the same responsibility of children toward their parents. In practice, older parents only rarely accuse their children of not taking care of them. In fact the old parents are always ready to protect their children and to make excuses for them. The law on the relationship between parents and children is important not solely because it calls for economic support. By making such a regulation "legal," the government gives this obligation a moral sanction which may have been lost in the rapid social changes of recent years.

The law on pension and invalid insurance (social security law) is one of the most important of the bureaucratic mechanisms which impinge on the life of older citizens, both individuals and their families. The basis of pension insurance in Yugoslavia is individual contributions achieved through past work and specific insurance payments. Social security funds are grouped in the various self-government organizations and are used for payments from the pension and sickness insurance. These rights, among others, are assured to workers: the right to sickness insurance, old-age pension, and family insurance; the right of the user of the pension to minimal insurance and a "protectional" addition, e.g., the right to additional money for help and nursing of other persons.

Men are entitled to old-age pension insurance at the age of sixty, women at fifty-five, when they have been insured for twenty years. Men who have not had twenty years of insurance are entitled to their pensions at sixty-five, women at sixty, when they have had at least fifteen years insured status. Men with forty years of insurance coverage and women with thirty-five years of coverage are entitled to insurance without regard to age.

The recipient of an old-age pension achieved through being insured forty years for men, and thirty-five years for women, as well as the recipient of disability insurance granted because of crippling at work or a work-related illness, is entitled to a minimal insurance payment which cannot be less than 85 percent of the smallest personal income for the current year in his republic.

Because the bases for old-age insurance are the contributions made by the employer on the individual's behalf and the latter's payments for this insurance, it is clear that the economic status of a person in advanced age depends on the kind of work that he has performed throughout a major part of his life.[22] The exact nature of his work career, however, depends on his

22. E. Palmore, "Sociological Aspects of Aging," in *Behavior and Adaptation in Late Life,* ed. E. W. Busse and E. Pfeiffer (Boston, 1969), p. 43: "Socioeconomic differences also persist among the aged, although there is some evidence that these differences become somewhat attenuated in comparison with younger groups, i.e., income differences become smaller because the income of the upper groups is reduced with retirement and the income of the lower groups is supported with social security and welfare payments. But the general stratification patterns remain among the aged: those with less income had less education and came from blue collar or manual occupation; they have less adequate diets and poorer housing; they see doctors less often; as a result, their health is poorer, they are more incapacitated, and they have a higher death rate; they are more likely to double up and live with their children; and they have more serious unmet needs. . . ."

education, his work opportunities, and especially on the success of the enterprise or organization where he was employed. As a result of the self-government system workers within different enterprises, even though they may have identical jobs, may earn different salaries. If an enterprise makes more profit the workers may have greater salaries and thus greater pensions in old age.

The data show that even after World War II 93 percent of all aged people did not change their work.[23] It is obvious that an old person's social status and place in the social hierarchy depend on the circumstances of his youth — whether he is properly educated; whether there exists a possibility of employment, that is, a choice of the most suitable job; and whether housing needs and other problems are solved. The possibility of obtaining the proper qualifications at younger ages depends on a number of economic and social conditions and the possibility of employment depends on the given economic state of the society. Systematic education of older people to enable them to change their occupation and to continue at work hardly exists. After retirement the old people are left with only the everyday duties within the family or in some voluntary social organizations.

The social and legal norms are adjusted in such a way as to motivate the individual to work in a single occupation throughout the whole period of his work career, e.g., until his retirement.[24] Society is not interested in older people remaining active after retirement but instead tends to encourage them to leave the work force and thus to free jobs for younger persons.

Many persons who are in good health but who may have low incomes wish to continue working after the pensionable age in order to maintain their standard of living. An increasing number of retired persons whose income decreases abruptly after retirement, with no possibility of continuing their activity or of additional income, consider themselves discriminated against in comparison with the rest of the population. Even those who are healthy and who have a high income after retirement have a hard time adjusting to the loss of their work habits and the social status they had when working. All that is left for them to do is to turn inward to their families, and this reengagement in family life can only be achieved if they have maintained good relations with their family throughout their lives.

Working women tend to be more content in retirement than men. Their work had not relieved them of the usual tasks of housekeeping, shopping, and laundry. In retirement then they have only a single rather than a double job. Further, their pension, as did their wages, continues to supplement the

23. Nedeljković, *Old People*, Table 1–28, Book I of analytical tables.
24. K. W. Back, "Ambiguity of Retirement," in *Behavior and Adaptation in Late Life*, ed. E. W. Busse and E. Pfeiffer (Boston, 1969), p. 111: "Hannah Arendt has in *The Human Condition* demonstrated how the meaning of work has changed in the last few centuries. The central figure in today's society is no longer the contemplative, thinking man, nor even the manufacturing man, but the laboring being (animal laborans). Life and values are oriented around activity, the act of working, and all other activities are made subordinate to this central concern. . . ."

family budget. In somewhat the same way farmers and worker-farmers differ from urban industrial workers. The farmers, even if they receive a retirement pension, keep on doing the work on the household farm which they had been doing all of their lives.

It is interesting that there now appears to be an increasing need among the urban population for a return to the peasant way of life – freedom, fresh air, "my own garden," the weekend house at the seaside, fishing – which especially shows itself after retirement. But in order to fulfill this desire after retirement the urban worker has had to achieve certain financial resources during his work life. The occupation, the social status, and role he had as a worker, the firm at which he worked, the part of the country he lived in, whether it was more or less developed, all these things throughout the work life thus determine the opportunities and status available to the urban worker after his retirement. The social structure thus dictates the specified style of life within which the individual has freedom of choice, and this has a far-reaching effect on the complete life cycle of the individual as well as on his family of origin and on the family that he creates for himself.

The law on social protection of the elderly (social welfare) focuses on financial aid mostly to single persons, those without kin, those whose children are unable to support them, or those with special housing problems.[25] Although the self-government society is conceived as one in which citizens participate directly in decisions, nevertheless people still encounter complex and delaying bureaucratic mechanisms. In order to receive financial aid or to be able to enter a home for the aged, it is necessary to submit various documents to the social administration.

The following documents must be presented in order for a woman aged sixty and over, or a man sixty-five and over, to receive social aid: (1) a formal request for aid, either oral or written; (2) (for those who do not have pension insurance) a certificate of the board for social insurance that the applicant does not have a pension; (3) a certificate as to whether or not taxes have been paid; (4) (if the person has children) a certificate of the income of all children and information as to whether they are employed or not; and (5) proof of residency based on official registration.

For admission to a home for the aged the certificate from the board of social insurance is required plus (1) a medical certificate from the medical center in the territory where the person lives that the person does not suffer infections or mental disease, involving a specialist examination (blood, urine, lungs, heart) and a report that the person is capable of placement in the home for the aged; (2) a birth certificate (issued in the birthplace); and (3) (if the person has pension insurance) the last pension check and pension certificate

25. The law on social protection – SRCroatia – *Narodne Novine* No. 19/1969 SRH.

in order to see on what basis the pension is established (personal, family, war veteran, invalid, etc.).

Such documentation often is difficult for the old person. The bureaucracy seems unable to take into account the capabilities of an older, often sick and poor person, and to simplify its usual procedures or make them easier for him.

The problems connected with the social protection of older people most frequently arise from the slowness of the determination of persons who have needs and secondarily because of the limited number of institutions for the care of the elderly. Social services in the villages where many elderly live are not sufficiently developed. A house or the possession of land may disqualify the peasant for aid whether or not the land is cultivated. In the same way the aged peasant continues to be liable for the payment of taxes on his property, whether or not the land is used for farming.

The Yugoslav Constitution clearly states the duties and obligations of its citizens, individual versus individual, and individual versus society as a whole: "The citizen is obliged to help persons in distress according to his possibilities."[26] This constitutional principle is the foundation of various mechanisms and organizations based on "solidarity." These organizations, in turn, fund projects such as housing projects for workers, or operate various financial funds which raise money for financial and other aids, pensions, health, and social care.

Theoretically the self-government agreement of the producers in organizations of workers should insure each man that his needs are taken care of inside the existing bureaucratic organization of society. In this way, for instance, funds would be raised for institutions for child care, for aid in schooling, and for health protection, as well as for the security of the aging. This would mean that the work organizations would provide for all of the human problems of their workers. When this goal is achieved, the family, with the needs of all of its members met, may one day be capable of organizing its life and its future in a more realistic way.

Contradictions of the Bureaucracy and the Needs of the Aged

A feeling of insecurity and instability may be present at any time in a man's life, regardless of where he lives. Many persons find comfort in a bureaucratic structure since such systems serve to organize their lives. They hope that by operating in accordance with bureaucratic norms that their needs will be fulfilled both as younger and older persons. But very often it is those who adhere to the bureaucratic frame most strictly (most frequently motivated by fear) who, in old age, find themselves with a feeling that they

---

26. Ustav (Constitution) SFRJ i SRH, *Narodne Novine* (Zagreb, 1963), p. 36.

are not getting that for which they had hoped, who are disappointed in life, and who lean most heavily on the younger members of their family. The younger members, in turn, are bound by mutual needs to those elderly family members and feel responsible for them. However, the young also are forced to find an optimum style of living within the bureaucratic set of rules. Regardless of the ideology that organizes the society, bureaucracy grows and flourishes. If one member of the family attempts to escape the accepted norms, the existence and social status of other members of the family are affected. The young may oppose existing bureaucratic frameworks but they are counseled against such opposition by older family members. The elders cannot bear the risk of finding themselves on new pathways which are not accepted by the well-lubricated bureaucratic machine. Not to conform means that they would not have peace of mind. They would be the subject of criticism and rejection. It would be understood by all that somehow they had not succeeded in life.

Bureaucracy in any country develops a conviction among its citizens that its mechanisms and models of life are the only ones which are real, allowed, acceptable. People are made to believe that to conform to the bureaucracy is the chief part of human existence as a social being. The constant fear of the inability of satisfying their basic needs forces people to feel safer when surrounded by bureaucratic mechanisms. Bureaucratic mechanisms, however, become increasingly more complicated. The knowledge of norms, rules, laws, and all forms of bureaucratic organization has become a necessity for existence in a contemporary society.

The roles of various members of the family are more and more focused outside the family network. Parents, for example, must go to work, even if it means leaving a child locked in the house, because the bureaucracy cannot permit absence from work though it does permit a child to be locked up alone in a house. An old man must remain alone in the village because his children seek employment in factories in the cities.

Bureaucracy is not capable of coordinating family, individual, and social needs because it is essentially oriented towards "society" as an abstraction.[27] Marx analyzed bureaucracy within the whole of socioeconomic relationships. According to Marx, bureaucracy represents the greatest possible alienation of man.[28,29] Bureaucracy is so constituted that it promotes obedience within "social norms," and human relations, including family interactions, must conform to such social norms.

Since the social system places its highest value on the productivity of its individual members, the dominant bond between family members tends to reflect this value. Thus an old person who is no longer productive is discriminated against by both family and society. To illustrate, as the data

27. K. Marx, *Kritika hegelove filozofije državnog prava* (Sarajevo, 1960), pp. 194, 197.
28. K. Marx and F. Engels, *Rani radovi* (Zagreb, 1961), pp. 210, 214.
29. Četković, *Savre mena birokracija*, pp. 33, 141–42.

indicate, when an old person in a rural area has not been active in work, he makes decisions about the household only 20 percent of the time, while his children make such decisions 49 percent of the time. When he is active on the farm he is the decision-maker 55 percent of the time, his children 14 percent.[30]

In a society which is developing economically, whatever its ideology, bureaucracy develops, thus resulting in a conflict between societal demands and individual liberties. When the goal is to accelerate the development of society, individual needs are usually placed in an inferior position. The proclaimed philosophy of the society may be antagonistic to the life philosophy of individuals. The primary wish of the individual is to live his short life in happiness and pleasure, but the bureaucratic mechanism restricts him to living within a certain framework, whether he finds it congenial or not. In fact, only a part of the population identify themselves completely with all the rules of bureaucratic conduct and are content to live within them. The rest of the population must somehow develop mechanisms for manipulating bureaucracy and bureaucrats in order to achieve their desired ends. It is only the stubbornness of individuals which can effect changes in the bureaucratic mechanism, and these changes take place very slowly. It takes many years, for example, to change the laws on such matters as retirement and health care, which have a vital meaning for the elderly. Thus those persons who were retired in a year when the law was generally not congenial to them have to wait for years until this law, however bad, is corrected.

People have learned through the centuries to live with bureaucracy, regarding it as something unavoidable. Life does not "seem right" without it. It is accepted as a "given," a part of life, that reality within which man is born and within which he dies. Psychologically, the young are most prepared to challenge the contradictions which may appear in any system. In Yugoslavia the younger generation of farmers have proven themselves capable of adapting to the social system. They keep and cultivate their land, while at the same time they work in factories, accumulating savings and health and pension benefits. There is a constant demand for their services abroad, where they can earn good wages and accumulate savings. The young farmers use the advantages bureaucracy gives them to achieve a better standard of living. Old people in these so-called "mixed households" help to keep the farm going. Their status is higher than in purely worker or farming households.[31]

As persons age, they may indeed become more tolerant of the usual ways of doing things. Moreover, some persons become convinced that there will be financial and other rewards to them if they adhere to the approved modes of behavior. Only those retired persons whose pensions are relatively small

30. Smolić-Krković, Milinković, and Visinski, *Social Protection*, p. 71.
31. Ibid., p. 88.

consider themselves unjustly treated and feel like resisting bureaucracy, while the same bureaucracy is protected and favored by those who have benefits because of its existence.

Educated clerks comprise the greatest number of functionaries in the bureaucratic machinery of administration. Although they are the main effective organs of bureaucracy, they are also the greatest obstacle to the development of self-government and democratic relations. Because of the effect of the bureaucracy on the personality, the bureaucrat develops inelastic ways of doing things. Because power is especially important to them, bureaucrats have a mentality that is basically the same regardless of the ideology of a country.

Conclusions and Problems

Laws and common practice in Yugoslavia both assume that the family is able to give all necessary protection to its elderly members. Even old people themselves, when asked "Who, in the first place, ought to help the aged in case of need?" answered: "children" (73 percent), "family" (12 percent), "society" (7 percent), "social welfare" (6 percent), "neighborhood" (2 percent).[32] Family cohesion when it exists is manifested through mutual assistance. Old people who live with their children and grandchildren receive from them upkeep, financial aid, and care if they are ill. In the same way, older parents help the adult children with whom they may live. The help given by the old is more often in the form of work, that is, in performing various household duties and chores, than in the form of financial help.[33]

Facilities and services are needed, however, for those old people who are living alone, without family members who can take care of them. Such facilities and services for the aged, however, are both sparse and expensive. For example, they are almost nonexistent in villages. Because the need is very great, institutions for the elderly persons are being built (there are now about 150 homes for the aged in Yugoslavia). These institutions are of various types, ranging from the classical home for the aged which provides complete care and nursing to modern hotel-apartments for the elderly. Admission to these institutions depends on the sociomedical and economic status of the older person. All of the institutions require payment for the care of the old person. Either he, his children, or the social welfare organization must assume the cost of his care. The quality of care offered is often reflected in the level of required payments.

Much more could be done for the aged if a more realistic appraisal were made of the relationship between their needs and the possibility of satisfying these needs. Adult children, old parents, and society itself through its

32. Nedeljković, *Old People*, Table 3/61: analytical tables, Book 1.
33. Smolić-Krković, Milinković and Visinski, *Social Protection*, p. 73.

institutions, social service, social welfare, and social insurance, should collaborate in solving these problems. Though suggestions are given for the solution of these problems, the difficulties of establishing the necessary services, in the cities and even more in villages, most frequently are the result of both inadequate funds and complicated administrative procedures. Every action taken in these areas in some way has to be recorded on paper and to go through the official administrative channels in accordance with the existing laws. When persons become aware of what they are obliged to do just to avoid the pitfalls of bureaucracy, they frequently give up attempts to implement many ideas which would be helpful to the aged. Furthermore, it sometimes appears that if they were to proceed to implement their ideas, they might have to spend more time dealing with the necessary administration than with the activity itself.

There are many examples of bureaucratized institutionalized thinking in programs for the elderly. Staff members of homes for the aged repeatedly refuse to provide any services to old people living in their areas. They are not able or do not want to change the accepted rules by which they operate because there are a number of bureaucratic barriers which have to be overcome. The medical service, so important and frequently used by the aged, is so bureaucratically organized that the elderly patient spends needless time and effort in making his way from the general practitioner to the specialist and to the hospital. A great number of certificates and documents have to be obtained for even a simple intervention in the life of the aged person.

Bureaucratic mechanisms are present in the organization of every contemporary society regardless of its ideology. Such mechanisms are becoming more complicated instead of simpler. Viewing the whole life span of a man, those bureaucratic mechanisms which affect his old age should be made simpler, in accordance with the ebbing of his strength and capacities. They should facilitate the satisfying of his vital needs, provide him with more choices, and permit him an organization of his life which enables him to maintain self-confidence and self-respect.

Empirical Studies

6. Linkages of Old People with Their Families and Bureaucracy in a Welfare State, the Netherlands *Joep M. A. Munnichs*

Introduction

The older person in the Western world lives his life surrounded by a complicated set of influences that determine his place and position in society. The older person himself is only partly aware of this. Often what appear to be minor changes, the moving of neighbors, for example, can have far-reaching yet unsuspected consequences for the way of life of an old person. The factors which push the older person in a certain direction, for example, to an old people's home, are not yet at all clear. Probably the most important factors in this context are the person's health, the presence of adult children nearby, the quality of the relationships with the children, and the existence of such a home. However, the old person's worry about future dependency may also make him seek admission into a home. The groups of factors which determine when an appeal will be made for general assistance and which indeed may differ from person to person are only partly mapped out. The most important factors most certainly include (1) the health and marital status of the older person; (2) the presence of adult children and the geographical and psychological distance from them; (3) in the absence of children, the presence of substitute-family relationships; and (4) the image of old age held by professionals in the area of aging.

The linkages of older people with their families and bureaucracy can perhaps be best understood in terms of a choice. On the one side, the old person has the choice of help from his own family; on the other side, from the welfare services. In fact, however, this choice seems to be one the old person is increasingly unable to make. The possibility of falling back on the family for help and support is decreasing, so that the older person often must turn to the help of professional and societal organizations which form part of the bureaucratic system. Questions about the intervening role of children and other family members seem in this respect very relevant. To these questions gerontologists are adding others: (1) What would be the best solution for the older person in the light of changing societal developments? And, from the point of view of those who must administer the services of the bureaucratic system, (2) How far is present society to go in this provision of services?

How meaningful the gerontologists' questions are impresses us whenever we investigate whether the characteristics of the usual kind of bureaucratic

Author's Note: Appreciation is extended to Dr. Peter Coleman for his assistance in translating this study and to Dr. Gerrit Kooy for his helpful comments on the first draft.

system, such as is described by Weber (1972), link up well with the characteristics of older citizens. Without expressing a value judgment—and neither does Weber—I must point out that bureaucracy means impersonality in social relations, routinization of tasks, centralization of authority, rigid rules and procedures, and the emphasis of the means to an end instead of the original goal. Apart from some positive characteristics such as rationality, the splitting up of goals in well-defined tasks and systematics, the bureaucratic system has a pejorative sound. Therefore we may also raise the question whether as a result of its own characteristics the bureaucratic system has produced further social services and questionnaires, for example, the "social adviser" who exists in the Netherlands to rebuild the linkage with beneficiaries. The basic question to be considered is not only how would the relationship between older parents and their children affect the demand for services from society, but also how the existing services should be optimally applied. For the time being the possibility of changes in the relationship between parents and children seems more limited than the possibility of changes in the social services. Thus it can be seen that the question concerning alternative solutions to the needs of the aged is very complex. A second consideration must be the type of society in which old people find themselves. Bureaucracy is a qualitative trait of a society, but it is not identical with its purpose. The purpose of society determines whether the bureaucratic system will carry more or less weight. For example, dependent on the role played by the governing ideology, bureaucracy in Western Europe works differently from that in Eastern Europe. Therefore it is necessary to identify another important characteristic of society involving the problems of older people, family, and bureaucracy.

One can characterize the Netherlands and a great part of the Western world as welfare states. We can adapt M. Penelope Hall's definition: "The distinguishing trait of the welfare state is that the society in the shape of the state takes upon itself the responsibility that her members are guaranteed a minimum of health care, economic security and civilized living and can participate in accordance with their mental capacities in the social and cultural advances of this society" (Hall, 1952, p. 6).

Naturally the actual content of the activities of society will change in accordance with the general level of welfare. Moreover, welfare states are more and more governed by the principle of costs-benefits. The purchasing power of the individual therefore may get more stress and attention at some periods than collective expenditures, which may be much more useful from a social standpoint. The slow rate of clearing slum dwellings and the existence of a housing shortage are good examples. The failure of concentration on better social circumstances is also connected with the absence of a commonly accepted ideology covering the whole life of society (see van Heek, 1972). Therefore the welfare state as it actually operates gives rise to ad hoc accommodation to group aspirations and individual desires and the related complaint that there is barely any long-term planning. The system only "treats the symptoms."

The bureaucracy and the welfare state can have a negative influence on each other. However, a well-run welfare state should be able to contain within limits the negative effects of the bureaucracy. What is clear is that the welfare state has too little room for maneuvering to make fundamental corrections.

These remarks about the welfare state can be related to our subject as follows: What is the present state of development of the welfare state and the bureaucratic system in Dutch society, and how does this development affect the older population and their relationships with their children?

The implications of the above questions are too numerous and too many-sided to fall within the range of social scientific methodology. They must be split into separate parts and afterwards the parts must be fitted together again like the pieces of a mosaic or a jigsaw puzzle. There is a danger that by the choice and the presentation of different research data a certain element of prechoice by the social scientist may result in a misrepresentation of reality. This danger is certainly present in our analysis because hardly any attention has been paid to some aspects of the questions which concern us.

The relationship of old age to the family and bureaucracy in each society has its own character. It therefore seems necessary to restrict ourselves to one system, that is, to one country. The provisions developed in one country within that system can have a completely different influence upon family relationships from the provisions in another country. Further, what appears to be most useful is to stress the developments which apply to particular measures in the country in question. What is most striking in the Netherlands, in contrast to other countries, is the very high percentage of older people – 10 percent – living in homes for the aged. In nearby countries, for example, Belgium, the percentage living in such homes never rises above 4 percent. Living in an old-age home is certainly dependent on the old person's relationships with his children. Special analysis of this development in living arrangements in particular should yield insights which can be useful in other countries where old people's homes may be in great demand.

In light of the above discussion the remainder of this chapter concerns successively a short sketch of some social traits of the Netherlands, and especially of the provision made for old people's homes, the development of this provision, and its nature. In the following paragraphs I shall further explain the high percentage of old people in old-age homes. I shall present data on the older population of the Netherlands and on the aging of the Dutch population as a whole; on the living arrangements of older people; on the existing provisions for social and financial support for old people and some history of these developments; data on the role adult children play in the application of these provisions; and, finally, a discussion of attitudes about old age in Dutch society, particularly attitudes of social workers and policy makers. I shall close with a short account of research needed in this field and with some general conclusions.

General Characteristics of the Older Population of the Netherlands

Some Characteristics of the Dutch Population

The Netherlands is a small country, 12,850 square miles, about one-fourth of the size of New York State. Within this territory live more than thirteen million people, making the Netherlands one of the most densely populated countries in the world. During the twentieth century the Netherlands experienced rapid population growth because of a very low death rate and, simultaneously, a relatively high birth rate. Together with increasing industrialization after the Second World War, this has resulted in increasing urbanization of large parts of the Netherlands. The Netherlands then is a small, densely populated, and urbanized country. In this small country, however, distances seem greater than they may appear to residents of larger countries such as the United States. A distance of fifty miles is a long way for a Dutchman, both physically and psychologically; for an American such a distance may be merely a trip to dinner. This psychological set has important consequences for the nature of family relationships in the Netherlands.

Another aspect of the Netherlands which is important for an understanding of the country and its people is its great religious diversity. This results in differing political convictions, educational practices, and, in short, differing *Weltanschauungen* among the population. These differences affect all aspects of daily life. One of the consequences of differing religious practices is that the Netherlands still has a very low percentage of working married women, about half that of the surrounding countries. In 1968 the Netherlands had the lowest level of female employment of all EEC countries: 26.3 percent as compared with 33.6 percent in neighboring Belgium. Only 22.8 percent of all women workers in the Netherlands were married, compared to 62 percent in Belgium. According to the 1971 census, the number of working women in the Netherlands has risen substantially and the number of working married women has more than doubled since 1960, rising from 173,000 to 483,000.

Special Housing for the Elderly

Since the last World War the proportion of older people living in old people's homes has increased steadily from 5 percent in 1950 to something over 10 percent in 1972. By a home for the aged I mean a building for the accommodation and care of old people who, because of their physical or mental condition or owing to social circumstances, are no longer in a position to maintain themselves independently in their own homes but who, in general, need only little or incidental medical and/or nursing care. The home for the aged in the Netherlands is not strictly comparable with a retirement home or an old people's home in the United States. In the latter there may be only provision for accommodation and communal meals. The homes for the aged in the Netherlands combine some of the characteristics of both independent community living and sheltered care. A home for the aged in the Netherlands is a relatively self-supporting world with a general managing director, a nursing head, and other supportive personnel. The mean number of personnel is one staff member to three residents. The mean age of residents is about eighty years and, in order to be admitted to the home, at a minimum the residents must be unable to manage their own household. The residents get whatever care they may need. In the case of serious treatable illness the residents go to a hospital for a short period and then return to the home. If they are very frail and necessarily bedridden, however, they go to a nursing home. Unless the resident requires continuous nursing care he can stay in the home for the aged as long as he lives. In general these homes contain one hundred residents, all of whom have their own rooms with facilities such as a kitchenette with light cooking arrangements, a toilet, etc. A communal meal is furnished which can be eaten in the resident's own room if he prefers. At the end of 1972 the Netherlands had about two thousand such homes. As we shall see further, the government has discovered that alternatives other than homes are necessary to meet the needs of the aged.

The Demographic Structure of the Dutch Population

Of a total population in 1970 of 13,119,430 inhabitants the Netherlands possessed 1,339,749 persons aged sixty-five and over. The preponderance of women compared to men is already present in the group of sixty-five to sixty-nine years and increases steadily through the age group ninety-five years and older. (See Table 1.)

In Table 2 the sex composition of the older population of the Netherlands is compared with that of some other countries. The effect of the First World War in countries such as Belgium, Great Britain, France, and West Germany may be seen in the extremely high proportion of women to men. The Netherlands, on the contrary, is similar to Sweden and Norway in its sex distribution.

The Netherlands has a mean life expectancy of seventy-six years for women and seventy-one for men, one of the highest life expectancies of any country in the world. With a lower life expectancy there would be less necessity for provisions for the very old. Table 3 shows the life expectancy of the Netherlands, compared with culturally similar neighboring countries.

Table 1. *The Dutch population, sixty-five years and over, according to age and sex on January 1, 1971*

Age group	Men		Women		Total	
	Number	%	Number	%	Number	%
65–69	219,645	45.3	265,300	54.7	484,945	100
70–74	161,024	43.6	208,526	56.4	369,550	100
75–79	109,853	42.7	147,156	57.3	257,009	100
80–84	62,674	42.7	84,117	57.3	146,791	100
85–89	25,992	41.8	36,175	58.2	62,167	100
90–94	6,881	41.2	9,832	58.8	16,713	100
95 and over	983	38.2	1,591	61.8	2,574	100
Total	587,052	43.8	725,697	56.2	1,339,749	100

Source: *Yearbook 1972* (The Hague: Central Bureau for Statistics, 1973).

Table 2. *Number of women per one thousand men in the older age groups in 1967–69 in the United States and some West European countries*

Country	Year	Age			
		65–69	70–74	75–79	80 and over
Sweden	1967	1129	1209	1307	1385
Norway	1967	1175	1217	1307	1413
The Netherlands	1969	1201	1276	1317	1334
United States	1969	1199	1347	1448	1557
Belgium	1967	1265	1432	1531	1668
England and Wales	1969	1272	1650	1904	2448
France	1968	1276	1675	1954	2351
West Germany	1967	1367	1689	1836	1692

Source: *United Nations Demographic Yearbook, 1969* (New York: United Nations, 1970).

Table 3. *Mean life-expectancy at birth in some countries of Europe around 1963*

Country	Year	Men	Women
The Netherlands	1961–65	71.1	75.9
Denmark	1964–65	70.2	74.7
France	1965	67.8	75.0
Great Britain	1963–65	68.1	74.2
Belgium	1959–63	67.7	73.5
West Germany	1964–65	67.6	73.4

Source: *Mortality Tables for the Netherlands, 1961–1965* (The Hague: Central Bureau for Statistics, 1967), p. 33; *United Nations Demographic Yearbook 1967* (New York: United Nations, 1968).

Table 4. *Percentages of married men and women, sixty-five years and over, of the sum total of each age category in the period 1899–1969*

	Age							
	65–69		70–74		75–79		80 and Over	
Year	Men	Women	Men	Women	Men	Women	Men	Women
1899	67.4	46.3	57.1	34.3	45.6	23.3	30.2	11.8
1930	70.9	52.4	60.8	39.5	48.2	26.2	30.5	12.6
1947	74.2	56.3	64.4	44.1	51.9	30.3	30.8	12.6
1969	83.2	57.6	77.4	46.0	66.5	33.4	39.3	14.7

Source: Data from Central Bureau for Statistics, The Hague.

The large number of persons over eighty-five years of age, more than 80,000 in a total population of only 13 million, the high mean life expectancy, and the preponderance of older women, who are usually widows, all mean that a large proportion of the aged need social services. Marriage among the elderly or living together with another person prevents institutionalization of the aged in many cases. In each age category from sixty-five to sixty-nine to eighty and over, for both men and women, there is an obvious increase in the percentage of married persons since 1899. Among the youngest men (sixty-five to sixty-nine years) the proportion married rose from 67.4 to 83.2 percent; among the youngest women, from 46.3 to 57.6 percent. Among the oldest group of men (eighty and over) the proportion married rose from 30.2 to 39.3 percent; among the women, from 11.8 to 14.7 percent. From Table 4 one can see how great is the number of single people, that is the unmarried, divorced, and widowed, among the elderly. On January 1, 1972, 741,369 (55 percent) of older people were married and 598,380 were single. In this latter group 73 percent, 435,056 persons, were women. However well the Netherlands contrasts with its neighboring countries in its proportion of men to women, these data suggest that the problem of old age is still to a large degree a problem of unmarried single and widowed women.

Living Arrangements

The living arrangements of older people have a major effect on the kind of life the old person experiences. Housing developments have a great influence on living arrangements during old age, and therefore on the needs for homes for the aged as well. One must not underestimate the influence of housing design on the form of the family in any society. The one-family home is presently popular in the Netherlands, but its consequences upon the living circumstances of older people are difficult to trace out precisely.

Table 5 gives the number of persons living as heads of households or as

Table 5. *Number of persons aged sixty-five and older living as heads of household or as primary individuals*

Living arrangements	Heads of households				Single persons				Total			
	1960	%	1970	%	1960	%	1970	%	1960	%	1970	%
Living independently	325,700	79.9	484,600	93.4	97,500	57.5	212,400	83.3	423,200	73.3	697,000	90.1
Householder with others sharing accommodation	54,700	13.4	21,000	4.1	42,900	25.3	30,200	11.8	97,600	16.9	51,200	6.6
Living with other people	23,500	5.8	10,800	2.8	25,800	15.2	9,600	15.2	49,300	8.5	20,400	2.6
In accommodation other than houses (ships)	3,600	0.9	2,600	0.5	3,400	2.0	2,800	2.0	7,000	1.1	5,400	0.7
Total	407,500	100	519,000	100	169,600	100	255,000	100	577,100	100	774,000	100

Source: *Nota Bejaardenbeleid, 1970* (Rijswijk: Ministry of Culture, Recreation and Social Welfare, 1970), p. 32; *Woningbehoeftenonderzoek* (The Hague: Central Bureau of Statistics, 1970), Table 6.

primary individuals living alone or with others in 1960 and 1970. First of all we must point out that the total of 774,000 persons in these living arrangements is barely 59 percent of the total elderly population in the Netherlands in 1970. The missing 41 percent of the elderly population is composed of women not heads of the family living with their husbands who are heads of households (±240,000); older people in old people's homes and in homes for the aged (125,000); people living in nursing homes, mental hospitals, and in monasteries and convents. A more detailed presentation of living arrangements of the elderly is given in Table 9. There are a number of changes between 1960 and 1970 among these 59 percent of the elderly reported in Table 5 which are very important. There has been a very large increase in the total of those living independently both as heads of households and as single persons living alone, but the relative increase in the latter group is proportionally greater. Related to this is a decrease in those older persons living with others in their own households and also a decrease in those older persons living in other people's households.

There is a clear trend in the Netherlands to smaller family units. This trend may be seen in the data on the living arrangements of married couples by the age of the head of the household. (See Table 6.)

The total number of households consisting of married couples living alone increases steadily as the age of the head of the family increases. Only 10 percent of married couples with a male head forty to forty-nine years live alone, compared to 81 percent of married couples with a head aged seventy-five years and older. Where the head of the family is fifty to sixty-five years old, more than 35 percent of the married couples have no unmarried children at home. By the time the head of the family is sixty-five to sixty-nine years of age, 73 percent of the couples have no unmarried children at home.

Table 6. *Number and proportion of married couples that maintain a household, alone, with unmarried children (possibly others) or only with others, according to age of the head of the family in 1971.*

	Household arrangement							
Age of the head of the family	Couple alone	%	Couple with unmarried children and possibly others	%	Couple without unmarried children, but with others	%	Total	%
40–49	69,600	10.3	600,000	88.9	5,600	1.8	675,200	100
50–64	264,400	33.2	512,600	64.4	18,800	2.4	795,800	100
65–69	130,800	70.9	49,200	26.7	4,400	2.4	184,400	100
70–74	99,200	78.9	23,800	18.9	2,800	2.2	125,800	100
75 and over	87,600	81.3	17,600	16.3	2,600	2.4	107,800	100
Total	651,600	34.5	1,203,200	63.7	34,200	1.8	1,889,000	100

Source: *Woningbehoeftenonderzoek*, Table 5.

Table 7. *Number and proportion of single persons, who as head of a household maintain a household alone, with unmarried children (and possibly others) or only with others, according to age and sex in 1970*

	Household arrangement and sex							
	Alone		With unmarried children and possibly others		Without unmarried children but with others		Total	
Age	Men	Women	Men	Women	Men	Women	Men	Women
40–49	13,400	22,200	6,600	32,600	4,600	3,800	24,600	58,600
50–64	31,200	93,000	14,400	60,200	15,200	19,600	60,800	172,800
65–69	12,600	61,800	4,000	12,600	5,400	9,000	22,000	83,400
70–74	12,200	59,000	3,800	11,400	6,400	7,000	22,400	77,400
75 and over	25,800	83,600	7,400	18,400	6,200	9,400	39,400	111,400
Total	95,200	319,600	36,200	135,200	37,800	48,800	169,200	503,600
(In percentages)								
40–49	54.5	37.9	26.8	55.6	18.7	6.5	100	100
50–64	51.3	53.8	23.7	34.8	25.0	11.4	100	100
65–69	57.3	74.1	18.2	15.1	24.5	10.8	100	100
70–74	54.5	76.3	17.0	15.3	28.5	9.4	100	100
75 and over	65.5	75.1	18.8	16.5	15.7	8.4	100	100
Total	56.3	63.5	21.4	26.8	22.3	9.7	100	100

Source: See Table 6, p. 100.

When the data for 1960 are compared with those for 1970, once again one can see an increasing decline in family size among the elderly. In 1960 almost 32 percent of the married couples in which the man was between sixty-five and sixty-nine years had unmarried children at home; in 1970 this figure was only about 27 percent. In those households with a male head seventy to seventy-four, those with children at home decreased from roughly 23 percent in 1960 to about 19 percent in 1970.

In all age categories a larger proportion of single women than of men maintain their own households. As Table 7 shows, three of every four unmarried women in the age groups sixty-five and over live alone, compared to about half of all unmarried men. The unmarried man is likely to introduce "others" into his household — housekeepers and other persons — in contrast to the older woman who maintains her household alone.

Single persons who have one-person households live alone either in a house or in part of a house. They are the ones who would be first likely to fall back upon social services (e.g., old people's homes) in case of need. The total number of single persons with a one-person household in their own accommodation has increased faster between 1960 and 1970 than might have been expected on the grounds of the general population increase (see Table 8). Beginning at age forty these persons increased from 302,940 to 414,800 during the decade. The most important factor in this increase, how-

Table 8. *Number and proportion of single persons who maintain a one-person household, alone in a house or in part of a house, according to age groups in 1960 and 1970*

Age	1960			1970		
	Alone	Alone in part of a house	Total	Alone	Alone in part of a house	Total
40–49	14,580	16,860	31,440	29,800	5,800	35,600
50–64	57,420	44,860	102,280	101,400	22,800	124,200
65–69	30,660	21,260	51,920	63,400	11,200	74,400
70–74	30,420	20,760	51,180	61,200	10,000	71,200
75 and over	40,140	25,980	66,120	90,600	18,800	109,400
Total	173,220	129,720	302,940	346,400	68,400	414,800
(In percentages)						
40–49	46.4	53.6	100	83.7	16.3	100
50–64	56.1	43.9	100	81.6	18.4	100
65–69	59.0	61.0	100	85.2	14.8	100
70–74	59.4	40.6	100	86.0	14.0	100
75 and over	60.7	39.3	100	82.8	17.2	100
Total	57.2	42.8	100	83.5	16.5	100

Source: *Algemene Volkstelling 1960* (Population Census Data) (The Hague: Central Bureau for Statistics, 1964), Table SH 1; *Woningbehoeftenonderzoek*, Table 6.

ever, is that many more housing units have come into existence. However, one must also consider changes in attitudes toward the living arrangements of older people between 1960 and 1970. Otherwise, the relatively stable percentage of those living alone in the separate age groups in 1970, about 80 percent in each group, is not explainable. Whenever problems in old age make their appearance, the elderly person must then give up his one-person household either by taking in others, or going to live with others, or entering an old people's home.

To what extent older people are living with their children or with others is not exactly known. On the basis of the data presented here and additional data available to us we are able to assess this number fairly closely. The group living in the households of others, which previously was an extensive one, is led to live with others because of the difficulties of old age. One may assume that these people especially, by declining to live with their children or others, are directed to general institutional services. Table 9 presents the living arrangements of older people.

As will be apparent further in this discussion, it appears that old parents, even in case of need, prefer to live independently rather than to live with their children. To fully understand the more than 120,000 old people living with children or others, it must be pointed out that there are a large number

Table 9. *The living arrangements of older persons*

Living arrangement	Number	%
Independently living married persons	725,166	54.1
Independently living single persons	356,000	26.5
Older people in old people's homes	117,000*	8.8
Older people in nursing homes (geriatric clinics)**	16,500	1.2****
Older mentally ill patients in mental hospitals***	5,000	0.3
The number of older people probably living with children or others	120,000	9.9
Total number of old people in the Netherlands	1,339,749	100

Source: *Statistiek van Bejaardenoorden 1970* (The Hague: Central Bureau for Statistics, 1972); M. Wimmers, *Verpleeghuizen in Nederland* (The Hague: Central Bureau for Statistics, 1972); B. T. G. de Jong, *Jaarverslagen 1970, van de geneeskundige hoofdinspectie en milieu-hygiene* (Yearbook of the Ministry of Health) (The Hague: Ministry of Health, 1971); *Yearbook 1970* (The Hague: Central Bureau for Statistics, 1971).

* Includes 16,406 married persons.

** We assume that only three-fourths of older people resident in nursing homes have their domicile there. Patients who stay less than three months are not classified as residents.

*** This includes the aged mental patients who entered the hospital at earlier ages.

**** There is a remarkable agreement with data from E. Shanas, P. Townsend, D. Wedderburn, H. Friis, P. Milhøj, and J. Stehouwer, *Old People in Three Industrial Societies* (New York: Atherton, 1968) for Denmark and the United States, respectively 1.4 percent and 2.3 percent.

of religious communities in the Netherlands with relatively many older persons among them. These persons are reported as living with others. When this is taken into consideration, the number of older people living with married children and/or "others" in the household will probably amount to no more than 6 to 8 percent.

From data in the city of Rotterdam collected in 1965, it appears that barely 6.7 percent of all old people are living with children and/or others. Moreover, 90 percent of these persons who live with children are unmarried. The same picture emerges from studies made in a middle-sized town in the south of the Netherlands.

From the above data the "individualization" of the older family in the Netherlands appears obvious. Many more older married couples were living alone in 1970 than in 1960; many more single persons were living alone in 1970 than in 1960. Is this increase in couples and individuals living alone accompanied by an increase in social services for the aged and, especially, by a marked increase in the number of institutionalized older people?

Services for the Elderly in the Netherlands

In the Netherlands until recent times caring for old people was almost exclusively seen as a task for private organizations. Apart from a few large old people's homes in the great cities comparable to the workhouses in other countries, charities took care of the aged. With the development from an agrarian to an industrialized society voluntary forms of communal help to the elderly disappeared into the background and a more professional service became prominent. In the beginning such service was especially in the field of public health. After the Second World War, however, professional service to the elderly extended into the field of home care and general social work. The major reason for the increasing attention of the government to the problems of the elderly has been the rapid growth of this population, especially since the Second World War. As Table 10 shows, while the population nineteen years and under doubled between 1899 and 1969, the population sixty-five and over increased fourfold. Estimates of the future growth of the population indicate that the youngest population will increase by about one-quarter by the year 2000 and the oldest by about one-half.

Bureaucratic elements exist within institutions run by both the government and by private organizations. A few words must suffice for these private organizations as they affect the elderly. District nursing care as well as family-care services are organized locally with local committees deciding the policy of these organizations. As a result, the development of these services as well as their policies can differ sharply in the various towns. Therefore not only are the bureaucratic characteristics of these organizations different but also their problems. While the waiting list for family care is long in one town, in another, because of better organization, help can be given almost immediately. Efforts are now being made to coordinate the policies of these organizations on a regional and national level.

The growing attention of the government to the problems of the elderly

Table 10. *The growth in the population in the Netherlands according to age-categories (1899 = 100)*

Year	0-19	20-49	50-64	65 and over	All ages
1899	100	100	100	100	100
1909	114	117	109	117	115
1920	129	142	135	132	135
1930	140	168	168	161	155
1947	160	208	227	237	190
1960	194	225	298	342	226
1969	206	262	326	428	254
1980	218	295	359	522	282
1990	241	335	381	606	315
2000	268	359	473	680	351

Source: *70 jaren statistiek in tijdreeksen, 1899–1969* (The Hague: Central Bureau for Statistics, 1970); *Calculations about the Future Growth of the Population in the Netherlands, 1970–2000* (The Hague: Central Bureau for Statistics, 1971), lijst 16.

in Dutch society is immediately demonstrable in the financial support for every older citizen given after the Second World War. This provisional act was replaced in 1957 by the General Old Assistance Act. Since 1957 each older person from the age of sixty-five on receives a basic pension related to the level of prosperity of the country. In recent years an attempt has been made to raise the pension to the minimum income level. In 1954 a single person received monthly about 50 Dutch florins, a married couple about 100; in 1973 a single person received about 550 florins, a married couple about 750. The enormous increase in monthly payments is obvious. Some of this increase is related to continuing inflation. The financial position of the elderly has been improved by this pension, which to a large degree has promoted the independent living of older people. However, as a result of independent living parents and children have involuntarily been set apart from one another, at least in the geographical sense.

Further, the government increasingly is turning its attention to other aspects of the life of the elderly. In the beginning such attention was mainly directed to housing policy, influenced by the explosive increase of the total population after 1945. The government stimulated the building of old people's homes primarily in order to increase the turnover in the existing housing supply. Facts and rumor about poor practices in old people's homes resulted, after a long period of preparation, in the passage of an Act for Old People's Homes in 1963. The act was designed especially to set standards for the technical aspects of the accommodation itself and to protect the privacy of the inhabitants. Through this law it also became possible to begin a register of all the available old people's homes in the Netherlands. Under government stimulation the number of places in old people's homes increased from 57,270 in 1960 to 118,088 in 1971. Although this accommodation with all services included was built for older people in need of care, the cost of such a residence was often too high for them. For needed money old people turn to the so-called General Assistance Act, which supplements their income. The amount of money which must necessarily be made available for older people living in old people's homes rose steeply, especially in recent years, so that the government decided to restrict the building of such homes and to put more stress on care for older people in their own homes. The actual amount of money given old people under the Assistance Act is shown in Table 11.

Between 1968 and 1969 in particular the government became aware that a solution for the problems of the elderly rather than the old people's homes was financially necessary. The government then began the development of part-time home helps. Table 12 gives the total number of places in homes per one thousand older people in each of the eleven provinces of the Netherlands and, further, the number of home helps for older people available in 1970 and in 1971. The rapid development in these programs is easily seen by comparing services for 1970 and 1971. At the same time it appears that

Table 11. *Amount of money (in guilders) spent per month for the General Old Assistance Act (Algemene Ouderdoms Wet) in the Netherlands for couples and single persons for several years*

Year	Amount of AOW per month	
	Couples	Single
1957	117,—	70,50
1958	132,—	81,—
1960	149,50	94,50
1962	179,50	113,50
1964	244,—	159,—
1966	342,50	241,—
1968	399,50	281,—
1970	477,—	336,—
1972	633,—	447,— *
1973	732,—	517,—

Source: Data from the Ministry of Culture, Recreation and Social Welfare, Rijswijk.
* Since 1971 an extra payment was given for holidays of f. 364 for a couple and f. 257 for a single person.

Table 12. *The number of places in old people's homes in 1970, the number of part-time home helps in 1970 and 1971, per one thousand older people in each of the eleven Dutch provinces and the Netherlands*

	Number of places in old people's homes per 1000 older people in 1970 and 1971		Number of part-time home helps in 1970	Number of part-time home helps per 1000 older people living independently 1970	Number of part-time home helps, Dec. 31, 1971	Number of part-time home helps per 1000 older people living independently as of Dec. 31, 1971
Groningen	77	84	1,536	25	2,499	44
Friesland	86	84	2,087	32	2,732	48
Drente	65	78	1,513	42	2,296	62
Overijssel	66	77	1,976	22	2,712	33
Gelderland	105	110	2,892	19	3,973	29
Utrecht	106	113	1,733	21	2,125	30
Noord-Holland	91	97	4,671	18	6,422	27
Zuid-Holland	66	64	6,985	21	10,170	32
Zeeland	86	93	714	17	1,012	27
Noord-Brabant	95	89	2,512	19	3,956	31
Limburg	78	79	976	13	1,545	20
NEDERLAND	83	86	27,595	21	39,442	32

Source: See Table 11, p. 106.

in most of the provinces, with the exception of Friesland, South-Holland, and North-Brabant, the number of places in old people's homes is growing relatively faster than the number of old people. In all of the provinces the number of home helps has made a sharp rise. It appears probable that this service for the elderly in their own homes can replace the old people's home in some part. That the use of other services too shows a clear correlation with the more individualized way of living, which is now being stressed, appears from the fact that in 1970 a total of 580,000 meals were delivered to the elderly by the Union of Women's Voluntary Service (UWV) compared to 229,000 in 1964. The UWV is only one among the organizations which delivers meals to the elderly.

Further, the government has tried to develop "open" care for the elderly by establishing multipurpose centers for this age group. These now exist in about fifty towns. In the beginning the philosophy of the government was to integrate these in district centers intended for all age categories in order to stimulate the integration of the aged, but this approach was unsuccessful. However, the number of service centers in which all the professional attention is concentrated upon old people living in a district is still limited. Old people who are fully mobile can make use of such centers, but those who need services at home are scarcely or only partially assisted. In general, only about 16 percent of old people living in the particular district of the service center make use of it. More detailed data about who makes a request for service and how often and for what reason are still unavailable.

That there exists within the Netherlands an enormous need for help, information, and assistance on the part of the elderly appears not only from the above data on home helps and "meals on wheels," but also from the demands older people make upon the "social adviser." The position of the social adviser has been established to inform citizens about the provisions of social laws and the total field of social welfare. This position can be seen as an intermediary or perhaps as a sort of bridge for the no-man's-land between the bureaucratic system and the individual citizen in difficulties. National data about who makes use of the services of the social adviser and why he is called upon are missing. There are illustrative data available, however, for the cities of Amsterdam and The Hague.

The importance of the social adviser for old people in particular can be seen from the fact that of a total of 21,115 visits to the social adviser in Amsterdam in 1971 54.8 percent were from old people. These old people came especially to ask advice on financial problems, but secondarily they also had considerable problems concerning living arrangements. Nearly 5 percent came to discuss their relationships with other people. The same sort of data on the use of the social adviser exist for The Hague, except that there the requests of old people were about 30 percent of the total.

The social adviser as an institution has developed differently from town to town. In this connection the differences in the use of the social adviser between Amsterdam and The Hague perhaps may be explained. However, from the data of both cities it appears that many old people are asking for advice from outsiders — strangers — rather than from their families.

To conclude this discussion, there are clearly two developments in services for the elderly related to the changing composition of the family. On the one hand we see a rapid increase of the number of places in old people's homes while on the other a development of "open" care. In the last few years the latter has received more emphasis than the former, probably because of considerations of efficiency and finance. The high percentage of institutionalized old persons in the Netherlands, almost 10 percent, differs sharply from the percentages in Belgium, West Germany, and Great Britain, where only about 4 percent of older people are institutionalized. The central question which must now concern us is the role of adult children within this context of available services. Are children helping the elderly and, if so, how?

The Role of Adult Children

It is clear that there is an obvious trend to a "thinning out" of the family in the Netherlands; and at the same time the general services to the elderly (for example, in the form of the General Assistance Act) are being taken over by the welfare state. This change in family style is most apparent in the relatively high percentage of older people living in old people's homes. Because, in contrast to the past, more parents as widows and widowers live alone during old age, they are now thrown upon the general services in case of emergency. This depends on the closeness of and the quality of the relationships with their children.

In the Netherlands the husband determines the mobility of the family. The adult married daughter of older people holds a more intensive relation with the parental home than the adult son does. However, she may not be close enough to give help if it is needed. For about a quarter to a fifth of the elderly the geographical distance between parents and children is so large that the children cannot help in case of emergency. However good the relations between these older parents and their children may be, these parents cannot count on obtaining immediate and lasting help from their children. In such cases of geographic distance they must find other solutions for their needs. Where the relationships between older parents and adult children are less good, often as the result of an authoritarian attitude toward their children by the parents, which is not infrequent in the Netherlands, the combination of geographical distance and relatively restricted contacts with children can together be the reasons for old parents to seek to insure themselves for the future about which they may be increasingly concerned.

In the first instance, where the relationships between parents and children are good, there is probably mediating help from the children. In the second case, where relations between parents and children are less good, the problem confronting the old person is often dealt with without the children's presence. In both instances the result may be the same. The Dutch data on the family life of old people are especially sparse concerning the mediating role of adult children. The same is true for data on the quality of the reciprocal relations between the generations. Lowenthal (1968) has pointed out that the quality of relationship for an old person is indeed an important variable in mental well-being, but that day-to-day concrete existence may be unrelated to such quality. Further, the mediating role of children and the use made of general services, such as old people's homes, are also dependent on the societal patterns of expectation about the living circumstances of older people. This pattern is clearly influenced by an increase in the number of homes for the old and by the knowledge that living in a home is a common occurrence among the elderly and thus may be thought of as ordinary. These common societal beliefs which are shared by both older and younger persons stimulate old people to enter homes and cause other alternative living arrangements to receive less and less emphasis. In the following section I will give a brief summary of the available data on this topic. However, I must first point out another fact.

The present question of the relationship between old age, family, and bureaucracy rests on the assumption that each older person has one or more relatives who constitute a family. Nothing could be further from the truth. The Netherlands contains not only a substantial number of unmarried elderly people, 131,722 or 10 percent of the aged in 1971, but also a fairly large number of older married couples and widowed old people who are childless — somewhere between 10 and 20 percent. Together with the unmarried, these form a group of at least 260,000 persons. If only these single persons and married or previously married persons without children were to make appeals to institutional services, the existing institutional provisions would be insufficient. The question can also be put the other way around. Are the single and the childless, through the "individualizing" of the Dutch family, more likely to use institutional services than other old people? From the limited available data it appears that nearly 16 percent of the inhabitants in old people's homes are married, while almost 60 percent of all Dutch old people are married. For single men these percentages are 25 percent and 12 percent, while for single women they are 59 percent and 33 percent. Single people then are overrepresented in old people's homes. The same applies for patients in geriatric clinics and nursing homes (see Wimmers, 1970). Thus the supposition holds good that those who have no relatives or a limited number of relatives are earlier forced to use institutional services than those who have relatives. The first victims of the thinning out of the traditional family and of the decrease in the former patterns of informal help between neighbors and acquaintances are above all the unmarried aged or those single who have been married but are without children. This is confirmed by research in Breda where, of the old persons married or in widowhood, living in their own homes, about 15 percent had no children, while of the old persons living in homes for the aged almost twice as many had no children (unpublished data, Gerontological Centre). Dooghe has reported similar data for Belgium. In a sample of 3,025 people living in their own homes, 22.3 percent of all older persons were without children (Dooghe, 1970).

This impression is further intensified when we look at the scarce Dutch research data on the relationships between older parents and their adult children. Unfortunately, we cannot draw upon national representative sample research equivalent to that of Shanas et al. (1968) in Denmark, Great Britain, and the United States which was later replicated in Belgium, Poland, Yugoslavia, and Israel. There are a number of local and regional investigations, however, worth mentioning in this connection. From the Rotterdam research of 1965 referred to earlier, which involved a random sample of more than three thousand older persons living in their own homes, it appears that the percentage of children who regularly visit their old parents once a week corresponds fairly well to the reports from such neighboring lands as Denmark, Great Britain, and Belgium (Dooghe, 1970). Old persons living in Rotterdam are visited at least weekly by 91 percent of their children who live in Rotterdam, while only 76 percent of the children living outside of Rotterdam visit their parents this often. The number of old people who wish that they had more visits from children is only 6 percent. For these persons decreased visiting by children leads to feelings of unrest and loneliness which may cause them to enter homes for the aged perhaps earlier than they would otherwise. It appears from other data in this inquiry that there is a clear connection between financial help from children and the frequency of their visiting. Nonetheless, when old people were asked who is responsible for their financial support, the degree to which things have changed in the last few decades is apparent. In only 8 percent of the cases are children said to be responsible and in 70 percent, the local authority. The same trend is evident when the questioning turns to the housing choice old people would make in case of emergency. Only 10 percent of old people in Rotterdam prefer to live with one of their children in case of emergency, and 60 percent prefer to go into an old people's home.

Research findings from a 1971 study of almost six thousand old people, the members of one of the largest associations for old people, living for the most part in the south of the Netherlands, show the same sorts of trends. The old people in this research live in the less urbanized areas of the Netherlands. Table 13 shows the places where the elderly, living in their own homes, would most like to move in case of emergency. As Table 13 shows, only a small number of old people in this study want to move in with one or

Table 13. *Where the elderly wish to move in case of emergency**

	Number	%
To one of the children	97	1.7
To other relatives	9	0.2
To an old people's home	1215	21.1
To special housing, flats	1086	18.8
Prefer to remain in own home	1332	23.1
Would not know	328	5.7
Not applicable:		
Live with children	363	6.3
Live with my grandchildren	3	0.1
Live with others	165	2.9
Live in an old people's home	631	11.0
Live in a nursing home	12	0.2
Live in a monastery/convent	184	3.2
Unknown	51	0.9

* A sample of old people living in their own homes.

another of their children. A similar low percentage answered "yes" to the question, "Would you like to live with one of your married children?" Only 1.4 percent said, "Yes, I should like to." Only in case of emergency did 13 percent even want to consider living with a married child.

Some exploratory research has been done on whether children participated in the decision of old people to enter a home for the aged. Of 50 old people who had lived for a year in an old people's home, 26 said that the decision for them to enter the home was made by children, other relatives, or friends. The choice of which home to enter, according to 36 of the aged, was also determined to a large extent by children, other relatives, and friends.

From a recently completed pilot study on 151 older people living in a random sample of eight old people's homes it appears that only 9 percent had entered on the advice of their children, 6 percent on the advice of other relatives, and 3 percent on that of friends. The general practitioner had advised entrance to 29 percent, but as many as 49 percent said that they had entered the home with no outside advice. Thirty-four percent of these elderly said that they had entered a home because of health, 35 percent because of anxiety over the disabilities of old age, and 15 percent because of family circumstances. Here again children appeared to play a very limited role in decision making.

Data on the quality of the relationships between old parents and their adult children are especially scarce. A partial impression was obtained in 1967 in an inquiry with 679 students, from which it appears that nearly 11 percent of these college freshmen reported that there was an old person at their parental home. This older person could be their own father or mother, one of the grandparents, or another old person. The students were asked if they had regular contact with the old people living at home and whether this contact was intimate or more impersonal. About three-quarters of the students who had an old person at home said that they had a regular and intimate contact, while only about one in ten of the students who did not have an older person at home reported regular contact with an old person.

Images Concerning Old Age

There are many prejudices toward old age among old people as well as among those people who are not old. How these prejudices operate is less well known. It is clear that because of the large number of single old persons and their necessarily limited contacts with children, the fear of the handicaps of old age which are stressed in these prejudices drives elderly people into old people's homes. Although it may be difficult to obtain reliable data about this process, the scarce data are at least very indicative. In a study made a number of years ago older people as well as younger people appeared to overestimate the number of chronically ill among the old by a factor of about 50 percent. Even today in the Netherlands many are surprised at the low percentage of older people living in old people's homes. Most people expect that it must be at least 20 percent, twice the real figure, which is 10 percent.

From fairly recent research among employees from the social welfare services, especially from the sector of care for the elderly, it appears that these employees in general have a favorable conception of various aspects of old age. The original attitude scale used in this research concerned physical and mental status, personality, time perspective, social contacts, and financial circumstances. But only twenty-two of the sixty-eight items in the scale proved useful. These were items dealing with personality and social relations. The same questions were also administered to a control group, and the most important differences between the experimental and control groups on the stereotypes of age can be seen in Table 14. The experimental group (employees from the social welfare services) is in general more positive about older people than the control group. The former consider older people as valuable human beings who possess both positive and negative features, while the control group tends to associate old age with sickness and senility. The images of old age held by the two groups are in marked contrast to each other. Informal interaction with old people in the bureaucratic network of services as well as in the family and the household thus appears able to influence people's beliefs about the aged in a more realistic direction.

Table 14. *The percentage of positive or negative (−) answers in an experimental and a control group*

	Experimental group	Control group
In general I find old people pleasant	71.5	46.7
I find most old people are admirable in the way they handle money	57.1	33.9
In my opinion the large majority of old people possess good health	46.6	21.0
In my opinion many old couples can still have a full sexual life	56.4	27.4
Many old persons should be more critical about themselves	48.2	24.2
In my opinion many older people become meaner as they grow older	−67.9	−46.7
To be old seems to me a heavy burden	−82.1	−61.3
It seems to me dreadful to be old	−69.6	−45.1
I find most old people finally become senile	−73.3	−33.8

Research Needs

In this presentation I repeatedly stressed the gaps in our knowledge of old people in the Netherlands. The Netherlands lacks research into family structures, divided into the aging individual, the aging couple, the aged household and the extended family, and the extended aged household (Bloom and Monro, 1972). We know very little about what use old people make of general services from private organizations as well as local authorities. There is scarcely any interest in sociological studies of the family which relate the sociological theories of the family with the older age groups. It goes without saying that there is even less interest in more subtle studies in which the central theme is the geographical and psychological distance of old people from the children and the relationship of old people with bureaucracy. An obvious example of this neglect of old age is the Dutch study, *Making Known and Getting Known: An Evaluation of the First Five Years of Government Information on the Public Assistance Act (1962-1967).* Although it is precisely old people who make major use of the benefits under this act and who often have considerable difficulties using the services provided by this act, there were no old people included in this research (cf. van der Haak, 1972). It is clear that the Netherlands is seeking a balance between what the governmental bureaucratic system and the private organizations associated with it can do and, on the other hand, what the family, other relatives and, incidentally, neighbors can do for the elderly. There seems to be an increasing tendency to use general services rather than to fall back on informal forms of help. This tendency is undoubtedly connected with the particular situation in the Netherlands in which there is less emphasis on old people living independently than there may be in other countries, for example, in Great Britain. Cross-national research would be desirable into what are these thresholds of tolerance which in one country lead old people into institutions and in another lead to the development of supportive community services.

Bureaucracy and Old Age: Provisional Conclusions

The discussion to this point has described a social development. It is not yet obvious whether we have reached the terminal phase of this development. What may we then conclude? Until relatively recently the care of older people was not a matter of central interest in the Netherlands. It was first assumed to be primarily a housing problem, but little by little it became seen as much more of a social problem because housing also came to mean the provision of security and care. A great part of the modern anxiety about old age was removed both from old people and the general population by the entrance of the old person into an old people's home.

The improvement of their financial circumstances provided many old people with longer independent lives, much more so than was possible in the past. Undoubtedly an improved financial status increases the proportion of people living alone. The resulting independence associated with living alone makes it very difficult for the old person to call in the help of his children in case of emergency. For old people an appeal to their children is seen as a decline. Especially among those living alone, people will seek an old people's home when they experience the infirmities of old age. Thus, from the new emphasis in living arrangements in which a large number of aged couples and individuals live alone we see an enormous increase in the demand for places in old people's homes.

Another reason why the relationships of old people with their children has become less one of material help is the fact that everyone in the Netherlands has the right to support if in need, in accordance with the General Assistance Act. Children are no longer responsible for the support of their parents. This can ameliorate the relationships between parents and children, but it can also stimulate the dissolution of the family. Relationships between parents and adult children may improve because reciprocal financial responsibility has become superfluous. A more personal emotional relationship may appear which can give reciprocal satisfaction. This satisfaction presupposes a filial relationship, as described by Blenkner (1965). But if it fails to appear, we see a fading of the relationship between parents and children. Especially in the Netherlands, in which in the recent past the relationships of parents to children were highly authoritarian, reflecting the influence of certain religious attitudes, the possibilities for individualism introduced by the General Assistance Act has not strengthened the relationships between older parents and their adult children. The obvious conclusion of Reuben Hill (1970), in speaking about the relation between old parents and their adult children, may be repeated here: "In short, there appears to be support for the generalization that dependency does beget avoidance. . . ." (p. 76).

It is obvious that the bureaucratic welfare and support systems of the government have certainly underestimated the above-mentioned developments. The government itself has realized only lately that the family of the past is vanishing, that an old people's home has appeared as a substitute, and that this substitution is attended by an enormous increase in national expenditure. The requirements for entering an old people's home have become so nominal that many more enter than was previously thought possible. Even worse, many who in the past would have rejected life in a home are accommodating themselves to the idea of living in a home in the future. This new phenomenon was not perceived by the bureaucrats. Nor did they fully comprehend the consequences to the elderly of living in an old people's home.

It now appears that lack of attention by the government to the social process involved in the institutionalization of older people in homes, as well as inadequate information about this and the offering of inadequate alternatives to institutionalization, all make it seem that it will be well-nigh impossible to correct or to change the trend in the Netherlands toward institutionalization. The relationships of old people to their children will change only very little as a result of this trend. Good relationships will not suffer as a consequence of this trend; poor relationships will not be improved. What aspect of the bureaucratic system in the Netherlands is responsible for this? The impression is that the impersonal, businesslike characteristics of the bureaucratic system in a welfare state is the major reason that a policy has been followed which, once underway, is difficult to stop or reverse. The government had no realization of the social implications of its building and housing policy. Housing was considered a solution to the "problems" of the elderly. That changes in the living arrangements of the elderly would affect all aspects of their lives was neither anticipated nor planned by the government nor by anyone else. Yet housing changes have initiated revolutionary changes in the life of the elderly and their children.

References

Bierkens, P. B. "Psychologische aspekten van het kinderloze echtpaar." 1972. Mimeographed.

Blenkner, M. "Social Work and Family Relationships in Later Life with Some Thoughts on Filial Maturity." In *Social Structure and the Family*, ed. E. Shanas and G. F. Streib. Englewood Cliffs, N.J., 1965.

Bloom, M., and A. Monro. "Social Work and the Aging Family." *Family Coordinator* 21 (1972):103–15.

Borst, A. G. "Attitudes van niet-bejaarden en oudere werknemers." Scriptie, University of Nijmegen, 1968.
De Rotterdamse Bejaarden, Deel I, 1968; Deel II, 1970; Deel III (in press).
Dienstencentra Oktober 1970. Report, Department of Social Welfare. Den Haag, 1972.
Dooghe, G. *De struktuur van het gezin en de sociale relaties van de bejaarden.* Antwerpen, 1970.
———. *Bewoners van bejaardentehuizen, sociologische doorlichting.* Antwerpen, 1972.
Hall, M. P. *The Social Services of Modern England.* London, 1952.
Hill, R. *Family Development in Three Generations.* Cambridge, Mass., 1970.
Kennis en heeld van de sociale dienstverlening. Ministry of Culture, Recreation and Social Welfare, Deel I, Deel II, 1967.
Kooy, G. A. *Het modern westers gezin.* Hilversum, 1970.
———, and het klooster van Wingerden. "The Aged in an Urban Community in the Netherlands." *Human Development* 11 (1968):64–77.
Lehr, U., and H. Thomae. *Konflikt, seelische belastung und lebensalter.* Köln and Opladen, 1965.
Lenior, T. M. J., and J. M. A. Munnichs. *Integration en evaluation.* Report 24, Gerontological Center, Nijmegen, 1972.
Litwak, E., and Figueira, J. "Technological Innovation and Ideal Forms of Family Structure in an Industrial Democratic Society." In *Families in East and West,* ed. R. Hill and R. V. König. Paris, 1970. Pp. 348–96.
Lowenthal, M. F. and Haven, C. "Interaction and Adoptation." In *Middle Age and Aging,* ed. B. Neugarten. Chicago, 1968. Pp. 390–400.
Mast, F. A. C. de, P. W. M. Remmerswaal, and J. M. A. Munnichs. *Atlas van de ouder wordende Nederlandse bevolking.* Nijmegen-Deventer, 1972.
Mol, F. "Beinvloeding van ouderdomswaardering, een experimentele studie bij eerstejaarsstudenten." *Gawein* 16 (1968):86–128.
Nota bejaardenbeleid, 1970. Ministry of Culture, Recreation and Social Welfare. Rijswijk, 1970.
Oosterberg-Volker, J. P. "Rijp beraad? Onderzoek naar factoren, die het beslissingsproces om in een verzorgingstehuis voor bejaarden to gaan wonen, beinvloeden." Scriptie, University of Wageningen, 1972.
Rapport onderzoek naar levensomstandigheden van bejaarden enz. Hilversum, 1965.
Sauer, R. B. L. "Satisfactie met tehuisbewoning bij bejaarden in drie verzorging-stehuizen." Scriptie, Universiteit van Groningen, 1971.
Shanas, E., and G. F. Streib, eds. *Social Structure and the Family: Generational Relations.* Englewood Cliffs, N.J., 1965.
Shanas, E., P. Townsend, D. Wedderburn, H. Friis, P. Milhøj, and J. Stehouwer, *Old People in Three Industrial Societies.* New York, 1968.
Staps, A. C. J. *Probleem inventarisatie bejaarden en bejaardenvraagstuk.* Report G.I.T.P. Nijmegen, 1972.
van der Haak, C. P. M. *Bekend maken en bekend raken.* (*Making Known and Getting Known: An Evaluation of the First Five Years of Government Information on the Public Assistance Act, 1962–1967*). The Hague, 1972.
van Heek, F. *Verzorgingsstaat en sociologie.* Meppel, 1972.
Weber, M. *Gezag en bureaucratie.* Rotterdam/Antwerpen, 1972.
Wimmers, M. *Onderzoek verpleegtehuizen.* Deel II, 1970.
———, and J. van der Bom. *Sociale relaties, sociale situatie en relatiepatroon van oudere mensen.* Report 22, Gerontological Center. Nijmegen, 1972.

7. The Household, Intergenerational Relations, and Social Policy *Hannah Weihl*

Various research projects carried out in different countries (Shanas et al, 1968; Rosenmayr and Köckeis, 1965; Blume, 1968; Townsend, 1957) during the last several decades have shown that the family has not withdrawn its support nor shed its responsibility for the elderly in spite of the growing tendency of parents and adult children to maintain separate households. In both industrialized and developing countries there usually exists some recognition of society's obligation toward its aged population (Goode, 1963; Schorr, 1960), but the distinction between what is familial responsibility and what is societal responsibility is blurred and indistinct. Both society and the family regard each other, as well as themselves, as responsible for their aged members, yet often there is no clear delineation of the scope of responsibility of each of them. This situation results in some confusion, the state expecting the family to provide services that the family, in turn, regards as the state's responsibility. In Israel, for example, on the one hand there exists a law recognizing the state's obligation to provide all aged with a basic income regardless of their children's income, and this allowance is increased when the old person has no other source of income.[1] On the other hand, there exist two laws that define the responsibility of children and grandchildren to support their parents financially.[2] There is no legal provision obligating the state to extend its services to the elderly other than to provide them with basic income; and at the same time there is no formal obligation of the family to support its aged with anything but financial aid. In some instances adult children use this confusion between government and family responsibility to ease their own burden. They threaten to withdraw their support from the aged parent, other than the financial support required by law, in order to force the state to intervene.

In this chapter I will consider the effect of the living arrangements of older people on their relationships with their adult children, and how the state, via its social policy and bureaucratic structure, influences this relationship.

Author's Note: This paper is partly based on research carried out in 1967–70 under grant number W.A. ISR 12–64, Department of Health, Education and Welfare, U.S. Government.

Unless specifically stated, all data on Israel referred to in this paper derive from this project and appear in the mimeographed research report.

1. National Insurance Act, 1967. The old-age allowance for a single person amounted in 1971 to 12 percent of the mean income. (Information obtained from Research Department, National Insurance Institute.)

2. Social services law, 1958; family law, 1959.

Living Arrangements of the Aged

Family relations originate and develop in an ecologically defined unit whose attributes are cohabitation, domesticity, and sexual consequentiality (Ball, 1972). Without going into the problem of how relations between household members develop and become patterned through time, I must point out that the division of labor (or the allocation of domestic tasks) in the household strongly affects the patterning of relationships between members. Cultural prescriptions of task allocation delineate the type of relationship between the members. Thus, for instance, the relations in households in which the decision-making authority is vested in a single family member differ markedly from the type of relationship prevailing in households in which this authority is distributed among various family members. A discussion of societal constraints on family relations of the aged has to recognize that the division of labor in households differs among groups, and that the universalistic institutional arrangements of societies affect these groups differently. The provision of income to all elderly persons improves the status of these persons but may well change the power structure of those households in which the wife never had any income of her own. Generational relations of different cultural groups thus may either be strengthened or weakened as a result of the same program.

The investigation of the differential effect of institutional arrangements for aged persons on the relations of old people with their children is important for theoretical as well as for practical reasons. Such investigations should enable one to gain a better insight into the processes of change in family relationships. Further, by a better understanding of the impact of policy provisions on different types of family relations, one may be able to prevent some of the unintended and undesired effects of certain social policies.

The households of old persons may be described in terms of two basic variables: marital status and whether the household is shared by persons of more than one generation. Four basic types of households emerge from the cross-tabulation of these two variables (see Table 1). Each of the four types of households may be subdivided into a number of subtypes, the most important ones being subtypes of Types III and IV, "living with children." There are aged persons who live with dependent children, persons who live

Table 1. *Household structure of old persons*

| | Marital status | |
Living arrangements	Married	Not married
Living alone or with siblings	I	II
Living with children	III	IV

Table 2. *The proportion of old persons in Israel living with children in different types of households*

Household	%
Living with dependent children	18
Living with adult unmarried children	22
Living with married son	21
Living with married daughter	23
Living with widowed children	8
Living with others	8
Total	100

with adult unmarried children, some of whom may be quite young; those who live with adult middle-aged children; those who live with married daughters who may have children of their own; and those who live with divorced or widowed children, both male and female. The numerical importance of each of these subtypes in Israel is given in Table 2. Each of these structural subtypes probably has a different impact on the life of the aged parent and on his relations with his children. For instance, living in a two-generation household differs from living with grandchildren; living with a widowed son and his family differs from living with a married son and a daughter-in-law.

The discussion in this chapter is confined to two main types of households —the one-generation household consisting of married or unmarried aged and/or other aged, such as siblings, and the household consisting of at least two generations. Reference to subtypes will be made when necessary.

The relations of aged persons with their children are differently structured depending on whether they live apart or with their children. Old people living apart from children are an economically self-sufficient unit although they may be receiving financial help from the children or the state. Persons living in such households are not dependent in the management of their daily lives on children or other relatives, nor are such relatives dependent on them. The aged in such households may live much as they have been living all their adult life: independent in their decisions, managing their own affairs, their own space, and using time at their own discretion. Their relations with children are thus independent of problems of living together and of domestic functions.

Relations with children in the second type of household—the one consisting of two or more generations—revolve very much around precisely the issues mentioned above. Aged persons living with adult children, even if they have never lived apart from their children, usually do not continue to live as they had most of their life. The old person has less authority over domestic and financial functions. In fact, in such situations, very often a man has lost the status of "head of household" and a woman the right to make major household decisions. The old person may participate in household chores but he is seldom given the authority for decision making. Such old persons are less autonomous than others in the use of time and of living space. For example, they may retire to bed earlier than they would like or eat at a less convenient time in order to meet the needs of the younger generation. They have given up or lost a great part of their autonomy, and their relationship with their children, or at least with the children with whom they live, is very much affected by how dependent they are upon them (Kalish, 1968).

Parents living apart from children are free to decide if and when they are prepared to extend and to accept services from any of their children. These parents are free to decide what and when to give or accept. In short, they are managing the relationship with their family without the constraints imposed by common living space. Aged parents living with children, however, are very much restricted in their surroundings. They cannot behave as they wish in their home without first considering the effect this would have on other members of the household and on their own position in the household. They often have little freedom of choice in how they maintain relations with "outsiders," including their own children. Israeli data show that the aged living with children have less social contacts than the aged living alone, one of the reasons being that the former feel that they cannot freely entertain visitors.

The discussion to this stage describes most of the two-or-more-generation households but not all of them. The aged parent who lives with dependent children — either children who are not yet of age or children who cannot live independently, such as adult children who are physically or mentally impaired — usually has not lost status and autonomy and carries on all or most of the household responsibilities. This subtype of household constitutes as important category when it is considered as an object of welfare programs and social services.

The different types of households of aged persons and how these households affect basic differences in relationship with children have been described. The effect of various institutional arrangements on the aged living apart from children and the aged living with their children will now be considered.

Institutional Constraints and Living Arrangements

The household may be viewed as a unit of consumption and as a unit of provision of services to its members. Income is the resource needed for the fulfillment of the first of these two functions, and manpower is the resource needed for the second. Both of these commodities tend to become scarce in old age. Income is reduced because of those social provisions which remove older people from the labor force and thus reduce their resources; manpower diminishes because physical capacities diminish with age and older persons often experience difficulties in performing ordinary household tasks such as cleaning, shopping, and ironing, as well as difficulties in performing the routine activities of daily living such as washing and dressing.

Both resources, income and manpower, can be augmented from sources other than within the household. Society may provide additional income to the old person as in the instance of old-age pensions, and it may provide substitutes for missing manpower via different social services. On the other hand, the family may help the old person, both by extending financial help and by replacing failing manpower within the household. Both society and family will replace resources only if they feel a moral commitment to do so — and if they have resources available to use for this purpose. The first condition is more important than the second, because without an accepted value position neither society nor family will allocate resources to the elderly, and the aged will live — as they often do — in poverty and neglect with diminished respect for themselves as persons.

In developed countries society only reluctantly recognizes its obligations toward its aged population. Though there is a general recognition of the obligation to provide a minimum income for the elderly, there is often no consideration of the fact that financial needs indeed may increase in old age because of the restriction of manpower available from within the household for the provision of domestic services. There is also little recognition that other needs, such as the need for more heating in winter, medical need when there is no health insurance, and the need for transportation, increase and often cannot be adequately met by old age allowances and pensions.

In the area of services society clearly delegates all responsibility to the family. Within those public agencies that provide manpower services, such services are mainly extended to the childless aged and to those old people whose children are considered to be unavailable. The bulk of the aged population, however, has children and does not qualify for public assistance. Many old people, however, do need help in carrying out domestic functions but do not have the means to hire such help.

The Effect of Restricted Income

The lower level of income of old age often prevents old people from carrying on their previous life style. Reduced income restricts their consumption, their leisure activities, and their ability to help their children when the latter need help, or when the parent would like to do so. It also diminishes or cuts out the possibility of buying services. Thus the lower level of income reduces, or threatens to reduce, not only life style but independence. Independence is here used in its widest sense—financial, emotional, and physical. How, then, does the loss of income, often resulting in old people having to "be a burden to my children," affect the relationship with children?

The two types of households, the single generation and two generation, differ in response to income constraints. Consider first the one-generation household consisting of aged persons only. Restriction of regular income (unless the loss is small compared to general wealth) in this type of household results in a general cutback of consumption. Households of aged persons differ from those of younger persons in that an effort is made to maintain a standard of living that approximates the highest level achieved during the working life, however long past, while the younger generation develops new needs and a higher standard of living.[3] The longer the period that old people live in retirement, the wider the gap between the prevailing standard of living and the standard of the household of aged persons. As Juanita Kreps (see Chapter 2) has pointed out, the purchasing power of income from pensions tends to diminish over the years, while the income of the working population rises with the cost of living. Pensions are usually defined as a proportion of the last salary, and this sum is not raised every time future salaries rise. Those aged who live apart from children have less up-to-date furniture and household goods than those who live with children. As things wear out, they are not replaced.

One would expect, therefore, that the claim on children's financial help increases with age or the length of time in retirement, as indeed it does, according to the evidence from cross-sectional studies in Denmark, Britain, and the United States as well as in Israel.[4] On the other hand, one would also expect differences between countries in the proportion of persons who are financially dependent on children, because of country-by-country differences in social and economic structure and social security provisions. The difference between the three above-mentioned societies and Israel in this respect is striking: 12 percent of all aged in Israel receive regular financial help from children, as compared to 2 percent in Denmark and 4 percent in Britain and the United States.[5] Among those in Israel who live apart from children about 16 percent receive regular financial aid from children and another 8 percent receive irregular aid. Among those who are not assisted by children there is a high proportion who stated that they actually needed

3. The differences in the standard of living between the two types of household, measured by the availability of durable goods in the household, are striking. Thus only 77 percent of all widowed aged living alone in Israel in 1967 had a wireless set, as compared to 93 percent of the widowed aged living with children. The figures for modern cooking facilities (gas or electricity) are 68 percent and 94 percent respectively for the two groups of widowed aged.

4. E. Shanas, P. Townsend, D. Wedderburn, H. Friis, P. Milhøj, and J. Stehouwer (1968), Table VII-24, p. 214.

5. Ibid., Table VII-28, p. 222.

help but children cannot, or would not, help them. One tends to suspect, therefore, that the need for financial help is greater than the actual help extended (this may very well be true for the economically advanced countries as well) and that there are comparatively few claims on the children for help because, in spite of the strain they feel, old people do not want to interfere with the lives of their adult children.

What the children feel about this is not known, but there are indications that children tend to ignore the financial problems of their parents or to state openly that the parent's time is passed and that their own obligations must focus on the advancement of their own families.[6] This argument was also often used by the aged poor when they were asked why their children did not support them. There is a definite strain felt between parents who have to live on a reduced income and children who realize the parents' difficulties, but do not—and often cannot—interfere. The strain becomes much more acute, and thus better voiced and better documented, when the financial resources of the older generation are not sufficient to meet some undefined minimum. One would assume that such a minimum income might be culturally defined, but it probably is also a function of the type of emotional relationship between the two generations, as well as some compromise between the child's feelings towards his parents and his own familial commitments. Parents resent the loss of independence because whatever their situation they wish to retain the self-image of the "parent," the provider, the one who decides, and because financial dependency very often means actual loss of status in the family. If their lack of income has long ago restricted their options to develop meaningful activities and relationships in retirement, it now becomes a threat to their self-image and changes their relationship with their family. The adult children of such parents have more options open to them. First, they may choose to disregard the situation and to do nothing about it, or even to disappear from the parents' lives altogether. Empirical evidence shows that this does occur, although rarely.[7] The other alternative for children is to interfere, either by taking all or part of the burden of support upon themselves, while at the same time seeking to enlist help from various other sources. The strain this engenders in their relations with their parents has numerous sources: the nature of the children's own resources and the effect of helping parents with other family goals; the attitude of spouses and of the children's children to the aged parents and to the situation of the parent's dependency; the children's emotional ties with the parent; the ability of the children to cope with the role reversal that now occurs; the strength of the norm of filial responsibility in

6. Quite a few children of middle income parents had no idea about the size or composition of their parents' income. (Data from an ongoing study.)

7. This is an uninvestigated area which seems to be of primary importance for the understanding of the structure of intergenerational relations. Blume states that 6 percent of the aged have lost contact with children (p. 50).

the society; the participation of other siblings or kin in the burden of support; and the children's information concerning availability of other possible sources of support and their ability to react and to manipulate these sources.

The empirical evidence available shows that usually there is at least one child who accepts the responsibility for the aged parent, and who helps, though often the help extended is scarcely adequate, mostly because the child may lack financial resources.[8] One would like to know more about the distribution of help to parents among siblings and about the differential use of available familial resources.

In households shared by two or more generations, the problem of restricted income is different in nature because of the structural diversity of this household type. The majority of such households are families that have never separated into two households because there are still children either underage or adult but still dependent, or because a widowed housewife continued to live with one of her married or unmarried grown-up children, or because there were no means available to either the parent or the adult child for maintaining two separate households. There is very little evidence of parent or parents moving in with children, or vice versa, after the generations have lived separately for some years, or of newly widowed parents joining children. It seems that the main characteristic of the aged living in this type of household is their lower income compared to the aged who maintain an independent household (Blume, 1968; Weihl et al., 1970). Most of those who share households are women (Blume, 1968, p. 51; Weihl et al., 1970, p. 36).

Restriction of income has a different meaning for those persons, usually men, who are still providing for a family than for those who have grown-up children but have never been physically separated from them. In the first group restriction of income means poverty for all family members and loss of status and authority of the parent often accompanied by resignation and despair. Here the inadequacy of institutional arrangements for income at old age is felt most keenly, for it feeds the often already existing generational strain and acts to punish the older person for being a father or mother and the children for having an older parent. Institutional constraints, instead of helping the older parent to maintain at least a previous standard of living and so to maintain his position in the family, force both a lower living standard on the old person and a lower status.

Most of the remainder of the aged who live with children are widows, have a low income, and have never separated from their children. Thus it can be assumed that most of these women have been dependent on others,

8. Israeli data show that there is a relationship between level of income of parent and financial help extended by children. Low-income aged are more often supported than the better-off aged. Some low-income aged stated that they are not supported by children because the children lack means. It seems reasonable to expect that the children of many low income aged are themselves not financially affluent.

husband and/or children, before becoming subject to income maintenance programs at old age. Curiously enough, their financial position is sometimes strengthened on receiving old-age pensions. Where before they had no income of their own, they now have some. Quite often, when the children with whom they live are themselves none too well off financially, this income is of importance to the family. It serves to confer status on the old woman. Moreover, she may now be able to show gratitude and give rewards for services rendered. Thus her standing in the family changes and her options widen.

It has already been seen that old people who live with adult children share the higher standard of living of the younger generation. This is certainly a positive point to remember. On the other hand, one ought not to forget that if the aged parent has little or no means for sharing the expenses of the household and/or his personal comforts in the form of cigarettes, sweets, some clothing, small gifts, and other such items, he may feel uncomfortable even if the family he lives with provides him with pocket money and supplies his needs without suggesting that this is a burden. Instances have been found where old people during interviews have voiced their unhappiness with this situation. In some few instances children outside of the household give money to their parents, either for their personal needs or as a contribution to the household expenses. In other instances such a contribution is being paid directly to the sibling with whom the parent lives. The enormous symbolic importance the older person attaches to his financial independence, to the value of being able to maintain himself, cannot be better illustrated than by the demand of members of Kibbutzim (collective settlements) that a pension fund be established to which each member contributes during his working life in order to enable persons to make personal contributions to the Kibbutz in their old age. This idea has been widely discussed and is advocated by many members. It has been passed on to an executive level of the various Kibbutz movements and probably will be officially accepted and enacted in the near future.[9]

For the adult children of aged persons the economic support of these elderly may involve a serious financial burden. Those in the work force, the younger generation, are already supporting the retired generation via taxes paid to the government. In addition to this, many adult sons and daughters are directly supporting aging parents, either by caring for them in their own homes, or by supporting them financially in separate households. Thus a certain proportion of those still in the labor force carry a double financial burden that is not equally distributed between income groups. There is reason to assume that parents with low income very often have children with low incomes. It is the low-income children on whom this financial

9. Discussions on this subject have been published in journals of the various Kibbutz movements as well as in Israeli newspapers. See, for instance, D. Attarr, *Pensions for Aged* (Hakevuza, 1971).

burden is greatest because of the effect of limited funds on the children's own family, a fact which ought to interest those who are responsible for shaping social policy. There is no evidence in Israeli research data, however, that this double burden of direct and indirect contributions causes strain on generational relations, probably because most persons of both generations are not aware of this double taxation. Many aged persons believe that their contributions towards pension funds and old age pensions are accumulated at some bank, and that there exists somewhere a certain sum of money earmarked personally for them.

There is one further item related to restriction of income which must be mentioned here. In some instances, and differing from society to society, aged persons need to apply to public or private agencies for financial help or for other services which they cannot finance themselves because their resources are insufficient to cover essentials. This occurs among the aged who have no savings, or where pensions from work are small or nonexistent, and with those aged whose main or only source of income is their old-age allowance. It probably occurs more among the childless aged than among those who have children. Becoming clients of the welfare services is a new role for the aged, and for many a very difficult one. To become dependent on welfare is regarded by some aged persons as the last degradation, and some refuse to ask for help even when in great need. Having to learn the rules associated with a new role, a role which one dislikes and considers inferior, is difficult for anyone. It is especially difficult for the old. The aged person in need is thus threefold burdened: with a heavy financial problem, with a painful decision to ask for help in order to alleviate some of the financial difficulties, and with a need to adjust to the demands of a bureaucratic system new to him. In many instances, because of the reluctance and sometimes the refusal of the old person to ask for help, it is the children, and in their absence other relatives, who approach the bureaucracy for help. But there may be younger persons, too, for whom the bureaucratic structure is strange and bewildering. One would like to know if the relevant bureaucracies have given enough thought to the problems of communication with their potential clients.

This discussion of the impact of restricted income on relations with children cannot be concluded without pointing out that not all aged need financial aid and/or services from children. In all countries there are people who manage to save substantially during their working years, and some who go on working after the usual retirement age. Israel, however, is an example of a society in which relatively few of the aged have resources other than old age allowances and sometimes a pension from their former work.

Restriction of income then has more than an economic effect on old people. It affects the composition of households and the interrelationships of generations within households. It forces changes in the social roles of the elderly, in their modes of life, and in the expectations of the old person.

Restriction of Manpower

Some of the problems arising from the restriction of manpower for providing household services to the aged have already been mentioned in the above discussion. Manpower for all services can be hired if money is available, although even those aged who are financially well off sometimes can find no suitable manpower available in the labor market. Such situations do occur because manpower to help aged persons often needs special training and preparation that potentially suitable persons do not have. In Israel as in many other countries services to the aged are not attractive to the average person seeking employment.

As a result, even for those aged who can pay for services, the problem becomes one of lack of suitable personnel. This point must be reemphasized because in the more industrialized societies domestic and other household help is very difficult to obtain and unless some specific effort at recruiting is made many needs of the aged cannot be met (Blenkner, 1968).

The problem of needed manpower for domestic services arises in both the household types discussed earlier even though its actual manifestations may differ. As has been stated, old people who live apart from children are either married, and thus there are two persons to share household tasks, or they live alone. The problems of the single old person are greater than those of the married. When an old married person becomes unable to perform household tasks, or tasks of personal self-maintenance such as washing or dressing, these tasks are usually taken over by the spouse. The instance of both spouses being unfit to perform most household and self-care tasks are probably rare, though some men may feel incapable of performing what they consider female tasks and thus refrain from doing so. The impression from the data, however, is that if it is necessary many of the aged men do perform many household tasks.

Available data indicate that there are numerous informal and unpaid sources of help, both to the two-person household and to the old person living alone.[10] Help is given by a child or some member of a child's household, by siblings and siblings-in-law, by nephews and nieces, and by neighbors and friends. The same household may use different helpers for different tasks, one doing the shopping, another the preparation of food, etc. Thus we sometimes observe a cluster of helpers active in one particular household. The division of labor in such a voluntary unit is not necessarily fixed, nor is it permanent. It may consist of various members of the family, such as some or all of the aged person's children, or it may consist of nonrelatives, or be a mixed structure, including welfare services. In the ultraorthodox community in Jerusalem, a closely knit community bound together by an ide-

10. Data for Denmark, Britain, and the United States in Shanas et al. (1968), Table V-7, p. 118, and pp. 117–23. Data for Israel, in Weihl, Nathan, and Avner (1970).

ology that emphasizes the value of extending charity, one finds poor or sick people who are served by a relatively permanent cadre of women.

Little is known about the emergence and dynamics of such networks of help resources in different types of societies. Are they self-appointed or do they emerge as the result of the initiative of somebody? What are the relationships between such helpers? How does such a network reorganize after the dropout of one link? What happens in crisis situations? What changes, if any, occur at the intervention of some welfare agency? Leichter and Mitchell (1967), in their study, *Kinship and Casework*, point out that caseworkers of the investigated agency tended "implicitly and explicitly" to help aged parents to "realize their children's right to independence in their new families," thus holding up as ideal the "norms of the nuclear family."[11]

As already mentioned, cases are known where the service available from a welfare agency has been incorporated into the help pattern without breaking up the network; on the other hand, social work evidence in Israel indicates that sometimes the voluntary support system more or less disappears once welfare services have shown an interest in the person. Glazer has warned against the "development of social policies that sanction the abandonment of traditional practices." He goes on to say that "every piece of social policy substitutes for some traditional arrangement, whether good or bad, a new arrangement in which public authorities take over, at least in part, the role of the family, of the ethnic and neighboring group, or of the voluntary association. In doing so, social policy weakens the position of these traditional agents and further encourages needy people to depend on the government, rather than on the traditional structure, for help."[12]

Turning now to the other major type of household, aging parent(s) living with married or unmarried children, one finds much less need for help. Domestic services are usually carried out by the younger generation only. The need for manpower replacement arises only in those cases where the aged person is unable to perform some of the necessary tasks of self-care, when he needs attention, and where the younger generation is temporarily or permanently unable to perform the necessary domestic activities. In most instances the aged person in this household, even when incapacitated, is served mainly by manpower available from within the household.

As one views the situation of the aged in such households two things become apparent. These are: first, the absence of helpers outside of the family; and second, the differential application of the normative value of filial responsibility. Although there are instances of aged persons in such households receiving assistance from persons outside the household, such assistance comes only from relatives, mostly children and children-in-law not living with the aging parent. Government and nongovernment social agencies have withdrawn from the situation as if in silent consensus that

11. Leichter and Mitchell (1967).
12. Glazer (1971).

once an old person lives with children his needs are being looked after. This may indeed be true because most families do not neglect an aged parent living with them even if the care of a parent constitutes a heavy burden on their material and emotional resources. Families who share households with ailing parents are left very much to their own devices unless a crisis situation occurs in which they are forced to seek help.

Public welfare services in Israel, and the same might be true for other countries, tend to regard these aged persons living with children contrasted with the aged living alone as being much more the family's responsibility. This is expressed in the little thought and even less consideration given by public and voluntary welfare agencies to the needs of families with ailing parents. Services such as home help for families, care for an ailing, aging parent so as to enable the responsible child to have some respite, are rarely available. One ought to point out though that little is known concerning the demand for such services. It is quite possible that families rarely apply for this kind of service and that therefore it is not considered necessary. On the other hand, public welfare agencies apparently do not consider such needs as "legitimate."

Society in both its formal public services and in its informal voluntary aspects extends various kinds of manpower-replacing services to old people who live alone, regardless of whether the children of these persons do "their duty." Social services in Israel try to enlist available children as part of the support system for the old person but usually do not insist on such help even if backed by legal provision.[13] The arguments used by welfare agents for this purpose are many, such as the duties of children to parents, the plight of the parent, the emotional importance of the child's help to the parent, but these arguments are not strongly advocated and may be of little avail if the child does not feel obligated to give support to his parents. Thus society actually accepts that sons cannot be made responsible for extending various services to their parents, even though everybody agrees that, morally speaking, this ought to be the case. Having accepted this fact, society, both in the form of organized services and through voluntary bodies, proceeds to help where help is needed.

The children of those aged who share a common household are, however, measured with a different yardstick by the state bureaucracy and by society as a whole. These children are regarded and treated as the sole carriers of responsibility for the elderly. They have no choice but to volunteer whatever resources they may have, even at the expense of the basic welfare of their own children. They cannot withdraw from the situation in which they find themselves. It may be said that, in contrast with their own siblings, as well as with those adult children whose parents maintain a separate household,

---

13. An investigation into the actual application of the law in Israel has shown that social workers in public agencies do not adhere to the regulations of the Ministry of Social Welfare and that there is little application of the law. Doron and Rosenthal (1971).

they are not volunteers. They are not free to give aid when they feel like it and in a manner that they prefer. On the contrary, both the formal and informal system of support services expects these children to act in accordance with normative values of filial responsibility. The following example from the Israeli scene illustrates this point. Because of the scarcity of nursing home facilities only very few patients in need of such care can be institutionalized. The criteria for deciding who, among those patients needing financial assistance, will be admitted depends largely on whether the patient lives with relatives or alone. The inability or the unwillingness of the family to cope with the situation is considered only in the most extreme cases. The aged parent living in a shared household then is at a disadvantage because, by being just one other member in his child's household, he forgoes claims on welfare services he would have had available to him had he been living alone. However, his general well-being as well as his status in the household may be affected by the denial of such services. Ironically, it is almost as though society were punishing the family for having decided to care for the old person.

The above discussion of differential application of the norm of filial responsibility in the provision of services illustrates the existing confusion in social policy regulations regarding the target unit. When needs are discussed, measured, or defined, is it always made explicit whose needs are the subject of the discussion? A person in need of physical care living in a multigenerational household will have his needs fulfilled if adequate manpower is available in the household, but that same household as a unit may have need for help which is ignored. In this example, if the target unit were the aged individual alone, there would be no need to supply community resources. His minimal care and general welfare are more or less assured. If, on the other hand, the household is regarded as the target unit, the definition of needed services should be based on the welfare of all members of the household. On the basis of this definition unanswered needs may be detected and possible resources allocated. An analysis of the nonfinancial needs of households containing aged persons with the household defined as the target unit of social policy may prove fruitful for a clearer understanding of needs and for a more rational allocation of resources and delivery of services. This emphasis on the conception of the household as the target unit of social policy for the aged is not intended to overlook or underrate the existence of individual needs. These do exist, both on the emotional and material level. However, they should be evaluated and provided for in the framework of the more general needs of the household.

Summary

The structure of the household in which an aged person lives is an important factor in the shaping of the relations between the generations.

Even when the aged parent is physically dependent on others, living apart from children enables the continuation of relations of independence. The old person may still be his own master in decisions concerning domestic activities, allocation of resources, social interaction including his interaction with his family, and in the way he uses his time. Living with adult children always restrains the independence of the aged parent.

Institutional arrangements, such as income maintenance programs and domestic aid services, have a differential impact on aged living in structurally different types of households. Such institutional constraints affect the relations between the generations. In Israel bureaucracy tends to disregard the important needs of the elderly, its functionaries apply the moral value of filial responsibility differentially among households, and, restrained by laws and customs, bureaucracy fails to distinguish between the needs of different households and the needs of different individuals.

References

Ball, D. "The Family as a Sociological Problem: Conceptualization of the Taken-for-Granted as a Prologue to Social Problem Analysis." *Social Problems* 19 (1972):295–307.

Blenkner, M. "The Normal Dependencies of Aging." In *The Dependencies of Old People*, ed. R. A. Kalish. Ann Arbor, Mich., 1968. Pp. 27–38.

Blume, O. *Moeglichkeiten und Grezen der Altenhilfe.* Mohr Tübingen, 1968.

Doron, A., and R. Rosenthal. *Achrayut Kerovim Bema'arechet Hassa'ad Beyisrael (Kin Responsibility in the Welfare System of Israel).* Jerusalem, 1971.

Glazer, N. "The Limits of Social Policy." *Commentary* 52 (1971):51–58.

Goode, W. J. *World Revolution and Family Patterns.* New York, 1963.

Kalish, R. A. "Of Children and Grandfathers: A Speculative Essay." In *The Dependencies of Old People*, ed. R. A. Kalish. Ann Arbor, Mich., 1968. Pp. 73–84.

Leichter, H. J., and W. E. Mitchell. *Kinship and Casework.* New York, 1967.

Rosenmayr, L., and E. Köckeis. *Umwelt und Familie Alter Menschen.* Berlin, 1965.

Schorr, A. *Filial Responsibility in the Modern American Family.* Washington, D.C., 1960.

Shanas, E., P. Townsend, D. Wedderburn, H. Friis, P. Milhøj, and J. Stehouwer, *Old People in Three Industrial Societies.* New York, 1968.

Stehouwer, J. "The Household and Family Relations of Old People." In E. Shanas, P. Townsend, D. Wedderburn, H. Friis, P. Milhøj, and J. Stehouwer, *Old People in Three Industrial Societies.* New York. Pp. 177–226.

Townsend, P. *The Family Life of Old People: An Inquiry in East London.* London, 1957.

Wedderburn, D. "The Financial Resources of Older People." In E. Shanas, P. Townsend, D. Wedderburn, H. Friis, P. Milhøj, and J. Stehouwer, *Old People in Three Industrial Societies.* New York, 1968. Pp. 347–87.

Weihl, H., T. Nathan, and U. Avner. "Investigation of the Family Life, Living Conditions and Needs of the Non-institutionalized Urban Jewish Aged 65-plus in Israel," Research Report. Jerusalem, 1970. Mimeographed.

8. The Family — A Source of Hope for the Elderly?
Leopold Rosenmayr

In recent years a growing amount of intercultural and international comparative data have described such central problems as subjective health, intergenerational cooperation, and joint living of older people. These studies, by now almost redundant, leave us with the satisfaction that we have been able to destroy some general and crude stereotypes of the isolated, sick, and helpless old. Further, they offer evidence on certain types of emergency aid to the elderly and of the high frequency of interaction of the elderly and other persons as measured by visits.

Second thoughts, however, must arise when we review these data critically. In this chapter I intend to make such a review. The large number of studies — not to speak of their different theoretical and methodological design — makes it practically impossible for any individual researcher to present a satisfactory overview. I will try, however, to analyze broad themes and to suggest new avenues for research, based on critical evaluations of empirical findings and their interpretations.

This chapter will also add some recent findings to the evidence, which consists largely of unpublished materials. These are the result of Austrian studies, and it is difficult to estimate whether they have more than regional Central European significance.

There is a paucity of data, at least in Europe, on public social services for the elderly in their own households. We have little information — mostly only ad hoc remarks from the people who organize such services — on home help, food distribution systems, "meals on wheels," etc. This is only in part because of the general underdevelopment of these systems of aid, and of sociomedical services (massage, physical therapy, and other "rehabilitation," or psychiatric consultation). Research is needed to evaluate the efficiency, costs, and the acceptability of further development of these services to the elderly.

The theoretical perspective on family help and organized public social services is close to Eugene Litwak's and Gordon F. Streib's conception of shared functions, particularly to the statement that "although theoretical analysis is still incomplete and many of the applications must be worked out, the basic idea of shared functions is sound" (Streib, 1972, p. 6). Not just for semantic reasons but for more accuracy it is best to use "coordination of functions" or the need for coordinating and supplementing functions within a process of continued evaluation of the developing needs of the elderly, as these needs change sociohistorically, according to the phase of life of individuals and couples and families (family life cycle), and according to the social situations of these individuals and couples.

First I will review the results of research on the family, then discuss the problem of coordination of functions between family and society and the opening of options through linkage (Sussman, 1972), and finally I will present an overview of the social work organizations and the social security and pension systems in Austria.

Recent Data on "Joint Living" of the Elderly and Their Children

The smaller the community and the less industrialized the region, the greater is the frequency of a household shared in common by parents and their married children (Tartler, 1961) and the greater the preference for such a household (Friedeburg and Weltz, 1958). Joint living is usually, though not exclusively, correlated with occupational and economic factors (Kaufmann, 1966). Twenty-six percent of the agricultural households in Federal State Lower Austria are still three-generational. For the nonagricultural population of the same area this percentage drops to 6 percent and for Vienna, to only 4 percent.

There are also structural differences within these common households. In urban areas the three-generation households include complete couples in both generations (grandparents and parents both married) in 16 percent of all cases, whereas both generations are complete in 34 percent of farmers' three-generation households (Kaufmann and Rosenmayr, 1972). This supports the often-made assumption that the farmers' extended family maintains the three-generation household throughout the family life cycle for economic reasons and to maintain a rational division of labor. (See Table 1.)

Agricultural households tend to be patrilocally structured. Of those consisting of two married generations, 59 percent contained the husband's

Table 1. *The structure of three-generation households by marital status of adult members (percentage distribution)*

Marital status	Vienna	Lower Austria	
		Nonfarmers	Farmers
First and second generation married	16	23	34
First generation widowed or divorced, second generation married	47	52	48
First generation married, second generation widowed or divorced	14	11	5
First and second generation widowed or divorced	23	14	13
Total	100 (250)	100 (209)	100 (248)

Source: Leopold Rosenmayr, "The Elderly in Austrian Society," in *Aging and Modernization*, D. O. Cowgill and L. D. Holmes, editors, © 1972, p. 188. Reprinted by permission of Prentice-Hall, Inc., Englewood Cliffs, New Jersey.

parents. The nonagricultural households struck a balance in favor of matri-locality; only 39 percent were patrilocal (Rosenmayr, 1971). Living with a daughter is chosen more often for emotional reasons (Nimkoff, 1962), and living with a son is the pattern outlined by the social norms of heritage and by the traditional division of labor. From intercultural studies the finding is that widowed persons with sons only are more likely to live alone than widowed persons with daughters only (Shanas et al., 1968).

In Vienna more than 50 percent of women aged sixty-five and over (approximately 80,000), live alone, whereas only 7 percent of the aged females of the agricultural population of Lower Austria live alone. The peasant family – at least in certain areas – does provide a home for nearly all its aged members. This does not imply, however, that these aged feel integrated and have no complaints about their social relationship within the family.

In the urban family old people show an increased desire to live with their children only after they have lost their spouse (Rosenmayr and Köckeis, 1965). One should not conclude that reestablishment of joint households replaces the emotional losses. What these reestablishments show is that household separation has not entailed a breach between the generations, leading to their mutual isolation. On the contrary, we should speak of a revocable detachment. The theory of disengagement as formu-lated by Cumming and Henry (1961) does not have general application to family relations.

A positive correlation between common living and a mutual positive evaluation of existing intergenerational relationships was not found. Certain studies show that fewer tensions exist in member families of extended net-works who live in separate households. It is quite plausible that psychologi-cal independence of the younger generation can be more easily reached outside the physical omnipresence of parents and parents-in-law. Conflict is likely to be greatest in those circumstances where economic reasons force the old and the young together and when the traditional subordination of the young to the old are loosened.

It has been observed widely that the postponement of entry into the labor force for educational reasons, combined with trends toward earlier marriage, provides an open invitation for older parents, at the peak of their earning power, to subsidize their married children. This, of course, may mean psychological dependency and conflict.

We have to answer the question of how we can explain that only a minority of the elderly follow the pattern of joint living, yet the existence of family relations and exchange between the elderly and their grown-up children is a major social fact of theoretical and practical importance to social gerontology. How do the findings about household separation match with the emphasis on the cooperation within the extended three-generational family?

Part of the explanation, of course, is a marked tendency for children to settle in the vicinity of their parents' homes. The studies further reveal that the most frequent visitors of old people are members of their families. The aged are seen much more often by children and grandchildren, except when they live too far away, than by neighbors and friends (Rosenmayr and Köckeis, 1965; Langford, 1962; Pfeil, 1961; Sussman and Burchinal, 1962; Sussman, 1953). In the case of childless old persons, there are frequent contacts with siblings and other relatives. Langford (1962) and Shanas (1962) also found that old people in distress turned first for help to their children and relatives. In our Austrian studies there was less discussion of financial support than in some other countries, since such support was expected from government and welfare agencies rather than from children.

There is some evidence that parent-adult child relations are not fully reciprocal inasmuch as aged parents seem more attached to their children than children to parents. Old people, far more frequently than younger ones, consider that they see too little of their families (Reiss, 1962). Yet the children's feeling of moral obligation seems in general sufficiently strong to balance this emotional disparity.

The data suggest that the family relations of older people can continue to exist and to be operative even when they are not living in the same household with their kinfolk. Joint living in the same household seems to be readily accepted in cases where circumstances necessitate it, but it is by no means regarded as generally desirable. Before the results of such empirical research became available it was often believed that old people lived separately from their children only when they were obliged to do so, owing either to unwillingness on the part of the younger generation to accept them into their homes or to the fact that homes were too small to include two families. Yet, in the most widely differing countries, whenever such a question was asked, only a small proportion of the aged preferred intergenerational joint living.[1]

An Evaluation of Recent Austrian Data on Joint Living and on Help Patterns

Data from two Austrian studies (a 1971 microcensus, comprising approximately 19,000 interviews of the population sixty years and over; and

1. "Our findings reinforce the well known view that the majority of older people with married children prefer to live independently." I. M. Richardson, *Age and Need: A Study of Older People in North East Scotland* (Edinburgh and London, 1964), p. 60. As Margaret Blenkner says: "Most older persons under 75 are quite capable of taking care of themselves and their affairs. They neither want nor need to be 'dependent' but they do want and need someone to depend on, should illness or other crisis arise." M. Blenkner, "Social Work and Family Relationships in Later Life," in *Social Structure and the Family: Generational Relations*, ed. E. Shanas and G. F. Streib (Englewood Cliffs, N.J., 1965), p. 53.

1,500 interviews based on a public opinion sampling technique of the population fifteen years and over) are used in analyzing joint living and help patterns. First reported is the microcensus.[2]

The microcensus was based on a 1.3 percent sample of the 1,475,000 Austrian population sixty years and over, thus including some 19,000 persons who answered twenty-two questions in December 1971. There were 540 persons, 2.8 percent of the study group, who declined to give information. Institutional residents were not included in this microcensus and 41,000 persons sixty years and over in old people's homes were outside this survey.

Almost 90 percent (87.5) of the data was secured by direct questioning. In 12.5 percent of the cases the person to be interviewed could not be contacted personally by the interviewer. In these cases the information was given by another member of the household. As the distribution of information originating from informants does not differ in essentials from that originating from interview subjects, information from subjects and information from informants is given together in the description of the results.[3]

A general tendency towards an overlap of generations is apparent from these data. More than 7 percent of the elderly between the ages of sixty and sixty-five still have a living father or mother. Twelve percent of the persons sixty and over have one or more great-grandchildren, and among those aged seventy-five to eighty 22 percent have great-grandchildren.

Further international research on intergenerational continuity is needed to evaluate these figures. The theoretical point made earlier in this paper that the general tendency toward household separation between generations is not an "irrevocable detachment" is being substantiated by our data. (See Table 2.)

The data seem to confirm the general thesis of "emotional matrilocality" in the sense that the oldest persons, those over eighty, show a slightly higher probability of rejoining the household of their daughters than of their sons.

In the microcensus the interviewers asked those old persons who had children but who lived separately from them whether they would seek acceptance by an institution, entrance into a hospital or an old people's home or residence, or whether they would rather live in the vicinity of their grown-up children, or in the child's apartment or house.

2. The Austrian microcensus is a government survey carried out by the Austrian National Statistical Office. The author of this chapter was one of the consultants. The responsibility for the research, however, remains with the National Statistical Office. The data processing, tabulation, etc. can be influenced only in part by the consultants.

3. I should like to express my gratitude to the Austrian National Statistical Office for allowing me to use some unpublished material. I am particularly indebted to its president, Dr. Lothar Bosse, and to Dr. Zeller and Dr. Klein for their cooperation.

Table 2. *Old persons living in a common household with children* (*percentage distribution*)

Living arrangement	Number of cases	Age groups				Average	
		60–64	65–69	70–74	75–79	80+	60+
With a son	(485,500)	24	19	16	15	16	19
With a daughter	(569,400)	16	13	13	15	21	15

The data show clearly that living together or in an apartment in the vicinity of the grown-up children is conceived as an alternative to institutional care (see Table 3). One must also take into consideration, however, that the set of motives connected with the wish to move close to the children may be considerably different from the wish for hospitalization or institutionalization. Furthermore, the wish to move close to the children is nega-

Table 3. *Preferred living arrangement of people over sixty if move necessary* (*percentage distribution*)*

Type of household of old person	Hospital	Old persons' home	Old persons' residence	Vicinity of children	Apartment of children	Number of cases
One-person household	10	20	15	12	10	358,700
Two-person household (couples only)	9	6	10	13	7	510,900
Two-person household (parent and child)	1	1	–	1	1	41,000
More-than two-person household	8	4	3	4	2	485,500

* Percentages do not total 100 because the categories "no desire to move" and "no answer" are omitted. The absolutes are estimates on the basis of the microcensus of 1971 comprising 19,000 cases.

tively correlated with the size of the community. It is expressed most often by old people in communities of less than 2,000 inhabitants; least often by those in cities of more than 250,000. (Vienna is the only Austrian city of this category.)

We now turn to a study of 1,500 persons of fifteen years and over to investigate joint living from the point of view of different age groups (see Tables 4, 5, and 6). In this 1972 Austrian study we asked about actual joint

Table 4. *The proximity of persons aged thirty or more to older relatives (percentage distribution)**

	Age of respondent		
Proximity of relative	30–44	45–59	60 and over
In same apartment	26⎱66	16⎱51	14⎱50
Living nearby	40⎰	35⎰	36⎰
Living further away	34	49	50
Total	100	100	100

* Total sample comprised 1,500 persons fifteen years and over; the age group fifteen through twenty-nine, however, is not included here.

Table 5. *The proximity of persons to older relatives according to size of community (percentage distribution)*

	Size of community		
Proximity of relative	Less than 2,000 inhabitants	2,000–50,000	More than 50,000
In same apartment	52⎱80	34⎱74	21⎱52
Living nearby	28⎰	40⎰	31⎰
Living further away	20	26	48
Total	100 (406)	100 (388)	100 (346)

Table 6. *The proximity of persons to older relatives according to frequency of attendance of religious services (percentage distribution)*

	Frequency of attendance			
Proximity of relative	Regularly	Frequently	Rarely	Never
In same apartment	45⎱77	41⎱69	33⎱63	23⎱63
Living nearby	32⎰	28⎰	30⎰	40⎰
Living further away	23	31	37	37
Total	100 (333)	100 (240)	100 (201)	100 (372)

living with older relatives. Eighty-five percent of these "older relatives" are parents or parents-in-law.

Our finding that joint living is caused primarily by economics must be supplemented by the statement that the smaller communities with generally still more powerful religious traditions tend to exert some social and ideological pressure toward joint living.[4] In Austria a solid correlation exists between the size of the community and the frequency of attending church, largely but not exclusively caused by the higher percentage of the agricultural population in the smaller communities.

The chance to build one's own house in the smaller communities is much greater than in the cities. Financial contributions from both generations toward building a home are not infrequent. In cases where the older mother or mother-in-law loses her husband, or, less frequently, the husband his wife, joint living has a better chance to develop in the smaller communities where there are likely to be independent individual homes.

A comparison between the reality of intergenerational living patterns and preferences suggests that the preference structure deemphasizes both "extremes": living in the same apartment and being widely separated. The data point toward a reconfirmation of the theory that modern intergenerational structures tend toward an optimal mixture of intimacy and distance. Extreme closeness and extreme distance do not attract more than relatively small minorities of choices—in all relevant groups. The author's theory of "intimacy at a distance," first developed in 1956, is reinforced by recent research.[5]

Types of Help to the Elderly from Their Families

Intergenerational help patterns are analyzed as a next step. Among the aid given to the elderly by their adult children we may distinguish three categories: (1) help in the household, (2) assistance with shopping, and (3) nursing in case of sickness. This is a preliminary way to study the enormously complex problem of giving and receiving help in intergenerational exchange. Further studies will have to differentiate between services which provide substantial physical and psychological assistance to an aged person and the kind of emotional back-stopping which occurs when one simply drops by the aged member's home for a few minutes. Which of these is more significant or important to the sustenance of the aged person is a question for research.

4. Intergenerational living is economically functional in agriculture. Eighteen percent of the active population in Austria are working in agriculture, according to the 1971 census. In various empirical studies I undertook in Austria I found that smaller communities have more powerful religious traditions. L. Rosenmayr, *Familienbeziehungen und Freizeitgewohnheiten jugendlicher Arbeiter* (Family Ties, Social Relations and Leisure Habits of Young Workers, with an English summary) (Wien, 1963). A recent study of young married women, of which some data are published in English, is found in L. Rosenmayr, "The Underdeveloped Position of the Woman in Industrial Society," *Social Change: Journal of the Council for Social Development* 4 (1974):4–14.

5. L. Rosenmayr, *Alte Menschen in der Grosstadt.* Mimeographed (Wien, 1958), describes this research started in 1956. It was summarized by L. Rosenmayr and E. Köckeis in "Propositions for a Sociological Theory of Aging and the Family," *International Social Science Journal* (UNESCO) 14 (1963):410–26.

Table 7. *Household help given by children or children-in-law to older people who live apart from children (percentage distribution)*

Frequency of help	Sex	
	Male	Female
Daily	3.0	4.3
Several times a week	3.4	5.2
Once a week	2.3	3.3
Less or never	91.3	87.2
Total	100	100

The results on help in the household for persons in Austria aged sixty and over who live in households separate from their children show an interesting difference according to sex (see Table 7).

Women tend to receive more help than men. Further research is needed to determine whether this is due to the considerably higher proportion of women who are widowed and therefore live alone in a one-person household. Several results point in this direction. Persons living alone in a household receive significantly more help, even if this assistance in household work is irregular and occurs less than once a week. One out of five persons sixty and over who live alone receive such help. The amount of help given to aged parents by children is strikingly low and raises questions regarding the discriminatory power of categories. The category "less than once a week or never" unfortunately taps at least two possible responses and does not differentiate between them.

Another important aspect of help to the elderly is assistance in their regular provisioning with daily goods, particularly food. Our data show that in this dimension of daily living the elderly receive roughly twice as much support than in the housekeeping dimension. In small communities the elderly who have children are to a much lesser extent forced to shop by themselves. Instead, grown-up children buy the necessary consumer goods for them. In communities smaller than two thousand inhabitants, one-third of the mothers and mothers-in-law are provisioned with daily consumer goods. This is because of the higher rate of common living in one household but also because of a greater sense of obligation to elderly parents found in the less urbanized areas. As with help in the household, assistance in shopping tends to be more frequently extended to aging women than to men.

We now turn to the expectancy of the elderly to be nursed in case of sickness. Tables 8 and 9 permit an overview (last column) and a juxtaposition of two main regional types for the population aged seventy-five and over.

Table 8. *Nursing expectations of elderly males according to residential location (percentage distribution)*

Will be nursed by	Males age 75–99			60+ Austria
	Communities up to 2,000	Vienna	Austria	
Spouse	48 (3)*	62 (2)	54 (2)	74
Children	30 (35)	14 (24)	24 (31)	11
Other relatives	8 (11)	4 (12)	7 (12)	5
Other persons	10 (36)	10 (30)	9 (30)	5
No one	4 (15)	10 (32)	6 (25)	5
	100 (100)	100 (100)	100 (100)	100
	36,574	28,750	113,179	590,700
	(4,769)**	(6,623)**	(18,689)	

* Figures in brackets relate to people living in one-person households.
** The two absolutes at the bottom of the first two columns do not add up to the sum of all persons of this age group in Austria (third column) as the communities from 2–20,000 and 20–250,000 were omitted.

Table 9. *Nursing expectations of elderly females according to residential location (percentage distribution)*

Will be nursed by	Females age 75–99			60+ Austria
	Communities up to 2,000	Vienna	Austria	
Spouse	9 (0)*	13 (0)	10 (0)	26
Children	59 (56)	34 (29)	49 (36)	39
Other relatives	18 (18)	16 (15)	17 (15)	13
Other persons	10 (16)	15 (22)	12 (24)	10
No one	4 (10)	22 (34)	12 (25)	12
	100 (100)	100 (100)	100 (100)	100
	62,846	69,111	219,226	879,025
	(14,691)**	(41,114)**	(93,979)	

* Figures in brackets relate to people living in one-person households.
** The two absolutes at the bottom of the first two columns do not add up to the sum of all persons of this age group in Austria (third column) as the communities from 2–20,000 and 20–250,000 were omitted.

In small communities, with a higher proportion of intergenerational households, the proportion of elderly who expect *not* to be looked after in case of sickness is lower than in the urban areas. In these same communities grown children are more frequently expected to nurse parents than in Vienna. The higher frequencies of expected help patterns of this kind — nursing in case of sickness — is not only due to intergenerational household structures and "living under one roof," but also to different types of family relations beyond the limits of the household.

A possible explanation is that family cohesion in the small community in Austria is more than a function of the intergenerational system of the economically based agricultural family. Immovables such as family property do play a greater role. But more important are expectations of care of the elderly because of their control over resources. The younger generation responds to this institutionalized expectation and looks after the old when they are ill or in need of help. Intrafamilial relations are more visible in small communities and towns than in the metropolitan areas, and information and communication about family networks are more articulated. Accepted moral standards – and care for the elderly by family members is such an accepted standard – become reinforced by such communication networks.

Finally, our data corroborate the common notion that the expectation not to be nursed by one's children in case of sickness augments the desire to be accepted by an institution. Also, the unavailability of help when in poor health tends to increase the desire to be accepted by an institution.

The Need for New Departures in Intergenerational Research

Our survey data have shown that the degree of help desired by the elderly equalled the amount the young generation was willing to give and actually gave. Whereas this finding is congruent with other data on intergenerational relations, it may be that experience with reality shapes the "wish" structure of the aged and reduces or limits their expectations. Furthermore, a certain hesitancy to put demands on the younger generation because of resultant anxiety from unfilled expectations may contribute to a picture that looks more harmonious and integrated than it really is.

A revision in the interpretation of results of studies on intergenerational relations is in order. Most studies have taken help patterns as the core of data for the established positive interaction patterns between the generations. Although help certainly is a very important criterion, it may not and cannot generally exclude conflict. Even the attitudes that accompany help may be of a kind to invite conflict, and such exchanges may create conflict. In addition, help, as we know from recent data on home help services, tends to be perceived differently by those who give it and by those who receive it.

Gordon F. Streib has made an attempt to go beyond the analysis of help patterns. He reports a relatively high self-evaluation of "family cohesion"; 74 percent of the parents and 60 percent of the adult children say that they form a "close family group," yet only 40 percent of the parents and 24 percent of the children want a good deal more interaction with each other (Streib, 1965; for similar results Lehr and Thomae, 1966; Bergler, 1966). Both the relationship of those two statements to each other and their independent value seem to indicate that the declaration of family cohesion (in questionnaire replies) tends to correspond to a certain expected standard.

Future research on family relations should study the communicative content of the interaction between the generations: patterns of information, influence, and sentiment. The following are sample questions: What is the degree of interest that adult children have in talking with their aging parents? What topics are of common intergenerational interest in various educational and occupational groups? How strong is the influence of the parents on their adult children and in what areas of decision making?

Family sociology has set the pattern for fruitful studies by falsifying prematurely developed "general theories" like the one of the isolated nuclear family and the isolated elderly. Research into the many dimensions that make up the bundle called "family relations" still lies ahead. It will eventually lead to a definition of the various types and qualities of these relations and possibly to an evaluation of their weight in other interactional systems. Cohesion and closeness may turn out to be preliminary concepts. This will be elaborated in the next section of this chapter.

In the future the relationships between the generations in the family will be still more complex through the appearance of a second generation in the age group of the elderly. Not the grandparents but the great-grandparents will be the oldest alive (Townsend, 1966), and grown-up children as well as grown-up grandchildren may contribute to help them.

Recent research from Eastern Europe indicates that patterns of interaction and help between the elderly and their adult children in socialist countries are similar to those found in Western countries. It is unclear, however, whether this is because of the survival of values and norms internalized before the political changes in postwar Eastern Europe, or whether even communist emphasis on loyalties outside the family, from the kindergarten through youth organizations to identifications with the party, now and in the future will not basically affect the dynamics of parent-child relations.

As the many gainfully employed women grow older, their readiness to act as the traditional "babushka" (the Russian grandmother who is most active in the household and family of her children or children-in-law and looks after the grandchildren) is being greatly reduced. The woman who has worked in the office, in the factory, or in the professions does not go back to the role of a homemaker, diffusing and sacrificing her energies and emotions for the young. This is most perceptible in some strata of socialist society where certain aspects of social change – the increase of employed women in industrial, administrative, and service jobs – came abruptly as a consequence of the political revolution.

Further research is also required on the differential effects of social class upon intergenerational relations in the family. The present emphasis is on similarities between classes with the qualification that joint living is more common in the lower classes. Urban working classes have fewer means to obtain separate apartments or houses for both generations. Also, among the lower classes there is greater employment of females because of economic necessity, and the grandmother in the household plays a central role in maintaining the household at least during the child-rearing stage of the family life cycle.

Patterns of exchange and help are not less developed in the middle and upper classes, yet the style includes more ecological (Braam, 1966) and social distance and more freely chosen and granted interaction. The elderly of the middle classes are much more mobile than the elderly with less resources. They travel more, have higher local mobility, and more extensive peer networks which are mutually reinforcing. Important changes take place during the aging process of the elderly. The younger grandmothers are more willing and able to accept a role in the extended family, not only because of their better health during the first phase of senescence but also because the grandchildren are more attractive to them and can more easily be disciplined as youngsters than as teenagers.

An area not yet explored is the effect of the relations between the marriage partners on intergenerational relations and vice versa. Equally important seems to be an analysis of family power structures in view of intergenerational relations (Blood et al., 1965).

Through the ages and across nations satire and irony have exploited the "mother-in-law complex"; yet no data on frictions or tensions with the mother-in-law shed any light on this question so that one is left with interesting and plausible, yet only general, hypotheses from the body of Freudian theory.

Although several avenues of refinement have still been open, only recently has it seemed as if the general picture of intergenerational exchange and interaction within the "modified extended family" would be outlined. It is not necessary to discard the idea of intimitization of the family (Kooy, 1970). It was coupled with processes of consciousness which redefined human relations within the family on the basis of values developed by the new urban middle classes as they grew in importance since the middle of the eighteenth century. Nuclearization was probably never as general as some theoreticians supposed; and, where it occurred, it did not necessarily prevent the reopening of relations to extranuclear family members on the basis of the newly established conditions of more equality, less formality of status, and mutual emotional support, or even economic exchange. The "new" extended or multigenerational family, however, developed more on the basis of conscious and rational regulation than according to strictly described or ritualized systems of allocation.

Help given by the modified extended family therefore has a greater chance of being accepted by the elderly without causing a feeling of self-diminution. Public action to give support to the aged has the innate danger of classifying them as marginal. It is the dialectics of societal organized help to a certain group that such a group becomes conscious of a certain deviance, whereas individual and informal assistance based on intimacy may avoid this sort of consequence. This is another reason for viewing family support as an important channel of social policy.

Future research efforts should focus, to supplement others, on the developmental aspects of intergenerational help by giving consideration to a sociology of life phases. To study one phase, knowledge about previous ones has to be obtained, as Lehr and Thomae (1966), Bergler (1966), Goldfarb (1965), and Shanas (1963) have demonstrated by their research. Earlier adjustments of conflicts determine later ones. This is in line with Goldfarb's statement (1965, p. 35) that ". . . behavior in old age is to a considerable degree related to early education and to socioeconomic status." The various types of alienation experienced by the elderly can be traced to their own early family experiences through life histories (Shanas, 1963).

Finally, limitations of age as an analytic variable should be emphasized. For some research problems the age variable is of crucial importance; for others it is less so. Quantities of activities, which are more easily measurable, may vary according to age. Attitudes towards symbols, areas of knowledge, and education and value orientations may be relatively stable over time.

Moreover, as has already been studied in other age groups, namely adolescents (Rosenmayr, Köckeis and Kreutz, 1966), social conditions of environment – "contextual variables" – direct the process of aging. In a culturally enriched environment age may lead to greater appreciation of music or literature. However, in a culturally impoverished environment, age may lead to a decline in the same area of activities (Lazarsfeld, 1955).

Family relations will have to be studied increasingly as an area of symbolic behavior, and they will have to be studied longitudinally. The sociology of aging should be integrated into a developmental perspective.

Historical Perspectives of Intergenerational Relations in the Family

To understand the present position of the elderly in the family, their integration and fulfillment of their physical and psychological needs by the family, it is important to first define certain patterns of present-day industrial society in Western Europe and in North America by a comparison with the past. Although evidence has been put forward by Murdock (1965) and Goode (1963) that the preindustrial family was not a predominantly large and complex family, a great number of sociologists stuck to the paradigm Durkheim developed. The contraction of the extended preindustrial family and the genesis of the nuclear family are functions of the modernizing processes of the industrialized world. Recent sociohistorical research refutes (or seems to refute) the thesis of Durkheim and the many variations in which it was presented since.

In the preface to a very well documented collective volume, *Household and Family in Past Time*, Peter Laslett (1972) says that the present state of evidence forces us to assume that the organization of the family "was always and invariably nuclear unless the contrary can be proven." According to Laslett, "the nuclear family household constituted the ordinary, expected, normal framework of domestic existence" (p. xi).

The contributions to Laslett's epoch-making criticism of the sociological cliché-evolutionism (from the complex and extended family system to its nuclear form) published in the work cited above merit careful study. Recent parallel research on rural communities in Austria in the seventeenth century (Mitterauer, 1973) reports results practically identical with the declarations of Laslett. They document the absence of joint living of two married generations in one and the same family-household for several historical rural communities.

A better perspective of present family relations of the elderly is likely to result by being informed historically about the widespread separation from the households of the younger generation. This reduces any regret we may have for certain past forms of living since we now know that they were only imagined, not real (Goode, 1968, p. 321).

The rise of individualism and the correct sociological observation of the formation of a personal and private sphere (Rosenmayr, 1965) since the seventeenth century led to the erroneous assumption of a parallel household reduction from a system of extended family cohabitation to a nuclear set. We now realize that—in order to "prove" a sociological atomization process —a nonatomized past was invented. This invention proved to be amazingly persistent against evidence.

One should not deny the fruitfulness of Peter Laslett's criticism. Yet it suffers from a lack of clarity in one important point, or maybe only from a misunderstanding on the part of those who now hail this new criticism of the traditional contraction-thesis. Laslett, in the introduction to his book, emphasizes that his findings relate to "the family as a group of persons living together, a household, what we shall call a coresiding domestic group" (1972, p. 1). Laslett is not concerned with kinship (family relations and positions) but with household units of family members. His criterion, even his object of study, is not the family but the household (of individuals from a family) or the "domestic group." The insistence is on residence, and the topic of Laslett's studies is the "coresident domestic group" (1972, p. 24); his emphasis is on a historical continuity of a type of coresidential family households which we may call "restricted," namely limited to a group with married members in only one of the two generations, and not comprising married parents and married children (plus, eventually, grandchildren). Laslett's entire argument, clarifying as it may be, still tends to blur the issue of *family* relations, as intergenerational relations are certainly not dependent on coresidentiality. As we are now led to believe that joint living of two married generations was a minority pattern historically, we need not and should not assume along with it that this separateness meant a lack of exchange and support between the generations.

A more succinct explanation is that "intimacy at a distance," taken in its most direct meaning, already existed in preindustrial society and even under rural conditions, and is not a product only of nineteenth-century urbanization and industrialization. One can question whether the exchange and aid patterns of noncoresidential nuclear family groups of agricultural preindustrial society deserve the term "intimacy." A reasonable posture is that intimacy is a product of the individualism and rationalism which developed, starting about the eighteenth century, and which defined special spheres of freedom for the individual, independent of his class position.

To better characterize premodern intergenerational relations within the kin group, the notion of an "exchange at a distance" is offered. Distances to be bridged may have been shorter—with the old couple living across the village street or in an annex building to the farm of the active generation or in an adjacent smaller house in town. Preindustrial society, with the exception of young students, young artisans, and seasonal workers, was less mobile residentially. To have a separate household for the younger generation on the farm or in the small town did not mean a great separation from the old family members.

The whole insistence on separate households of the generations of the historical family does not have a tremendous explanatory power for the understanding of family relations. The historian, particularly the one who uses social science methods, focuses on the household because he can methodologically better control findings in this sphere. The argument in this chapter is that the findings on separate residential groups are not valid for a historicosociological family theory. They do not carry theoretical power beyond a sociology of the household.

Although there is some significant evidence of "intimate" exchange patterns and aid systems of the present multigenerational family, it cannot be denied that in some cultures and subcultures of preindustrial society these patterns were still more intensive and catholic than they are now. From a point of view of residence—and this means household—the changes seem to be much less dramatic than the sociological stereotype of "contraction" would conjure. We hold to the hypothesis, however, that, with the atomization of modern individualism, standards and practices of intergenerational family relations have lost some aspects of mutual functionality.

Of course, such changes are difficult to measure, and needs have grown and developed so that historical comparison becomes a nearly impossible task in the field of family relations. Institutions and organizations of society have multiplied their power and influence so that their interference further diminishes the functionality of family relations for many areas of material and psychological support between the (married) generations in the family system. A certain reduction of kinship effectivity cannot be denied. Has it increased in some ways, e.g. as psychological support to the elderly, as a better understanding based on cognitive and emotional training?

Such problems, though strategically important, tend to be overlooked if we become too fascinated by the new findings of a somehow general and perpetual character of the nuclear household.

Shared Functions and the Emotional Dynamics of the Family in the Presence of the Elderly

In order to indicate problems and types of sharing or coordination of functions between family and society, it may help to outline a few theoretical ideas. Society, its culture and subcultures, prescribes and regulates need fulfillment on the basis of existing resources. In the process of optimizing need fulfillment, functions to fulfill needs are shifted from one institution to the other, for example, shifting certain functions of instruction from the family to the community, to the school system, to the mass media, to the peer society. Yet functions are shifted not only from the family to other institutions but also from prisons to hospitals; from curative to preventive medicine; from schools to mass media; from youth organizations to university seminars, etc. These shifts are emphasized because not infrequently in discussions on the transfer of functions from the family to other institutions, the "loss of family functions" is the sole focus. The family is by no means the only institution that "loses" functions, or from which functions have been shifted to other institutions, although, because of its centrality in society, the loss of functions by the family may be the most spectacular.

In the development of society, in the unfolding systems of production, need fulfillment and exchanges of functions are important elements of social change. The need-fulfilling functions of the modern family must be evaluated against the background of a great expansion of needs. It is doubtful whether a "scientific" comparison between preindustrial human needs and the role of the family in fulfilling them and need fulfillment through the family in postindustrial society can be made. Everyone – children, youth and the elderly – had less needs in the early historical period. The elderly in traditional agricultural society were viewed as groups with reduced needs; their average life expectancy was shorter; they were seen as approaching death rather than living in a phase of fulfillment, of "harvest."

As new needs were generated with the widening of areas of experience (such as mass traveling and mobility, mass information) new insecurities and imbalances (loss of homoeostasis) occurred. It became appropriate to view the family as an institution providing for the emotional needs of individuals in different phases of the life course, and assisting in their adjustment to changes due to the creation of new needs.

It is sometimes argued that the family should be particularly responsive to unspecific and diffuse emotional needs. It is a severe mistake, however, to classify emotional needs as generally unspecific. Emotional needs may very well be precisely "located" in certain types of external behavior or detailed internal attitudes expected from others, to changing or developing very concrete habits, and to forms of self-presentation.

It is a necessary, though not sufficient, function of the family to assist its "members" in coping emotionally with the expanding need system and the temporary frustrations which may be the side effects of this expansion. Further, the family has a necessary function in finding and organizing coordination between the institutions established to fulfill needs. This may particularly be the case for family functions related to aging parents and parents-in-law.

The needs of aging people of course are not always those arising from new technological or economic levels as, for instance, from new medical or leisure opportunities. "New" needs for the elderly may arise in emotional chain-reactions from the loss of certain abilities and positions. Retirement traumas, health tragedies, a long and painful dying create quite particular and indeed extreme needs a person has not had before. The family must be sensitized in order to detect needs or to find ways to implement solutions and gratifications.

The family in postindustrial society can be a detector of needs to be fulfilled mainly by other institutions. At the same time, the family is also seen as an institution which can serve to emotionally readjust individuals and relationships in view of their own or society's ever-changing needs. In taking care of this double function the family may very well lose other functions. The double function sketched above implies effective communication and cooperation with perhaps outside aids to support this cooperation.

The above is not a unidirectional/unilateral argument. Rather, in this presentation priority is given to macrosocial over microsocial changes. Changes in the system of production and consumption, of political organization and ideology, and of training and schooling have a higher order of generality and determine the main values according to which individuals are socialized within families. However, it must be taken into account that change is a reciprocal process involving many protagonists, and that individuals or families may be catalysts of change. To further desired change, or to block undesired change, the family must develop competencies. One of the competencies certainly needed in postindustrial society (which in many Western countries is a welfare society) is the set of capacities to handle the demands of bureaucracies. In the process of handling these demands families through their representatives, in fact, do both mollify and modify organizations and institutions (Sussman, 1973). This approach to social change and family functions already points to a certain concept of coordinating functions between the family and public social services for the elderly.

This concept would emphasize that various types of help in the households of the elderly could and should be taken over by well-paid and at least moderately motivated personnel. It is impossible to expect from women between the ages of thirty and fifty-five, who carry the heavy load of economically and emotionally supporting the members of their nuclear families, to extend further household assistance to their aging parents and parents-in-law or older relatives. In the case of certain stresses — for example, those of a woman who works for pay, or family stress due to babies or sick children, or those caused by problems with adolescents — conditions are such that we cannot simply assume that the de facto role of the woman within the family can be extended further to give help to the elderly. It might indeed be an overestimation of the functional capacity of the role of the woman to assume that if the care of old parents or parents-in-law were integrated into her role that this would not have a negative effect on her occupational or familial and marital role-segments. The existing and often urgently vocalized needs of the old tend to increase the psychic stress of the working woman and mother. They are an addition to what may be the already existing elements of intergenerational conflict. They strain the loyalties and emotional support of the woman towards her husband and children.

In particular, in the case of the woman under the stress of occupational work and middle age, important sources for aid to older members of the family should be found outside the family. At the same time, however, provisions should be made for leaving the older people in their familiar and accustomed surroundings. This requires an increase in home-help services for old people, organized by the federal, regional, and local authorities or by the churches or other voluntary groups.

An improvement of the system of aid must be well thought through. Various experiments have been carried out, for example, payments for members of the family willing to provide care for older members, the combination of such care with the services of sociomedical centers in the residential areas, and services and aid provided by a system of trained geriatric nurses. In order to provide help for older persons, the helpers must themselves receive help from institutions in a structural way; i.e., the individual role-holders in a family must receive material, psychic, and ideological support at the same time.[6] The connection in the system between the family and the institutions which may provide support of its functions in the care

6. M. B. Sussman, "Proposal: Incentives and Family Environments for the Elderly" (Unpublished document, Institute on the Family and the Bureaucratic Society, Case Western Reserve University, Oct. 1974), is an empirical study to test the feasibility of offering economic incentives and human service supports to members of extended family networks so that they can provide a creative living environment for elderly members. Similar studies were planned for Yugoslavia and Japan in 1975.

for the old must definitely be taken into account if we wish not to interrupt or destroy important human continuities.

A second concept from systems theory must be considered in social gerontology: the problems of the old must be seen as having a feedback effect. The stress caused by the care of the old has consequences on the persons providing the care. Gerosociology was considered a well-defined, limited field, simply the field of the various problems of the old themselves. But, in actual fact, it is a problem concerning the old and those who care for them alike. It also should be considered a problem of self-definition and self-understanding of those performing the care, not only for institutional providers, broadly defined, but especially the members of the old person's family.

The "bureaucratic" character of an aid system, its personnel and task organization, need not necessarily have "bureaucratic" consequences for the persons who receive the help. Cooperation with locally established organizations and groups for the recruitment of helping personnel might further diminish the danger of bureaucratic, nonpersonal contacts with the elderly. On the other hand, nonlocal help might be more acceptable to some elderly who may fear that details on their housekeeping, physical, or psychological handicaps would become generally known in the community. In addition, a further step in the development of public services would lead to physio- and medical therapy administered both at home and in day clinics, to specified branches of adult education, leisure clubs, etc. The aim of such services, however, should not be social "ghettoing" of the elderly but their stimulation through group activities and the individualization of social services. Such services should support the elderly in remaining outside old persons' homes and residences if they so desire, and if necessary encourage them to seek such "extramural," if supported, existence.

Social Security and the Role of the Family in Austria: Linkage and Options

In the 1860s when Austria was still a multinational monarchy, tied together by an elaborate system of public administration, that country developed the first basic layers of social security, which included legally guaranteed pensions for workers. Social welfare was introduced through a system of a controlled and restricted parliamentarism and could function only because of the extended bureaucracy of that time.

Pressures for change came from Catholic reformist social politicians who, for half a century before the Social Democrats began to be the decisive power in the development of social legislation, were ardent advocates for the proletariat. Several generations of workers and employees have benefited from a system of social and medical security developed since the end of World War I, when the multinational Austrian monarchy was dismembered. Since then the predominantly Social Democratic labor unions have been the main movers in the improving of social security coverage, supported by some forces in the political center and in the conservative political groups who sometimes even took the initiative in such legislation. Social security for the elderly — or more precisely economic security through pension systems and public health insurance allowing for practically free medical treatment, hospital care, and some rehabilitation — became nationally guaranteed. Social security is not only an organization which one counts on for financial support. It is part of the total value system of the society, an integrated element in the outlook on life and the generalized expectations of the people.

At present, practically every person in Austria has a legal right to a pension. Neither farmers nor small businessmen or self-employed artisans profited from social security until about a decade ago. But now the annual expenditures of the pension system, which is administered as a public fund outside the federal budget, amount to more than 30 percent of the total annual federal budget.

Whereas the economic and medical side of the social welfare system has expanded to a remarkable extent, without, however, abolishing poverty pockets, particularly among the rural isolated elderly and lower class urban widows, the sociopsychological aspects of welfare for the elderly have had a much less spectacular development. Social work and related aid systems as an important integral part of a welfare society are much less effective in Austria than the provision for economic security. "Care" for the elderly in Austria has a strong foundation, covering economic subsistence and guaranteeing health service and hospital treatment.[7] Such care is deficient, however, in the area of rehabilitation, home-help services, and recreational and cultural activities.

Sussman has outlined the problem of linkage and options (1972). In Austria this has four major aspects: (1) consultation of the elderly by family members to optimize economic benefits from the bureaucratically structured social security organization, e.g. the obtaining of special additional payment; (2) detection of health problems of the elderly family members and channeling the old persons through the network of diagnostic and therapeutic medical services — finding particularly scarce home-help services; (3) cooperation with these services — establishment of efficient help in the household, improvement of housing conditions; (4) provision of help in contacting friends, engaging in cultural and educational or sports activities (in this

7. It should be noted that if a retired person goes to a hospital all costs are taken care of by the pension system (with some exceptions in the instances of formerly self-employed persons). If the person goes to an old-age home or to a residence she or he will have to pay 80 percent of the pension toward the costs of stay in such an institution; 20 percent remains in the hands of the pensioner as pocket money.

dimension there is no strict boundary between linkage and encouragement).

Research currently under way on the quality of home-help services to the elderly provides bases for specifying hypotheses in terms of an analytic frame of linkage conceptology.

1. The better the quality of family relations, the higher the probability of functional linkage adequate to the needs of the elderly. Personality variables of the elderly under observation may account for some spurious correlation. For example, intensive contacts and verbal interaction between the elderly and other members of the family during the weekend contribute to a more thoughtful and purposive selection of doctors and medical treatment in the days to follow. Superficial, cognitively and emotionally less valuable contacts result in the elderly acting impulsively in seeking physicians and providers of services for diagnosis and treatment.

2. In view of certain economic, medical, and social needs of the elderly, linkage is a necessary function. The family is a nearly sufficient condition for introducing linkage processes in the case of economic and medical needs. Replacing the family in most cases implies additional energy. Linkage persons are then sought in the immediate ecological neighborhood and elsewhere.

3. The sharing of functions between family and home-help services has a certain probability of leading to conflict between the linkage person and the representative of the aid organization. This is likely to occur if the younger family member(s) establishing linkage for the older persons is not backed up by the family as a group, or because there is only one family member to perform linkage functions, or because the family does not as a whole support her or him in the linkage activities.

4. New qualitative methods of research reveal important differences in perception and evaluation of services performed. In order to approach the problem of shared functions of aid-giving by the family and organizations, such as home-help services, the differences in perception and evaluation may represent a decisive factor.

Research on home-help services to the elderly shows that home help is compensating for the lack of family help in old people's households. A majority of those who receive home help in the city of Vienna either have no family to assist them or are in conflict with their family. We may thus speak of a compensatory type of constellation between family help and aid from human services in Austria at the present time when such services are expanding. In other areas, relating to economic and health problems, the constellation seems to be rather cumulative. Those elderly persons who have qualitatively high-ranking family relations also have the better nonfamilial services. This results in optimal tapping of resources in bureaucracies. Further research is needed to determine the influence of personality variables versus the contribution of the family to effective linkages of the elderly with bureaucratic organizations. The educational and social class position of the elderly and the family in this problem area would need special sets of hypotheses. New data to structure such hypotheses according to the variation of social class have recently been presented by Anne Marie Guillemard and Remi Lenoir (1974).

Our sociopsychological emphasis on aging as a developmental process over the life span demands full attention to all barriers to options in later life. A democratic open society, beyond mere political equality, will have to consider carefully the opportunities and the qualitative life chances in the older ages as well as to conceive of this problem as an issue of social justice. The old should be compensated according to the achievements of the immediate present, else social change will work rapidly toward their relative deprivation. This goal cannot be implemented without preparing the institutions and organizations, as bureaucratic as they may be, to develop linkage services themselves. The offering of aid as such is not enough. Such programs need constant refinement in terms of training and retraining of aid personnel, and campaigning for the recruitment of personnel with new methods and increased efforts (Attias-Donfut, 1974).

Detecting the needs of the elderly—medical, cultural, and social—will have to be more actively promoted in the future. The role of social science in this respect will include action-oriented experiments. In a generalized sense, as one views the social problems of the elderly, empirical science itself has a linkage function or at least a function of clarifying existing linkage channels and their effectiveness.

The system of social security, which decades ago in Austria and in several other Western European countries developed into a very important element of social welfare, will have to be supplemented by other systems and subsystems that will take into account not only the increased life expectancy but also the human potential of the elderly. The revision of the general theory of decline in the aging process; findings on psychological crystallization and intellectual storage supported by training methods; rehabilitation and focused medical treatment allow for a further development of human potential (Rosenmayr, 1974). In view of these increased changes the idea of social mediation and connection through purposive focused action, namely linkage, will more and more become a central concept not only for the elderly but also for many other areas of social and cultural policy.

Summary

This chapter reviews research findings from several Austrian studies, designed, conducted and/or evaluated by the author, including a December 1971 microcensus comprising approximately 19,000 interviews of the population aged sixty and over, and a 1,500-interview survey based on a stratified random sample of the population aged fifteen and over. The Austrian data confirm the error of the older sociological theory of the isolated nuclear family of industrial and urban society. Although joint living of adult members of two or more generations in one household is a minority pattern for reasons of economic production (e.g. in agriculture) or because of particular support deemed necessary, "intimacy at a distance" in matters of housing, help, and communication corresponds to the wishes of both generations. More members of the middle-aged and elderly generations want to live close to each other yet in separate apartments than actually do so. Many grown children, however, either live in the same apartments or at a relatively great distance from their parents, living arrangements which do not correspond to their preferences.

Data on help patterns show that a small proportion of the elderly do not expect to be looked after by children or relatives in case of sickness. In small communities grown children are more frequently expected to nurse parents in illness than in Vienna, even if the children do not live in the same household with the parents, emphasizing cultural differences in values and beliefs.

Contrary to previous research, help with household work offered to aging parents emerged as a relatively infrequent form of aid, a result, however, which may be due to the measurement techniques applied. Assistance in shopping from children and other relatives, thus providing the elderly with consumer goods, significantly exceeded help inside the household.

This chapter finally emphasizes the necessity to revise findings on intergenerational family relations and to go beyond the present research on various help patterns. Although help is a very important criterion, it may not and cannot generally exclude conflict between generations. Ambivalence and the quality and content of communication must be taken into serious consideration when studying parent-child relations, particularly when parents have reached old age.

This chapter postulates a line of research which would emphasize the emotional dynamics of intergenerational relations viewed in various stages of the life cycle in order to include mental health aspects in the problems of the care for the elderly. The linkage concept provides an adequate explanation of relationships between family, elderly members, and bureaucracies.

References

Attias-Donfut, C. *Aide à Domicile.* Paris, 1974.
Bergler, R. *Psychologie Stereotyper Systeme.* Bern & Stuttgart, 1966.
Blood, R. O., et al. "Comparative Analysis of Family Power Structure: Problems of Measurement and Interpretation." Paper presented at the 9th International Seminar on Family Research, Sept. 14–20, 1965, Tokyo.
Braam, P. A. "The Situation of the Aged: Some Sociological Aspects." *Sociologia Neerlandica* 3 (1966):69–70.

Cumming, E., and W. E. Henry. *Growing Old.* New York, 1961.
Friedeburg, L. V., and F. Weltz. *Altersbild und Altersvorsorge der Arbeiter und Angestellten.* Frankfurt am Main, 1958.
Goldfarb, A. I. "Psychodynamics and the Three-Generation Family." In *Social Structure and Family Relationships,* ed. E. Shanas and G. F. Streib. Englewood Cliffs, N.J., 1965.
Goode, W. J. *World Revolution and Family Patterns.* New York, 1963.
————. "The Theory and Measurement of Family Change." In *Indicators of Social Change,* ed. W. E. Moore and E. B. Sheldon. New York, 1968.
Guillemard, A. M., and R. Lenoir. *Retraite et échange social.* Paris. 1974.
Kaufmann, A. "Demographische Struktur und Haushalts und Familienformen der Wiener Bevölkerung." Ph.D. dissertation, Vienna University, 1966.
————, and L. Rosenmayr. "Soziologische Grundlagen für die Entwicklungspolitik im Land Niederösterreich." Unpublished research report to the Provincial Government of Lower Austria, Wien, 1972.
Kooy, G. A. "Urbanization and Nuclear Family Individualization: A Causal Connection?" In *Readings in Kinship in Urban Structure,* ed. C. C. Harris. New York, 1970.
Langford, M. *Community Aspects on Housing the Aged.* Ithaca, N.Y., 1962.
Laslett, P. *Household and Family in Past Time.* Cambridge, Mass., 1972.
Lazarsfeld, P. F. "The General Idea of Multivariable Analysis: Interpretations of Statistical Relations as a Research Operation." In *The Language of Social Research,* ed. P. F. Lazarsfeld and M. Rosenberg, Glencoe, Ill., 1955.
Lehr, U., and H. Thomae, "Die Stellung des älteren Menschen in der Familie." Contribution to a discussion of the German Sociological Society, Frankfurt am Main, April 1, 1966. Mimeographed.
Mitterauer, M. "Zur Familienstruktur in ländlichen Gemeinden." In *Beiträge zur Bevölkerungs und Sozialgeschichte Österreichs.* Wien, 1973.
Murdock, G. P. *Social Structure.* London, 1965.
Nimkoff, M. F. "Changing Family Relationships of Older People in the United States During the Last Fifty Years." In *Social and Psychological Aspects of Aging,* ed. C. Tibbitts and W. Donahue. New York, 1962.
Pfeil, E. *Die Berufsätigkeit von Müttern.* Tübingen, 1961.
Reiss, P. J. "The Extended Kinship System: Correlations and Attitudes on Frequency of Interaction." *Marriage and Family Living* 24 (1962):333–39.
Rosenmayr, L. "Altersprobleme in der ländlichen Region." *Kultur-Berichte* (April 1971): 1–5.
————. "Die Revision der These vom generellen Leistungsverfall im Alternsprozess." In *Aktivitätsprobleme des Alternden,* ed. K. Fellinger. Eine psychosomatische Studie, Editiones "Roche." Basel, 1974.
————. "Wohnverhältnisse und Nachbarschaftsbeziehungen." In *Wohnen in Wien.* Der Aufbau, Monographie 8. Wien, 1965.
————, and E. Köckeis. *Umwelt und Familie alter Menschen.* Neuwied and Berlin, 1965. With English summary.
————, E. Köckeis, and H. Kreutz. *Kulturelle Interessen von Jugendlichen.* München and Wein, 1966.
Shanas, E. *The Health of Older People.* Cambridge, Mass., 1962.
————. "The Unmarried Old Person in the United States." Paper prepared for the International Social Science Seminar in Gerontology, August 1963, Markaryd, Sweden.
————, P. Townsend, D. Wedderburn, H. Friis, P. Milhøj, and J. Stehouwer. *Old People in Three Industrial Societies.* New York, 1968.
Streib, G. F. "Intergenerational Relations: Perspectives of the Two Generations of the Older Parent." *Journal of Marriage and the Family* 27 (1965):469–76.
————. "Older Families and Their Troubles: Familial and Social Responses." *Family Coordinator* 21 (1972):5–19.
Sussman, M. B. "An Analytical Model for the Sociological Study of Retirement." In *Retirement,* ed. F. M. Carp. New York, 1972.
————. "Competence and Options: A Theoretical Essay, Implications for Nutritional Research." In *Nutrition, Development and Social Behavior,* ed. D. J. Kallen. Washington, D.C., 1973.

————. "The Help Pattern in the Middle Class Family." *American Sociological Review* 18 (1953):22–28.

————, and L. Burchinal. "Parental Aid to Married Children: Implications for Family Functioning." *Marriage and Family Living* 24 (1962):320–32.

Tartler, R. *Das Alter in der modernen Gesellschaft.* Stuttgart, 1961.

Townsend, P. "The Emergence of the Four Generation Family in Industrial Society." *New Society* 8 (July 7, 1966):12–13.

9. Old People, Bureaucracy, and the Family in Poland
Jerzy Piotrowski

Introduction

The object of this chapter is to review the relationship of old people and their families, focusing on how bureaucratic organizations constrain or support the aged persons in assuming and using available role options and needed services. Attention will be given to the methods by which the kin network operates to link the aged with bureaucratic structures and how bureaucratic structures affect the quality of the relationship between the aged and their families.

The empirical material used in this chapter consists of findings from a study on the needs of older people in Poland, based on a nationwide representative sample of people aged sixty-five and over,[1] similar to the studies carried out in the United States, Great Britain, and Denmark.[2] First to be described are family relations, particularly the quality of generational interaction. The empirical findings are reported and the theoretical implications discussed. Then follows a discussion of the roles of family and society in meeting the needs of old people and in contributing to satisfactory living conditions in later life. Specifically presented are the services rendered to the old people by their families and by bureaucratic structures, and the interrelationship of the two. These services will be illustrated by reviewing the assistance required and provided during illness. The third part of the chapter contains a review of the role of the family as a link between old people and these bureaucratic structures. The scope within which public services are indispensable in order for the family to provide effective supports for the aged member and vice versa will be considered, and whether and to what extent the effectiveness of public services depends on the complementary services of a family. The concluding part of the chapter will be devoted to the transformations taking place in the family relations of old people and to the influence exerted by the development of services rendered by bureaucratic organizations in this emergent pattern of family relations.

With the materials available, a comparative analysis of relations and conditions of retired employees (white- and blue-collar) with older peasants (numerous among Polish old people) will be attempted. In Poland employees have rights to various social benefits such as retirement pensions and public

1. J. Piotrowski, "Old People in Poland and Their Vital Capacity," mimeographed (Warsaw, 1970); J. Piotrowski et al., *Miejsce cztowieka starego w rodzinie i spoteczenstwie* (The Place of the Old People in Family and Society) (Warsaw, 1973).
2. E. Shanas, P. Townsend, D. Wedderburn, H. Friis, P. Milhøj, and J. Stehouwer, *Old People in Three Industrial Societies* (New York, 1968).

health services; the farmers were at the time of this research (1967) without such programs, unless they were part-time farmers and primarily employees. Public health services free of charge have been available to farmers since 1972.

At this juncture the notions of the elderly, the family, and bureaucratic society need to be more carefully defined. Who are the old? (1) Are they people who are past a certain age, e.g., past sixty-five? (2) Is this chronological age used for men and women alike to describe the old? (3) Are they retired persons, regardless of chronological age? (4) Are they incapacitated persons for whom age is an important concomitant factor? In the majority of reported researches varied definitions are used to describe different populations, with the selection based on the theoretical inclinations of the investigator and the kind of research questions used. To what extent should one take into consideration differentiation according to age? There are great differences in perceptions, needs, mental and physical competence, services required, and family relationships when one is fifty-five, sixty-five, seventy-five, or eighty-five years of age. Such differences even exist between persons of the same age according to their occupations and whether they live in urban or rural places. Perhaps a definition covering all criteria—i.e., chronological age, retirement from the labor force, and capacity for self-care—is appropriate for most researches on the aged, the family, and bureaucracy. In this chapter all three criteria are used as indices of "old."

What definition of the family is most adequate for this research? Two basic units were used: (1) old people, children and their spouses, grandchildren and siblings, and (2) the family with which old people, whether as single persons or as couples, have real contact. Using the first definition, the existence and intensity of family contacts were examined. The findings were then used as a yardstick for the quality of family relations of the old. The concern with the nature and content of the existing relations between the elderly and the family indicates that the second definition, that involving contact and exchange, is of primary importance in this study. In the first case attention is focused mainly on the substitutional feature of social benefits and services; and in the second, on their complementarity, i.e., whether and how the support of the family and society is coordinated, adapted, supplemented.

It was found that the family circle of real contact varies according to the place of residence of the old, whether it is a farm, a village, or a town. The less modernized the place, the more numerous and multigenerational is family household composition. The range of activity and dependence on bureaucratic structures is limited in less modern places.

What is bureaucracy? Bureaucratic structures are those oganizations developed largely in complex societies to handle the differentiation found among people in response to industrialization requiring various technical skills and occupational training, and to provide rewards, status, and responsibility to all persons according to their position in the bureaucratic organization without reference to social or cultural characteristics. The bureaucracy rewards according to ability rather than family or lineage. To function appropriately, it has rules and regulations that cover every anticipated situation and that are universally administered. It is this part of society that obviously influences the fate and situation of old people through its support or constraint upon the quality of life desired by the elderly. Labor law, retirement norms and pension schemes, homes for the elderly, and various social services and institutions, all bureaucratic in nature and organization, affect the situation of old people.

The Modified Extended Family

The general theory dealing with the disintegration of the traditional extended family and its transformation into the isolated nuclear family with increasing modernization still prevails in much of the sociological literature. According to this theory, as societies take on industrialized/technical processes, the economic order requires mobile family units. This, it is claimed, leads to the disintegration of loyalty towards relatives, even to the closest kin of the nuclear family, including the parents of the married couple! So the traditional basic family bond — mutual loyalty — is now replaced by love between husband and wife, by the egoism of a nuclear family isolating itself from the circle of the extended family. The small nuclear family is characterized by many "reductions": reduction in size, in number of generations, and in bilateral extension, and, at the same time, reduction of its functions and social roles.

The above theory has static and dynamic components. The static version is dichotomic. It assumes that one pattern of family is typical for preindustrial times — the extended family with many and rich functions — while another pattern of family is typical for industrial times — the nuclear family with an atrophy of its functions. The dynamic variant is evolutionary. Both types of families constitute the two poles of the evolutionary process from the large extended family with a complex structure and functions to a small family reduced in its structure to the dyad, with or without children as its essential element and with a primary function — to love.[3] The evolution is from institution to companionship.

Present-day empirical researches on generational relations in the family and especially on the mutual services between old people and their children raise questions concerning the thesis that the contemporary nuclear family is isolated from its ancestors. It has been shown that the family still performs an important role in the life of old people, who continue to maintain lively

3. For example, P. Sorokin, *Social and Cultural Dynamics* (Boston, 1970): reduction of a family to a boarding house, serving mainly for sexual purposes.

relations with their families, especially with adult children, and who exchange many mutual services.

The theory of a nuclear family is contradicted by the theory of the modified extended family, which, though it less and less embraces three or more generations living under the same roof, vigorously maintains cooperation and a broad exchange of services ranging from economic to purely emotional.[4]

Research in many countries has revealed the existence of similar generational connections of older people. It seems, then, unquestionable that the static, dichotomic variant of the nuclear theory cannot be confirmed empirically. At the same time, however, these researches also revealed the coexistence of diverse types of generational relations in old age: living in a common household; living separately but maintaining active and frequent contacts; and living alone and eventually becoming isolated. One of the likely interpretations of these findings is the hypothesis that the parallel existence of these various types of family structures reflects a transitional stage in the process of the evolution of the family from the traditional to the modern. This interpretation can be supported by the fact that in this diversity some regularities can be observed. In Polish research certain relations could be observed between the number of persons and generations in the family and some specific traits such as the level of "modernity" of social classes and localities on the one hand and agricultural or nonagricultural living on the other. These findings suggest the existence of a modified extended family between the two polar extremes mentioned earlier. The modified extended family does not constitute any strictly determined social system and its variations include diverse social content.

It can be assumed, then, that the social content of the extended family system will change, moving more and more to the nuclear extreme. In such a case the services rendered by adult children to the old parents, quite frequent in many families, may be considered as a transitional phenomenon, remnants of the old tradition. The assessment of such a transition is somewhat difficult as we lack verified information on the traditional relations which might be compared with the results of contemporary research. Multigeneration as a dominating trait of the oldest type of family relations may be doubted in the light of what is known about the role of the nuclear family among farmers, craftsmen, and others. Polish ethnographers think that the multigenerational households appeared among Polish peasants relatively late, namely during the seventeenth century and at the beginning of the eighteenth, as a result of the exploitation of serfs. The services of serfdom

4. M. B. Sussman, "Family Continuity: Selective Factors which Affect Relationships Between Families at Generational Levels," *Marriage and Family Living* 16 (1954):112–20; Shanas et al., *Old People*; M. B. Sussman, "Relationship of Adult Children with Their Parents in the United States," in *Social Structure and the Family: Generational Relations,* ed. E. Shanas and G. F. Streib (Englewood Cliffs, N.J., 1965), pp. 62–92.

were calculated on the basis of homesteads, i.e., households, and not on the number of people. In the opinion of Jan Stehouwer, we may remember, there were no multigenerational farms among the Danish peasants in the old times.

On the other hand, social benefits and services can be considered as developmental elements. For instance, there can be observed a tendency towards a considerable reduction of economic values in the relations between generations outside agricultural localities, while a fairly lively exchange of services is maintained and the importance of services and emotional values is increasing. It is not known, however, whether in former times old people, especially the incapacitated, were really better cared for than they are now. Also, we know very little about the emotional content of their contacts.

The problem of the reduction of family functions is presented as a fact in sociological literature even more often than the reduction of structure. It is my opinion that, by virtue of its nature, the family now performs all the functions that were once performed by the traditional family. The tasks related to survival in modern society have increased, are more complex, and are being fulfilled cooperatively by the family and by society's institutions and organizations. It is obvious that the increasing division of labor in complex societies, the development of education, and other factors made the family alone unable to prepare its children for jobs. This fact has given rise to the social systems of education and learning. Society has also created its own institutions for other functions previously performed by the family, as, for example, organized education for sexual life. It has established clinics and regulates or at least attempts to regulate population through birth control. With regard to the procreational function, it deals with family allowances, medical assistance, maternity leaves, and so on. As far as the economic function of acquiring resources for the family is concerned, the productive component is residual, but its nature from the point of view of a family acquiring the means of subsistence is still maintained. Increasingly, both husband and wife work. However, it is the task of bureaucratic organizations to ensure jobs, the means of a livelihood. This collaboration between family and society is also clearly manifested in the protective function of the family. It is true that society establishes systems such as social security, national health service, and social welfare, but in this field the role of the family has not been eliminated nor has its influence been considerably limited.

With the rising level of culture and progress in all spheres of life, concomitant with the development of science and technology, the expectations and requirements in all the fields of family functions have increased. This has occurred to such an extent that the family itself cannot meet the demands upon it, and in order to perform its functions properly it needs the support of public institutions. Allowing for a certain degree of simplification, we can state that in sexual, procreational, protective, and child-rearing activities expectations have increased greatly. Also, within the scope of each of these functions, the number of services provided by public institutions is ever-increasing. So the family has lost its exclusive rights in all these fields.

Overall, the family has maintained and enriched its important role. Much more is now expected from families in all areas compared to families of a bygone era. Moreover, to fulfill all its functions, the family must cooperate with social institutions. This is particularly evident in education; families must take advantage of the opportunities offered to all persons by the educational system.

The above conclusion may also be valid regarding the attitude of the family towards old people. The present attitude may not differ greatly from the attitudes of the past. It is not easy to determine to what extent these attitudes have changed historically, but this must be dealt with on another occasion. In the next section I will trace some examples of the relations between family and society with regard to economic, protective, and emotional functions related to the elderly.

Family Relations of Old People

It can be said that in Poland today as in the past there exist two types of generational relations, urban and rural. The industrialization process in Poland is of relatively recent origin. In the twenties and thirties Poland still retained many features of the preindustrial period. Almost two-thirds of the population were agricultural; more than half lived on small family farms using traditional methods of husbandry. Outside of agriculture, small artisan workshops and stores predominated. Thus the most common type of family was the peasant family based on family farming, mostly multigenerational. In part, the multigenerational household resulted from the very limited possibilities of migration from the farms to nonagricultural occupations. Artisan and shopkeeper families too were often multigenerational, since artisan and trade workshops were family enterprises and were passed from father to son. Bourgeois families as well as those of the intelligentsia were more modern and individualized.

Since 1945 the social and economic revolution has transformed the country. The peasant population now constitutes only 25 percent of the population, and less than 45 percent of the population live in villages. The "working population," i.e., the white- and blue-collar workers and the intelligentsia, now constitute more than 70 percent of the population and mainly work in large-scale industry, such as manufacturing, trade enterprises, public administration, offices and services. During the last thirty years a vigorous urbanization and industrialization of the country have occurred. This has been accompanied by a mass migration of millions of people, especially of young adults from the rural areas to towns. Vertical as well as horizontal, occupational, and cultural mobility has also been very intense, due to increased access to education and the greater opportunities for social advancement by the masses of the population.

The impact of the processes here briefly outlined has produced differences in everyday culture and in the social position of old parents and their adult children in many families that could not fail to leave their mark on family relations, especially generational relations.

A special feature of family relations in Poland is the very high percentage of old people living with children (83 percent have children). Of people sixty-five and over having children, 67 percent live with them, compared to 42 percent in Great Britain, 28 percent in the United States, and 20 percent in Denmark.[5] Such a high index is to some extent accounted for by the fact that 76 percent of older peasants live together with their children. But even outside agriculture the proportion of old persons living with children remains high, 57 percent.

There are different reasons for sharing a household in the case of peasants and of workers. The common households of older peasants with their children are connected with the traditional family farm. The retiring peasant hands over his farm to one of his children, but as a rule continues to live in the same house and on the same farm, having his livelihood assured by custom or legal contract.

Outside agriculture, especially in towns, common households are mainly the result of housing difficulties following the tremendous destruction that Poland suffered during World War II and the mass migrations of people from the country to towns because of the intensive industrialization. Consequently young couples often live with one or both parents while waiting for an apartment of their own. The second main reason for living together is the fact that the old mother (less frequently the father, mother-in-law, or father-in-law) moves in with the children to help them in running the household and taking care of grandchildren and/or to be provided with the maintenance and care that the older person is not in a position to insure.

Thus there are two patterns related to common households of older people with their children: older people provide housing for their children or the children bring the old parents to their own apartments. In agriculture two-thirds of older men and outside agriculture somewhat more than one-third claim that it is they who provide housing for their children.

It happens not infrequently, especially when both older parents are still alive, that separate households are maintained in the same dwelling, but the contacts and cooperation between households are so lively and many-sided that it is difficult to determine whether these households should be regarded as common or separate.[6] About 30 percent of married older workers and 17

5. Shanas et al., *Old People.*
6. Piotrowski, "Old People in Poland."

percent of married peasants, although living with their children under the same roof, do not share a common household with them.

Also married older people live together and have a common household with their children less often than do widows or other nonmarried elderly. Among the nonmarried elderly, more women than men, more of the non-working than working, more of those restricted in their possibilities of independent existence than those economically secure, have a common household with their children. The elderly also prefer to live together with their unmarried than married children. Only in a little more than 60 percent of cases of common habitation with children do we find a three-generation family.

Living together with children or in their vicinity helps to maintain close contacts and exchange of various services. Eighty-eight percent of older people in Poland, 82 percent in Great Britain, 77 percent in the United States, and 75 percent in Denmark have children living no more than a half-hour's walking or driving distance. Living in the same household, of course, is more conducive to frequent contacts and services than living apart. Of white-collar workers who have children but who do not live with children, almost half (47 percent) did not see any of them in the week preceding the interview, and one-third had not seen them in the previous month; the percentages for the manual workers were 31 and 17 respectively, and for farmers, 30 and 17. The higher percentage of white-collar workers maintaining very loose contact with their children may result from the fact that in that group there are more elderly people with only one or two children; also less of them have a child living nearby. However, this difference between the family relations of old people of white-collar backgrounds and others may also reflect intergenerational cultural differences caused by the social and occupational advancement of the younger generation.

How can this pattern of relations between parents and adult children be evaluated? In reply to a direct question concerning how they evaluated the relationships in a joint household with their children, the overwhelming majority of the aged (about 80 percent) said they were good. However, such relationships are judged either as bad or varying from good to bad in 15 percent of those cases involving living together with a son or daughter and in 25 percent of those cases involving daughters- or sons-in-law. Generally family relations are worse between the adult children and elderly women than elderly men and worse also for elderly people living on farms than in towns. Complaints that relations in the shared household are not good are made most frequently by those groups of elderly people who are most likely to live together with their children.[7]

---

7. This corroborates the statement by Jan Stehouwer that "the proportion of people who respond negatively to their own situation is highest in those countries where we find 1) . . . high degree of help, and 2) . . . high degree of living together with children." Jan Stehouwer, "The Elderly and the Family," mimeographed, U.N. Symposium on Research and Welfare Policies for the Elderly (Herzlya, June 1969), p. 16.

Elderly people consider the best form of living arrangement to be separate from one's children (62 percent). Nevertheless, in Poland old people much more frequently declare a willingness to live together with their children than in the Western countries studied. This is especially the case for elderly people suffering from poor health and unable to support themselves financially. Certain differences can be observed in the various social strata. The largest proportion of persons who prefer to live with their children is found among farmers and workers in agriculture, the lowest among white-collar workers. More white-collar workers than manual workers, and especially factory workers, prefer to live in old people's homes to living with children.

The majority of older persons want to live near their children and the children in turn want to live near their parents. Family ties are strong, and the family remains the basic and accepted social environment for the aged, where advice or assistance can be sought when needed.

The importance of the family is confirmed also by replies to the question, Who should help an elderly person when in need, the family or society? The overwhelming majority say that it is the children who should help. Among people on the farms 15 percent of the men and 11 percent of the women, however, said that assistance should come mainly from society. Outside agriculture this view is shared by 35 percent of the men and 30 percent of the women. People with impaired mobility are much more often inclined to consider that it is the duty of society to come to their aid.

In our study the families of the adult-child generation had similar views on this question: 50 percent said the children should give their parents basic assistance; 40 percent, a certain amount of assistance; 6 percent, slight assistance; while 4 percent said that the parents should not expect their children to come to their assistance at all. On the other hand, when it came to taking care of elderly persons who are ill, 82 percent of the respondents said that children were largely responsible for providing such care.

The elderly were asked for whom they had the greatest respect and affection, and in whom they had the most confidence. In reply to each of these questions those living together with children pointed to their children after their spouses; the unmarried pointed overwhelmingly to the children with whom they were living. There was such a high unanimity regarding those questions that one wonders whether the answers reflect more ideal norms than the real pattern.

Contribution of the Family in Meeting the Needs of the Elderly

As confirmed by these studies, great numbers of old people are granted assistance from their children and, less often, from their more distant relatives. Generally speaking, these benefits can be divided into material aid and services. They vary depending on the individual needs of the recipient and the possibilities of the donor. Some kind of assistance was granted to 85 percent of the elderly by the children living with them, and many received some sort of material assistance. On the other hand, more than 50 percent of the elderly population under study gave some services and assistance to their children. This exchange of services occurs two-and-a-half times as frequently in cases where the old people live with their children.

The services rendered by the children to the old people are the following: providing lodging, 30 percent; providing full or partial maintenance, 50 percent; supporting old persons financially or in kind (helping in tilling the soil if the father is a farmer, taking care of everyday chores as well as of the sick), 15 percent. Among the services rendered by the old people to their children the most frequent were: managing or helping to manage the household, including cooking and cleaning (done mostly by women), 50 percent; providing lodging (more frequently rendered by the men), 40 percent; and, with decreasing frequency, babysitting with grandchildren, making small repairs, helping on the farm and taking care of the cattle, giving small presents, and providing the setting for official business.[8]

These data do not allow an assessment of whether these benefits and services met the requirements of old people or of their children, whether they were received by all in need, and whether the services received were sufficient. It is also not known to what extent these forms of assistance are required. In many instances old people and adult children living together and taking advantage of the family services are considered normal and highly satisfactory, not only because of the material benefits but also for emotional reasons. These services, however, when they become a necessity for the old may limit their options and freedom of behavior, forcing the old person to adapt to the preferences and ways of life of the children who are now masters of the house. This is all the more unpleasant when it is connected with a role reversal—the former breadwinners, protectors, and authorities become themselves subject to the authority of their children. The dependency on others especially makes itself felt in case of economic dependency. That is why the old people prefer to live separately. They appreciate Rosenmayr's "intimacy at a distance" and prefer material independence even if living independently means they are worse off.

Contributions of Society in Meeting the Needs of the Elderly

A wide variety of social services exist for old people: social security benefits, pensions and allowances, public health services, homes for the elderly and other benefits granted by social welfare, as well as various serv-

8. Piotrowski, "Old People in Poland."

ices such as home help and the provision of meals, nursing for the sick and incapacitated, and organized leisure time activities. Not all of these services are required by all persons and they are not available to everyone. Eligibility for social insurance benefits depends in the first place on having been a worker, and in the second place on the type of work and the sort of enterprise in which employment was held. During the time of this research in 1967 the peasants did not receive either old-age pensions or free public health services, both of which were available to hired labor. Thus the farm was the only protection for the peasants during sickness and in old age.

Public systems of services have different constraints and liberties. Within each old-age pension system, for example, one must be a certain age to be entitled to the benefits of a pension. Such an age limit is necessary due to the financial structure of a system and for the precise determination of the rights of the insured persons. Quite often this age limit becomes a penalty for the workers, as there is a widespread custom of firing employees who have reached retirement age. Loss of work is almost always unpleasant in itself, and in addition it is connected with the loss of material and social status. A mandatory retirement age can also operate in the opposite direction, forcing some employees who are not fully able to work to continue until reaching this age.

Peasants are not covered by the retirement system and since they work on their own farms they are not in danger of being fired. But there is no end to their work either because often they have no heir to take over the management of the farm and because by custom peasants are expected to work as long as they are able. On the other hand, if their children do inherit the farm, the parents become dependent on them for services, good will, and future success. These family services act in lieu of the old-age security institution and are a considerable burden for small farmers. This may cause family conflicts, and sometimes pressure is exerted on the old people to leave the farm. This phenomenon is not widespread because the control and sanctions of public opinion are still quite strong in favor of family responsibility for the old, but the old persons' fear of what may happen hinders the transfer of farms to their children as well as the modernization of the farms.

In urban areas too there are similar situations of potential conflict. One of the major reasons is the housing shortage. The unavailability of space can force the old people to leave their flats when their child's family increases its size. Another important reason for the breakdown of parent-child relationships is the problems related to taking care of the bedfast aged. Homes for older people or nursing homes for the bedfast, set up by social welfare, make it possible to move the old person from the home. According to the research findings, in most instances this results in a breaking of contacts with the next of kin.

A similar situation occurs as a result of the functioning of the old-age pension system. If an elderly person receives a pension, the children are inclined to stop giving any material services regardless of whether or not the pension is sufficient for subsistence. Peter Townsend is of the opinion that social services do not affect the services of the family because they are mostly concerned with cases where family assistance is lacking.[9] It seems, however, that in the field of material services the development of social services can accelerate the disappearance of services rendered by the family. Thus certain types of services can substitute for the family or for each other.

Taking care of a sick person is a good example of the complementarity of the services of family and society. The family is an important supplement to the hospitals. More bedridden old people (over sixty-five) are being cared for in private households in Poland than in hospitals and nursing homes for the incapacitated. In a severe illness most of the old people remain at home. The majority of old people who are unable to care for themselves or to perform household chores are living in private households. All these people rely mainly on the assistance of the family. In this respect the general pattern in Poland is similar to that of Western countries. If the person in need of attention is a man, he usually receives care from his wife; a woman is most often attended by her daughter or possibly the daughter-in-law living in the same household. The scope of nursing and medical care at home is much greater than in hospitals and dispensaries.

The care of the ill clearly illustrates the cooperation between family and social institutions. It also illustrates the necessity for such cooperation and the limited effectiveness of the services of each of them alone. This is also a good example of the problem that has been mentioned before, namely, the belief in "atrophy" of family functions. In spite of the great development of medical facilities such as hospitals, dispensaries, clinics, laboratories, and even private medical practice, the contemporary family does more for the care and medical treatment of the sick than the traditional one ever did.

Linkage

Increasingly in the modern era the family is serving as a link between its elderly members and societal institutions and organizations. In Poland as elsewhere there has been an increase in the number of social and welfare services available to the masses. These options for support from societal institutions and organizations when ill, chronically disabled, in failing health, or too old to work are concomitant with the development of complexity and differentiation in societies using technology in organizing their economic and productive system. Some of these third-party supports are limited to

9. Shanas et al., *Old People.*

certain population groups such as trade-union members, but many others are becoming – and undoubtedly in the future more will become – the "right" of all the people. This guarantee of services and aid when in need is a growing phenomenon in all countries regardless of political ideology.

One major task of the family – on behalf of its members who have health, educational, economic, and other needs – is to learn about available options for services and to help to develop competence in dealing with the bureaucracies established to provide these services and aid. The increasing assumption of responsibility by society as expressed through its legislation, policies, and institutions means a shift in the value of filial responsibility and a change in the expressive behaviors of younger family members that may appear unfair towards older ones. Especially in urban environments, as the demands as well as the aspirations and motivations of families increase, the possibilities of becoming family centered increase. The family, in this sense, really has the option of supporting the concept of traditional filial responsibility, of modifying it, or of rejecting it.

A family acting as an intermediary between the old father or mother and the home for the aged can either try to push the old persons out of the house or try to keep them (female in most cases) if somebody is needed to take care of grandchildren or for household work. It is worth mentioning that among the old people who have children about 65 percent prefer living alone or with just husband or wife but only 30 percent actually do live alone. Of the middle-aged women, nearly 50 percent did not want to have their mother living with them; and the remainder did so purely to have the mother take care of grandchildren and run the home. Seventy-five percent of the elderly agreed with the statement that children should take care of their parents only as long as they can benefit from the arrangement in some way. Even if this opinion is too pessimistic, it reflects the older people's suspicion that when children act for their parents, they are not motivated purely by the needs of their parents.

As far as material security is concerned, the family is not disinterested but proves to be an efficient linking agent in obtaining the benefits of social security or welfare for a father or mother who needs it. Such benefits release families from their obligations for the financial support of parents, notwithstanding the fact that social welfare payments are often insufficient for the parent's survival. Sometimes the family, for emotional or status reasons, attempts to prevent the older person from availing himself of social welfare, considering this to be a family disgrace.

Both the elderly and their children try to limit, if possible, economic changes which may result in heightened dependence of parents on children and loss of options and strive to develop instead emotional bonds and nonmaterial services and assistance. Among the latter can be found those services which help to maintain the capacity of the elderly to care for themselves, i.e., help in shopping, cleaning the house, and other functions that perhaps cannot be performed by the old themselves.

Conclusion

Our research shows that both family and bureaucratic services are indispensable for creating optimal living conditions for the old. In order to predict the future development of the family and its elderly members, a forecast analysis is needed, one which would cover societal, cultural, sociological, and sociopsychological factors influencing the patterns of development, with primary consideration being given to the problems associated with further extension of social and economic benefits. It is probable that further individualization of relations within the family will be observed in the future, together with the pluralization of family life patterns, and the economic independence of the old, the latter mainly due to wider scope and improvement of social security. There probably also will be a development of lively and enriched relations between the old parents and their children, supported by their similar interests and increasingly freed from financial worries.

For the old and, to a great extent, for the middle generation, the family continues to be the most important social environment in the foreseeable future. Mutual close contacts are desired by both sides as well, along with the need to maintain autonomy. A system is required whereby the family, according to the needs and values of distributive justice, could assist its old members in their contacts and relations with social organizations that could be useful for them. Finally, a harmonious development is also required between the benefits and services rendered by society and by family.

Interpretive Analysis

10. Implications of Telecommunications Technology for Old People, Families, and Bureaucracies   *K. Dean Black and Vern L. Bengtson*

Introduction

Throughout Western society the tempo of social change has quickened in recent years and the average span of life has increased. These changes, the consequences of profound technological innovation, in their turn have altered patterns of social organization in our culture. Service bureaucracies, for example, have proliferated in attempts to fulfill human needs which were traditionally the function of primary groups. And, in consort with all these changes, have come alterations in the normal course of aging. New patterns of old age have emerged together with a new type of older person who spends more of his years out of the work force, who is healthier and better educated, but who still faces many of the physical and social losses that create dependencies in the later years of the life span.

Two implications of such changes are of crucial import for social gerontologists. First, one must examine emerging technological innovations in order to better understand problems and prospects in meeting the needs of tomorrow's elderly. Developments which only recently were speculative visions — such as two-way telecommunications tied to service delivery systems — must be considered within the reach of mass audiences of older clients within the next decades (Ramm and Gianturco, 1973). Second, consideration must be given to the new social systems which may emerge as the result of such technology. Who will control the resources made possible by revolutionary technical developments? What will be the impact of such developments on current service systems? And how might technological breakthroughs affect interpersonal networks of older people?

The purpose of this chapter is to examine the future of the older person and his social networks in the light of one of the most dramatic of recent technological developments, two-way telecommunications systems, and to explore the sociological implications of such a technological advance. Two-way telecommunications systems may be defined as electronic communications devices which allow individualized, reciprocal, and immediate information exchange based on a shared-time computer network. The time is not far off when television sets in the home may be the vehicle for such information flow. Our focus will be on the impact of such systems on the

Authors' Note: Preparation of this paper was partially supported by grant "MH-18101, "Generational Differences: Correlates and Consequences," National Institute of Mental Health. The authors wish to acknowledge the help of Michael Furlong in much of the preliminary bibliographic work, and of Ingrid McClendon for typing innumerable drafts.

family network and on existing service bureaucracies—two quite different social systems upon which most older persons are dependent to fulfill certain needs.

Telecommunications, Aging, and Service Delivery Systems

Technological innovations affect the linkages of aged persons with bureaucratic organizations. For example, the telephone, air travel, and even the credit card have altered patterns of interaction and modes of interdependency among aged persons and their families. In this section we wish to introduce a technical development which has profound implications for the ways aged persons may be constrained or supported by bureaucracies and families in the year 2000. We will first describe the nature of that technological innovation, and then enumerate some of the problems in terms of existing social systems that may be created by such new technology.

Two-Way Television Technology

Recent developments in telecommunications technology seem certain to greatly change the nature of communication and information gathering. A primary example is two-way "cable" television, which allows the viewer to select his program from a vast array of possibilities and to exercise individual control of informational needs. Because of the needs of older people, as well as their reliance on television as a source of information, it seems likely that their style of life may be significantly affected by these changes.

Two-way cable television with computer interface promises the eventual development of systems involving (1) the storage of a wide variety of programs which may be accessed by code numbers and (2) viewer communication with the transmitting station, allowing individualized selection of programs or services. The viewer is able to scan a list of available materials and then select only *what* he wants to see, *when* he wants to see it. But two-way cable telecommunications is not limited to individualized programming of entertainment or education. What is most revolutionary is its potential application to human service. J. W. Ramey (1972) has noted some of the mundane but important functions two-way telecommunications may perform for the average citizen in the year 2000:

> It will read our meters and give us fire and police protection; it will operate the traffic lights and keep constant location of emergency vehicles and busses; it will give directory information and tell you what is the shortest route right now from here to Hartford in terms of traffic

conditions; and it will make possible doing your banking and some shopping if you want to . . . [in short] it will change the way a lot of human services are delivered. (pp. 21–22)

Ramey also gives an example of the way in which such telecommunications will allow greater ease in dealing with difficult bureaucratic details such as those associated with the death of a spouse. He points out how today, when a husband dies and the wife therefore becomes involved with the Social Security system, she must go through the routine of finding the correct office, perhaps discovering from interviewers that she did not bring the right information, then perhaps making another trip to bring the death certificate, or whatever was needed, and so forth. With cable telecommunications, a widow will use her television directory to find the right process to go through and will fill out all the forms sitting in her living room. The computer will be able to verify the various records involved: "You're still sitting in your living room . . . [where] you can fill out all the forms [by answering the TV screen] and the computer leads you [to whatever information is needed] to complete them. . . . The computer can probably verify [your marriage] and the death record. . . ." (pp. 21–22)

How far from reality are such technological visions and how likely is it that they may be developed to help the elderly? Two-way communications on a cable television system are now well within the realm of possibility and several prototype systems are already in operation (Parker and Dunn, 1972; Singer, 1971; Jurgen, 1971). Moreover, it is significant that nearly all such projects include serving the needs of the elderly among their stated objectives.

Because of cost factors and technical limitations, all of the services that a fertile imagination can envision for a two-way cable television system are not readily available. While the basic two-way communications capacity is now feasible, many of the more advanced applications await further developments. Certainly some advanced applications are even yet beyond our capacity to imagine, for, as Clarke (1962) points out, "We have known radio for barely a lifetime, and TV for barely a generation; all our techniques of communications must be incredibly primitive."

Technical considerations, of course, are not the only limitations to the application of telecommunications advances to provide services to the elderly. Another vital issue is cost. To be useful, a system must be within the ability to pay of those who most need what the system can provide.

There is reasonable evidence that telecommunications-based services and information systems will not be so costly as to prohibit their use by the majority of older people. Parker and Dunn (1972) project a national average cost for such systems of from four to thirty-seven cents per user hour, depending on the kind of information provided. And they estimate that the development of a national system of the type discussed here may "make the costs of information distribution in this form cheaper than other forms, such as classroom instruction or printed newspapers delivered by truck and bicycle."

Even more importantly, cost factors in developing telecommunications to serve the elderly will probably not be a deterrent once a sufficient number of policy-makers realize the magnitude of potential savings that would accrue when the system becomes effective. Salaries of personnel and the cost of office space represent the bulk of most service agency budgets. These could be substantially reduced if machines could do the work of information gathering. And especially given the increasing public demand for greater government support of social services, cost-effective service systems should increasingly become a high priority issue. The potential savings of employing telecommunications in service delivery are enormous; and the costs of development could be immediately underwritten if a miniscule proportion of current service agency budgets were earmarked for such exploration. Further, commercial television interests may come to see the advantage of developing telecommunication systems solely for entertainment—which may result in service systems applications later on.

An obvious conclusion to the above comments is that telecommunications developments seem a natural focus of interest to those who are concerned with the study of aging (Ramm and Gianturco, 1973). This is especially true since the field of gerontology is oriented not only to the solution of current problems of the elderly but also to those that may develop from changes in the future.

Social System Implications of the New Technology and Service Delivery

Given the current state of technical developments in telecommunications as well as the high level of interest in pursuing those developments in both governmental and private sectors, it is not unreasonable to expect that access to two-way cable television systems such as have been described will be available to the general public in the not-too-distant future. However, implementing the potential of such systems to provide needed services to dependent persons presents a number of problems unrelated to purely technological innovation. These problems have to do with the responses of individuals and groups to telecommunications advances—the potential impact of technological developments on existing social systems. Six issues are identified as particularly relevant to the problem of service delivery to the elderly in need; they will be introduced here, with the potential for their resolution discussed more fully in subsequent sections. These issues are (1) implications for the family life of older people, (2) reactions of existing service delivery agencies, (3) influence and control of telecommunications systems, (4) relations between professionals and clients, (5) privacy and the protection of human rights, and (6) the depersonalization of social life.

1. *Implications for the family life of older people.*   In traditional societies the family network has been the major vehicle for coping with the dependencies of elderly individuals. Although there has been considerable debate concerning the viability of a functional kin network in modern industrialized societies (Sussman, 1965), a number of recent studies have shown that elderly individuals are in close contact, exchange services with, and are aided by family members, particularly by adult children (Streib and Thompson, 1960; Sussman and Burchinal, 1962; Shanas and Streib, 1965; Shanas and associates, 1968; Hill and associates, 1970; and other chapters in this volume). In short, it is clear that when situations of need arise in the lives of elderly individuals, it is to their offspring that most turn for information and assistance. And the children respond, perhaps out of a sense of filial obligation, perhaps equally out of affection and sympathy.

How might an individualized, reciprocal, and responsive system of telecommunications delivery services affect such interaction? Would it leave the elderly individual even more isolated from kin, because children would feel less need to maintain contact with their aging parents? Would it further erode filial responsibility in an increasingly mobile society? On the other hand, might these innovations lead to a greater freedom in family interaction, with the focus of interaction less on assistance in crises and more on affection? Will such innovations free the family, however it might be defined in the year 2000, from the burdens of caretaking for dependent members to more expressive interaction? In short, will telecommunications service delivery systems represent a deterrent or an aid to the older person's relations with his family?

2. *Reactions of existing service delivery agencies.*   A major social development of the last century has been the institutionalization of specialized agencies for handling problems of dependency which once were the primary responsibility of the family. Such service agencies have developed into large-scale bureaucratic organizations with linkages to other sociopolitical institutions. The dependencies of older people — whether they relate to health needs, economic problems, housing, transportation, or even recreation — have increasingly become the domain of service bureaucracies, hierarchically organized and impersonally efficient.

What might be the response of the personnel of existing agencies to technology that allows the client to be in immediate and reciprocal contact with information that might alleviate needs? Would they welcome such innovation, acknowledging the potential human service advances it implies, or would they view it as a threat to hard-won budgets, prerogatives, and domains of influence and authority? Might the technology only serve to make the existing bureaucracies more powerful, to create an organizational superstructure built around telecommunications itself, more far-reaching than any present agency could ever be? Or will the result be more personalized, humanitarian, and immediate service than ever before?

3. *Influence and control of telecommunications systems.* The basic issue in the development and application of a telecommunications service system is who will decide how such technology will be used. This is a political issue. If the past is any guide, large-scale technological innovations have been produced by and for elites, with benefits gradually accruing to more and more members of the society.

Will the same pattern characterize telecommunications delivery systems — or do these, with their possibilities for feedback and individual control, represent a striking departure from previous technical developments? Might it be possible for the individual or the family to use such technology so it becomes the servant, rather than the controller, of persons in need? Is there the possibility of creating with this particular technology a truly client-centered service model in which there is a reversal of the traditional pattern regarding influence and control over information?

4. *Relations between professionals and clients.* The two preceding issues raise the question of professional roles in a telecommunications service delivery system. The special character of a professional occupation is its combination of technical expertise and the service ideal. The result is an unusual degree of both individual autonomy and status (Becker et al., 1961). The dependencies of aged individuals usually involve recourse to the services of professionals, from health practitioners to the more marginally professional social workers and Social Security caseworkers. The basic model of the relation between professionals and clients is a rigid superordinate-subordinate model as exemplified in service delivery bureaucracies (see Chapter 1 by Sussman in this volume).

Two-way telecommunications applied to service delivery will certainly have implications for the relationship between client and professional, and for the often tenuous interactions among types of professionals. Will professionals use technology to enhance their control — as another tool to *do* things to people? Or can instant feedback communication be a vehicle in developing greater parity between client and practitioner? Will the professional be in control or will he be in the position of service provider, lending his expertise only when needed? In a social climate increasingly characterized by tension between "professional autonomy and the revolt of the client" (Haug and Sussman, 1969), can the new technology be a means of involving clients in the system without threatening the service role of professionals? In short, can technology help both clients and professionals or will it exacerbate the problems of both in meeting human needs?

5. *Privacy and the protection of human rights.* Citizens in technologically advanced societies are increasingly concerned with the degree to which computerization of records creates a threat to individual privacy. Financial transactions, airline reservations, tax returns, arrest records, even grades in school — all have become computerized and therefore potentially

retrievable. Two-way telecommunications is made possible by the computer; and here the threat to privacy is increased by the potential of gathering information once available only with difficulty. Monitoring of television program choices, of blood pressure readings, of the nature of requests to mental health or marriage counseling services are a few possibilities two-way telecommunications suggests.

How can the issue of surveillance and privacy be separated from the need to obtain services? Is two-way telecommunications a step toward governmental control of fashion envisioned by George Orwell in *1984* or can it in fact lead to more direct citizen influence on the government?

6. *The depersonalization of social life.*   Television viewing has become the major leisure occupation of many Americans. It is especially important for the elderly (Glick and Levy, 1962). Two-way cable television has the potential of providing countless ways of gathering information that do not involve face-to-face interaction. The need to leave one's home and go into the outside social environment to obtain the necessities of life may be lessened.

Will this lead to a reduction of human interaction, to a depersonalization of social life? Might the increase in man-machine interaction even have personality implications, with man coming to resemble his electronic partner? Or will it lead to a wider range of information on which to base social contacts and to greater spontaneity in interaction?

This volume is concerned with the linkage of aged persons with bureaucratic organizations in industrialized societies and the role of family networks in such linkages. In this section we have discussed a revolutionary but attainable technological development, two-way cable telecommunications, which has the potential for dramatically changing information exchange and service delivery. We have raised many questions concerning the social implications of such an innovation, especially in the lives of older people. The basic issues seem to be this: What kind of social systems will be created by the new technology? To what extent can this technological advance be used to aid the dependent individual, to aid the family in relating to the older person, and to aid the service bureaucracy in providing better service? It is to these questions that we turn in the next section.

Linkages Between the Older Person, Families, and Bureaucracies in an Information-Based Society

In the previous section we discussed the current state of technical developments in telecommunications, noting that access to two-way cable television systems is likely within the next few decades. This suggests an "information-based" society—immediate, individualized, and reciprocal exchange of information – unique in the history of man. In this section we will discuss some ways in which the experiences of aging and being old in such an information-based society may differ from those of the current era. Three aspects of aging are considered. First is a treatment of changes on the level of the aging individual himself. Will personal characteristics be altered by the changes in the dominant mode of information exchange? The second issue to be considered concerns the ways in which advanced telecommunications systems may influence the nature of the relationship between the older person and those social systems, including the family and service bureaucracy networks, that he relies on in meeting the problem of aging. The third section is a discussion of possible changes in the political power of the elderly, both as individuals and as a voting bloc. This topic addresses directly the problems of influence and control over telecommunications systems discussed in the preceding section.

New Patterns of Adaptation

It is likely that tomorrow's elderly will exhibit more flexible adaptational patterns related to the new ways of information presentation. The way people think is undoubtedly influenced by the pattern and organization of the information that is regularly presented to them. This fact is perhaps best illustrated in the work of Bernstein (1961) and Hess and Shipman (1965) concerning the mechanisms by which cultural experiences are translated into cognitive behavior. From the perspective of this discussion, the implication is that the pattern and organization of information that is regularly presented to a person, particularly during the early years of development, is an important determinant of his capacity to understand and adjust to his world.

The technology being considered in this paper represents most fundamentally a significant change in the day-to-day mode of presentation of symbolic information. It is not surprising, therefore, that students of the social impact of the technology suggest that among the most important aspects of that impact are changes in man's capacity to represent and adapt to his world. Simon (1969) calls such changes "iconic changes" and describes them as "changes in man's pictures of his world, in the system of concepts and ideas through which he interprets his experiences" (p. 2).

Prior to the advent of television, information transmission was based on the spoken and the written word. Both present information linearly, item by item, with the items linked by some kind of logic. Only one such linear sequence is attended to at any given time. In contrast, televised information is not relayed as a single linear sequence but in a complex multidimensional pattern. As an artificial representation of reality, televised information is much more "real" than its verbal or written counterpart.

Hayashi (1972) suggests that the way of thinking imposed by automated and televised information is causing a change not only in the manner of thinking but in the manner of perception; the old mode, like spoken and written language, is logic-based, while the new depends not on logic but on sensibility to pattern among several simultaneously presented lines of information. "Synergy" is a term that is used to describe the way in which the complexly interrelated, simultaneously presented, lines of information combine to create a meaning that is not discernible from examination of any one of those lines independent of the others. The changes that Hayashi (1972) and Simon (1969) have described seem to point toward a greater comprehension of the synergy of natural process, or, in other words, a greater understanding of nature.

Technology, Human Services, and the Dependencies of the Aging

The picture just presented without question overstates the positive. Information technology is not likely to change the fact that aging is accompanied by many unavoidable losses. Old people will continue to encounter decreases in mobility, economic dependence, greater health needs, and social losses. And, as their needs increase their major resources for meeting those needs will probably continue to be focused within two major social arenas: formal service bureaucracies, and informal networks, particularly intergenerational relationships in the family (Blenkner, 1965).

Families and service bureaucracies are different in a number of important ways: "Bureaucracies are social structures which have an instrumental basis for operation, emphasize impersonality, are organized on the basis of formal rules, and stress professional expertise. On the other hand, a family as a prototype of primary groups is characterized by face-to-face judgments, stresses diffuse demands and expectations, and so on" (Streib, 1972, p. 6).

As an older person strives to meet his needs, he may often find himself in interaction with both the family and some formal service bureaucracy. As a result, whether or not he is able to meet his needs may not depend solely on his own competence nor on the independent characteristics of family and agency. The most important issue may rather be the manner in which the family and the service bureaucracy, with all of their diverse characteristics, articulate with one another (see Chapter 1 by Sussman in this volume).

Litwak (1965) has looked at this issue in depth and states his conclusions as follows: "First, in all areas of life there will be aspects of a given task for which the family will be superior to the formal organization, and there will be other aspects for which the opposite will hold. Second, in all areas of life the family and the formal organization must coordinate their behavior if the optimum achievement of goals is to take place" (p. 303).

According to Litwak, the particular areas of needs in which the family and the service bureaucracies might be expected to be strongest are determined by the sorts of characteristics that were described earlier. The four characteristics considered are expertise, resources, flexibility, and responsiveness. The most desirable system for helping old people would be one with high expertise, many resources, high flexibility, and high responsiveness. Both the family and the bureaucracies, however, have their strengths and their weaknesses. The family is flexible and responsive, but it often lacks expertise and certain resources that may be needed to serve the elderly. This is particularly true of such resources as expensive medical equipment which, to be cost-effective, must be ammortized across a number of years and many users. The bureaucracy, in contrast, is characterized by high expertise and many specialized resources.

These particular characteristics work together in such a way that the shared functions relationship described by Litwak tends to become a chronological one. The family is the first helper, meeting needs when they first arise with good responsiveness and flexibility. Family members will generally continue to support the older person until they run out of expertise and resources. At that point a negotiation is entered into with a service bureaucracy of some sort which then takes over the responsibilities that once were handled solely within the family.

The transfer from family to bureaucracy is important in many ways. Perhaps most obviously it represents a change for the older person from a personalized, familiar, and generally affect-laden situation into an impersonal, unfamiliar, and often undesirable situation. The contrast is particularly great when the older person is removed completely from the family setting and placed into an institution; but even if there are only periodic involvements with a service bureaucracy, the contrast is nonetheless there and likely to be disturbing.

A second consequence of the transfer of responsibility from family to bureaucracy has implications beyond the older person and his immediate situation. In an earlier section of this paper we discussed the need for greater cost-effectiveness in the provision of services for older people. That need is increasing because of the combination of the lengthening life span, decreases in the birth rate, and the increase in public demand for greater government support for services for old people. There are more old people and fewer young and middle-aged adults to support them. There is no service system more cost-effective than the family. Therefore the transfer of responsibility for services to the old person from the family to the bureaucracy represents an increase in cost to society as a whole.

There seems to be a compelling argument for instituting changes that may bring about an extension of the family's capacity to serve and an increase in the flexibility and responsiveness of service bureaucracies. This is one of the great promises of two-way cable technology.

One of the great innovations brought about by the computer in education is learner control of the instructional process. Is it possible that one of the benefits of the computer could be client control of the process of administration of his services? The following scenario presents one way in which services might be organized around a two-way computer-controlled cable television system to allow client control of that system and thereby to restructure, at least to some extent, the subordinate position that now characterizes the relationship of older people with those who provide their services.

This client in a client-controlled service system is considered not to be the older person alone, but rather the older person in the family context. With two-way communications, the family context need not be immediate. Although immediate personal contact is certainly preferable, the family could still provide a meaningful context for many services from a distance. It also seems possible that in the future a new profession may develop whose goal is to provide a family-like context for older persons in need of help. The older person with support from his family will locate the proper service agency using the diagnostic capacities of the computer. Since the system allows two-way "picture phone" communication, the first contacts with the agency will be with a human representative rather than the computer itself. The first task of the older person and his family would be the giving of information. The formal information is gathered directly and stored by the computer. Since many diagnoses require human judgment, the family, the older person, and the agency representative will prescribe what is needed to meet the problem in question. Rather than prescribing a service which is then carried out by the agency, the agency's responsibility will have changed, and its responsibility may be the *training* of the family to provide the needed service. The family will learn, through computer-assisted instruction, and then perform the service required.

The critical feature of this example is the change in the role of the service agency from performing a service to training the family to perform it. Thus the agency's major efforts are directed toward extending the family's capacity to serve. It would even be possible in this way to do away with the idea of service agencies as physical entities housed in buildings with secretaries and waiting rooms. The only requirement for centralization would be in the computer facility. The service agents themselves could work from their own homes or from anywhere else they might choose. The subordinate position of the client in the client-agency relationship is supported by the fact that bureaucracies are represented in people's minds more as places and buildings than as people helping people. The idea that institutions must operate from a single physical location is hard to overcome (Sarason, 1972), but it is necessary if client-helper parity is to be established.

Of course, only a portion of an older person's needs could be met within the family context, even with a system such as the one proposed here. There would still be occasions in which institutions would need to completely take over the care of the older person. But the point we are making is that there does seem to be a potential for extending the family's capacity to serve its older members far beyond what it is at the present, and to place control of at least a portion of services rendered in the hands of the client.

The above illustration suggests that information technology may make bureaucracies more flexible by placing them in a training mode, while at the same time extending the family's capacity for service. If these changes are realized, the outcome will very likely be improved performance in meeting the needs of the elderly with a decrease in cost. Moreover, there is an important interpersonal implication of such developments that may have profound consequences for the family life of older people. Many elderly individuals express concern about being a potential burden to their children; most wish to live independently (Blenkner, 1965). The technological support system may enhance family life by freeing both the family and the older person from those onerous and anxiety-producing caretaking crises which stem from a lack of information.

Aging and Politics: Channeling and Controlling the Technical Innovations

Of course, it is by no means certain that effective systems of human services delivery will emerge from the natural development of information technology. As we have indicated, there are many issues of influence and control that must be resolved if such client-centered systems are to be developed. Incentives must be found to direct industry into paths that will foster the growth of information-based human services. The same is true of existing service bureaucracies and of professionals in delivery systems.

The incentives involved may be economic, in terms of the market potential of specialized program audiences. Or, in the case of service delivery systems, the economic incentive must be made clear in terms of the potential for vast savings in information-gathering and delivering that would result from machines doing clerical tasks.

However, the incentives to the development of such systems may result from pressures that are not economic but rather political in nature. This raises some important issues regarding the political potency of potential consumers or clients, particularly the elderly and those who are concerned about meeting their needs.

Many who are currently working on the development of prototype community information systems see increased political involvement of the individual citizen as one of the major benefits of information technology. In describing the possible applications of their system, researchers at the MITRE Corporation have said: "At election time, a citizen can access-on-demand information on candidates, their position on issues, an explanation of referendum items (e.g., specific political platform positions for comparison). If desired, he may review this material prior to visiting the polls" (Stetten, 1971, pp. 3–4).

Although such innovations will benefit everyone, they will perhaps be of greatest help to the elderly. As information technology brings politics into the home, the physical immobility that so often accompanies aging may no longer be a deterrent to effective political participation. This will be particularly so when even voting may be done from a home terminal.

But limitations on political activity are not always physical in nature. There are important social-psychological changes as well that may be moderated by information technology. Havighurst, Neugarten, and Tobin (1968) have pointed out that withdrawal from social involvement is an accurate way of describing the social and psychological changes characteristic of aging in modern American society.

Political activity appears to be a frequent victim of such social disengagement (Gubrium, 1972), particularly as that disengagement is the result of involuntary losses of social support. A community information system might help to maintain political activity, if such a system could somehow mitigate involuntary losses of social support. Such a system could perhaps be designed to allow the individual to identify and interact with people of similar interests, thus increasing the probability of a restoration of some kind of meaningful social connectedness following a social loss. Gubrium's (1972) data suggest the possibility that this restoration of social support might indirectly help maintain political activity.

Many of the prospects for greater political potency of potential clients (particularly in old age) rest not with increasing individual political involvement, but rather with the development of a sense of group identity. For example, were the elderly to unite as a bloc behind a common cause, they would indeed be a powerful political force.

Current analyses, however, do not suggest this is likely under contemporary conditions. For example, the evidence shows that attitudinal differences between age groups are far less impressive than those within age groups (Binstock, 1972). As a result, bloc voting among the elderly is not likely to occur. Moreover, between 40 and 65 percent of those aged sixty-five and over do not even define themselves as old or aged (Riley et al., 1968). Those who do identify themselves as old are likely to be disadvantaged, and then it is not clear whether or not they attribute their many problems to age. It would appear then that there are two ways in which the political potency of the elderly as a group can be enhanced: (1) by increasing the political potency of those who now have the greatest sense of age-group identity, the disadvantaged, and (2) by increasing the age-group awareness of the elderly.

There is evidence that the disadvantaged stand to gain the most from information technology. A report prepared for the Los Angeles City Planning Department (Chesler and Derdick, 1968) showed that a very high percentage of ghetto residents use TV rather than newspapers as a news source. In other words, the broad range of printed educational materials — probably the primary source of usable information for the advantaged — is not being used by the poor. When two-way television becomes the primary source of information upon which political and social competence is based, the relative gain in opportunity for the development of competence may favor the disadvantaged who previously made little use of other major information sources. If the disadvantaged elderly, who feel the greatest age-group identity, gain in political competence, the result would seem to be an overall gain in political potency of the elderly as a group.

There are other aspects of the information revolution that may lead more directly to the definition of the aged as a special interest group. Earlier we referred to the likelihood that two-way cable television may increase the importance of the specialized audience. It seems likely that once the capacity to reach special interest groups has been developed, the telecommunications industry will try to better define the subgroups within society, to develop materials to meet the needs of those subgroups, and then to induce those in the subgroups to define themselves in the same way the industry does, and so become consumers of their product. In other words, when the telecommunications industry begins to see itself as serving the needs of special interest groups such as the elderly, it will probably also find itself in the business of using its considerable persuasive powers to define those societal subgroups.

The elderly already form a well-defined subgroup, and so the problem does not seem to be the acknowledgment of the existence of the elderly as a substratum of society; it is rather whether or not those who are societally designated as part of that subgroup actually have a personal awareness of membership — a "class consciousness" based on age. Most would argue today that there is little age consciousness among the elderly and that it is not likely to develop (Palmore and Wittington, 1971; Trela, 1971; Schmidhauser, 1968; Ragan and Dowd, 1974). However, if the telecommunications industry finds it expedient to promote that awareness among the elderly, many of those arguments may have to be reexamined.

The nature and extent of potential change in the political role of the elderly is unclear. There is little reason to believe that age-group consciousness will spontaneously develop among the general elderly, and yet a powerful and persuasive industry may find it to its advantage to foster the development of age-group consciousness.

It is as yet unclear whether political power on the part of the elderly as a group will be affected by the development of advanced telecommunications systems. However, such systems do appear to have the potential of allowing the individual older person to engage in reciprocal "feedback" relationship with those who serve him on a scale that has not existed heretofore. Whether or not such a reciprocal relationship does in fact develop depends on a number of social factors: (1) whether or not service professionals recognize those they serve as legitimate sources of "corrective" information; (2) whether it is considered economically feasible to develop institutionalized attention to what will likely be viewed as client complaints; and (3) whether channels for becoming aware of client-originated feedback are matched by effective channels for carrying out the suggested changes.

The obstacles to a reciprocal client-agency relationship are not imposed by the technology but by the social constraints that exist in bureaucratic systems. The information-flow that is demanded by such reciprocal interaction is provided by new information technologies. One of the most fruitful directions for the exercise of whatever political power might be available to older persons and professionals who are concerned with their needs would be toward assuring that the technology-based channels of reciprocal information flow are matched by social structural supports within the service agencies.

Making Possible the Ideal: Values and Implementation of Telecommunications Technology

The preceding sections have emphasized several positive potentialities of two-way information systems for older people. First, such persons may feel useful throughout life and experienced in the mastery of change. Second, bureaucracy, in its turn, may become more flexible and free its expertise to be used by the family which, in its turn, learns to be more expert in serving its older members. Third, the older person influences the shaping of the systems that serve him as he engages in a feedback interchange with bureaucracies that, freed by information technology, become more responsive to their clients.

In the enthusiasm that a development so seemingly beneficial can generate, it is often easy to forget that accomplishments are not as easy to achieve as they are to dream. The actual implementation of a telecommunications delivery system will create numerous changes in existing social systems. Successful implementation will involve the resolution of a host of obstacles, and resistances from a number of sources will be encountered. Six problem areas were identified in the first section of this chapter. In the second section we addressed in the context of a general discussion four of these issues: implications for family relations; the potential and problems for existing service agencies; political and economic aspects of influence and control over the system; and some aspects of relations between clients and practitioners.

In this section we turn to two additional issues, problems related more to values and mass opinion than to the observable aspects of social systems involving power, positions, and interactions. Arguments against the adoption of two-way telecommunications systems as the dominant communication mode in the year 2000 will probably center around two value stances. The first, one of the primary concerns of those concerned with civil liberties, is the invasion of privacy. Will the innovations discussed in this paper become a serious threat to individual privacy? The second is the possibility that such communication systems may deprive man of vitally needed human interaction and create a society of beings with characteristics that are less "human" than they are like those of the machines with whom they interact.

Such negative implications of telecommunications innovations are reasonable concerns and deserve serious consideration. In addition, there are general issues that arise whenever any new program of dramatic change is attempted. Implicit in any new system of doing things is a criticism of the old ways. Those involved in the existing order may respond to that implied criticism by directly opposing the innovations. These general issues regarding change and innovation, however, are beyond the scope of this chapter (Bennis, Benne, and Chin, 1969; Sarason, 1972).

Telecommunications and Privacy

The privacy issue became a topic of general public concern with the advent of computers, with their potential for mass storage of data and rapid dissemination of information. Computer technology, for example, made possible the credit-card industry. Individuals create data about themselves when they use their credit cards, and when such data are made available to others without the individual's consent or knowledge, the right to privacy is threatened. Two-way telecommunications, like the credit-card industry, is made possible by the computer. Here, the threat to privacy comes not only through the increased availability of stored information, but from the possibility of gathering information that has heretofore been available only with difficulty. Such information ranges from preferences in television viewing gained by monitoring a person's selection of viewing material through actual surveillance of a person's daily activities through television cameras placed in dwellings and public places. At present such direct surveillance is being considered in several instances as a means of achieving the obviously worthwhile purpose of monitoring the health status of patients in long-term care facilities. Some may feel that if direct television surveillance of patients for medical purposes is carried out, surely surveillance on a more widespread basis cannot be far behind. But the issue of surveillance, in any case, is perhaps more critical from the point of view of the elderly than from that of the population at large because if surveillance takes the form of monitoring the physical well-being of the dependent members of society, as has been suggested above, the elderly are more likely than most to become candidates for such practices.

It is important to note that the issue of privacy does not derive directly from a particular technology; it would exist even were we to revert to non-electronic means of information storage and transmission. Moreover, investigations of alleged invasions of privacy by computer data banks have failed to discover such abuses (Westin and Baker, 1972).

The Depersonalization of Social Life

Two-way cable television has the potential of providing new ways to perform many services. Many activities that used to require that a person leave his home and move personally into the outside world may be done instead from within the walls of his own home. Consider the following utopian possibilities: with no need to go to the grocery store, food can be ordered over the two-way television system. If a library book is wanted, just dial a number and get a video version. Many things that used to be done only with personal social involvement may become possible without face-to-face contacts. Such possibilities raise at least two questions having to do with values of interpersonal life and individual orientations. First, will the introduction of two-way communications systems reduce the amount of person-to-person interaction, with a negative effect on human social development? And second, will the increase in man-machine interaction create a new character in man, with man becoming less spontaneous and creative and more rigidly programmed, thus resembling his electronic partner?

Interaction with a machine may take the place of face-to-face human contact under two circumstances. In the first instance, when people need to interact with others, they may choose to do so via the two-way telecommunications system rather than through face-to-face contact. The second instance results from the capacity of computerized telecommunications systems to present video information that does not depend upon a human being on the other end of the system. For example, a person may choose between watching a movie and visiting with a friend. If telecommunications systems increased the opportunity of choice in seeking oriented information, will the amount of person-to-person interaction in fact be reduced?

In the first case, people interact with one another, but via the machine (similar to a telephone) rather than in immediate special proximity. There are reasons to believe that two-way cable television communications systems may in fact increase the amount of such interaction. Gestures and facial expressions are important forms of communication not possible with the telephone. For the elderly grandparent living at some distance from his or her offspring, visual as well as vocal communication would undoubtedly enhance interpersonal contact, and perhaps make such interaction more frequent.

However, many common forms of interaction may simply not be carried out through electronic communication. Consider, for example, the associational activities that are frequently included in studies of the interaction of the older people (Adams, 1968; Black and Bengtson, 1973). Family members give and receive help; they exchange gifts; they eat dinner together and go to church; they get together for reunions, holiday dinners, birthdays, and other special occasions; they engage in recreational activities such as picnics, swimming, hunting trips, and so on. The only activity that can be reasonably carried out via the two-way communications system is talking. Talking over two-way electronic communications systems has been possible since the invention of the telephone, and while people may rely more on a television-based system than the nonvisual telephone system, there is no reason to assume they would do so.

The second circumstance is perhaps more serious. Two-way cable television will provide alternatives to interaction with other human beings, whether face-to-face or via the cable television system. At present when someone is deciding whether or not to visit a friend or to stay at home, he may indeed look at the television schedule to see if there is a program that interests him. If there is not, he may visit his friend, but if there is a program that he is especially intrigued by, he may very well choose to stay at home. Under two-way cable television systems programs can be accessed and all interesting programs will always be available, and on a much wider range of topics.

The degree to which the viewing of video messages will be accepted as a substitute for interacting with people may be determined to some extent by the nature of the video materials that are prepared. For example, it would be possible to deliberately design video materials that will enhance interaction. They might teach people to do things for which interaction with other adults is essential. If television can be used for education, it can certainly be used to educate people to engage in social interaction. There are people today who are interacting with those who differ from them in race, religion, or ethnic origin precisely because television has helped to alter their picture of the social world. Certainly it is possible that the increase in alternatives to human interaction that will be presented by two-way cable television may tend to isolate men. But that is by no means the only possible outcome, and, with proper planning, two-way cable television may be used to increase the frequency of person-to-person encounters.

In short, it is unlikely that personal interaction will be reduced with the introduction of two-way television technology. Certainly individuals will have more opportunity to engage in stimulating activities that do not involve other people, but at the same time there are factors that would suggest that more avenues of personal interaction will also be open to them. In any event, telecommunications technology will allow greater individual selectivity in such contact—or lack of it. Someone once suggested to us that such technology could be devastating to men's social well-being. As evidence he cited the experience in a primitive village when water was piped into homes for the first time. At first, everyone appeared enthusiastic about the innovation; gradually, however, many women began returning to the village well for their water, ignoring the piped-in water. The reason, of course: they missed the social interaction at the common well. Telecommunications technology, like piped-in water, tends to draw people away from one another. But if the example is generally applicable, it illustrates what is perhaps an even more important point: if something is introduced which prevents people from getting together, they will refuse to use it rather than give up the opportunities for social interactions that are important and meaningful for them.

A common theme in the antitechnology literature is the notion that, as men begin to interact more and more with machines, they will come to take on machinelike attributes, losing their creativity and spontaneity and becoming creatures of patterned, regulated behavior. This argument has a superficial appeal because not only is it simple and easy to visualize, but it also is based on the view that most people today have of machines: mechanical devices given to repetitive, assembly-line sorts of actions. However, the technological advances discussed in this paper have to do with a means of transmitting artificial information that indisputably is capable of presenting that information in a far more complex fashion than has heretofore been possible given existing means of information transmission such as books, the radio, television as we now know it, and even human speech.

We have suggested earlier, citing the work of Basil Bernstein (1961) and others, that man's mode of thought and adaptation is dependent upon the nature of the information that is presented to him. If, through telecommunications and computers, information is presented in a more complex way, more synergetically as we have called it, thinking and perception will also become more synergetic and better adapted to a comprehension of natural processes.

In such circumstances the "robopath" seems unlikely. We are rather likely to experience greater spontaneity in people. In a world of logic the reasons for normal behavior are apparent; but in a world of sensibility to patterns within a complex reality, the reasons for eminently sensible behavior may no longer be obvious. Behavior appears to be spontaneous when its relationship to the immediate situation is unobvious and complex. As Simon (1969) puts it, "To explain spontaneity, we need not assume that behavior is uncaused, merely that its causes are multitudinous" (p. 295). Telecommunications may allow greater individual creativity and spontaneity on a mass basis than ever before.

Conclusion

In this chapter we have surveyed some recent developments in tele-communications technology and discussed the implications of these innovations for the elderly of tomorrow. We have reported that important technical break-throughs in two-way telecommunications have already been made, and that the time is not far off when many services now performed by way of visits to bureaucratic agencies may be handled by the older person in his home communicating with the agency via the television set. We have noted that a "new" older person is emerging in our society, and that two-way telecommunications may make service agencies into responsive training centers for the family, thus extending the family's capacity to serve. We have suggested that the problems of a possible invasion of privacy and a decrease in face-to-face interaction as the result of computerized two-way television are not insurmountable. In short, we have attempted to present a case concerning possible improvements of life in old age as the result of telecommunications technology which lie in the not-too-distant future.

Disraeli once said, "Man is not the creature of circumstances, circumstances are the creatures of man." In this day of rapid and complex change one may perhaps question that statement. However, it is nonetheless true that men do have the capacity to act in such a way as to shape their future, at least to some extent. Many groups are vying for their particular shape of the future. Confrontation and demands for action and change have become a common part of life. It is likely that in spite of one's best efforts no one's future will be precisely what one might wish. Nevertheless, it is undoubtedly true that those who invest themselves in guiding the direction of change are more likely to find themselves in a future that suits them.

Who will look out for the elderly? This is a challenge everyone should accept. After all, we all have a reasonable expectation of growing old, yet we have a remarkably lackadaisical attitude toward our own future; we often find ourselves so busy looking after the problems of today that we do not plan for the future. Nevertheless, it is to be hoped that a significant portion of persons concerned with aging will be interested in the possibilities for good that exist within the ever-increasing array of technological developments in communications, in that way perhaps lending their weight toward a better life for old people in the future.

References

Adams, B. N. *Kinship in an Urban Setting.* Chicago, 1968.
Becker, H., B. Greer, E. Hughes, and A. Strauss. *Boys in White: Student Culture in Medical School.* Chicago, 1961.
Bennis, W. G., L. D. Benne, and R. Chin. *The Planning of Change.* New York, 1969.
Bernstein, B. "Social Class and Linguistic Development: A Theory of Social Learning." In

Education, Economy, and Society, ed. A. H. Halsey, J. Floud, and C. A. Anderson. New York, 1961.

Binstock, R. H. "Interest-group Liberalism and the Politics of Aging." *Gerontologist* 12 (1972):265–80.

Black, K. D., and V. L. Bengtson. "The Measurement of Family Solidarity: An Inter-Generational Analysis." Paper presented at the annual meetings of the American Psychological Association, Montreal, August 1973.

Blenkner, M. "Social Work and Family Relationships in Later Life with Some Thoughts on Filial Maturity." In *Social Structure and the Family: Generational Relations*, ed. E. Shanas and G. F. Streib. Englewood Cliffs, N.J., 1965.

Chesler, L. G., and H. S. Derdick. *Communication Goals for Los Angeles: A Working Paper for the Los Angeles Goals Program*. Santa Monica, Calif., 1968.

Clarke, A. C. *Profiles of the Future*. New York, 1962.

Glick, I. O., and S. J. Levy. *Living with Television*. New York, 1962.

Gubrium, J. F. "Continuity in Social Support, Political Interest, and Voting in Old Age." *Gerontologist* 12 (1972):421–23.

Haug, M., and M. Sussman. "Professional Autonomy and the Revolt of the Client." *Social Problems* 17 (1969):153–61.

Havighurst, R. J., B. L. Neugarten, and S. S. Tobin. "Disengagement and Patterns of Aging." In *Middle Age and Aging: A Reader in Social Psychology*, ed. B. L. Neugarten. Chicago, 1968.

Hayashi, Y. "The Information-Centered Society." In *The Futurist*, ed. A. Toffler. New York, 1972.

Hess, R. D., and V. C. Shipman. "Early Experience and the Socialization of Cognitive Modes in Children." *Child Development* 36 (1965):869–86.

Hill, R., N. Foote, J. Aldous, R. Carlson, and R. MacDonald. *Family Development in Three Generations*. New York, 1970.

Jurgen, R. K. "Two-Way Applications for Cable Television Systems in the '70's." *IEEE Spectrum* 8 (1971):39–54.

Litwak, E. "Extended Kin Relations in an Industrial Society." In *Social Structure and the Family*, ed. E. Shanas and G. F. Streib. Englewood Cliffs, N.J., 1965.

Palmore, E., and F. Whittington. "Trends in the Relative Status of the Aged." *Social Forces* 50 (1971):84–91.

Parker, E. B., and D. A. Dunn. "Information Technology: Its Social Potential." *Science* 176 (1972):1392–98.

Ragan, P., and J. Dowd. "The Emerging Political Consciousness of the Aged: A Generational Interpretation." *Journal of Social Issues* 30 (1974):137–58.

Ramey, J. W. "Telecommunications Developments: Implications for the Family." Address delivered to the Groves Conference, Dallas, Texas, May 5–8, 1972.

Ramm, D., and D. T. Gianturco. "Computers and Technology: Aiding Tomorrow's Aged." *Gerontologist* 13 (1973):323–26.

Riley, M. W., A. Foner, and associates. *An Inventory of Research Findings*. Vol. 1, Aging and Society. New York, 1968.

Sarason, S. *The Creation of Settings and the Future Societies*. San Francisco, 1972.

Schmidhauser, J. "The Political Influence of the Aged." *Gerontologist* 8 (1968):44–49.

Shanas, E., and G. F. Streib, eds. *Social Structure and the Family: Generational Relations*. Englewood Cliffs, N.J., 1965.

Shanas, E., P. Townsend, D. Wedderburn, H. Friis, P. Milhhøj, and J. Stehouwer. *Old People in Three Industrial Societies*. New York, 1968.

Simon, H. A. *The Sciences of the Artificial*. Cambridge, Mass., 1969.

Singer, A. L. "Issues for Study in Cable Communications." Cited in R. C. Snider, "The Copius Cable." *Audiovisual Instruction*, 1971.

Stetten, K. J. *Interactive Television Software for Cable Television Application*. McLean, Va., 1971.

Streib, G. F. "Older Families and Their Troubles: Familial and Social Responses." *Family Coordinator* 21 (1972):5–19.

———, and W. Thompson. "The Older Person in a Family Context." In *Handbook of Social Gerontology*, ed. C. Tibbitts. Chicago, 1960.

Sussman, M. B. "An Analytic Model for the Sociological Study of Retirement." In *Retirement*, ed. F. Carp. New York, 1972.

———. "Relationship of Adult Children with Their Parents in the United States." In *Social Structure and the Family: Generational Relations*, ed. E. Shanas and G. Streib. Englewood Cliffs, N.J., 1965.

———, and L. Burchinal. "Kin Family Network: Unheralded Structure in Current Conceptualizations of Family Functioning." *Marriage and Family Living* 24 (1962):231–50.

Trela, E. "Some Political Consequences of Senior Citizen and Other Old Age Group Members." *Gerontologist* 11 (1971):118–23.

Westin, A. F., and M. A. Baker. *Databanks in a Free Society.* New York, 1972.

11. Social Systems and Social Facts *Kurt W. Back*

In the course of his life man interacts in many different associations. These associations are not only different in their composition and the situations in which he encounters them, but they differ also in rules, principles, and degree of emotional involvement. They are classified by scientists as well as in common parlance and understanding. Thus some of the classifications and typologies of sociologists may be abstractions, but the principles upon which they are based have definite meaning to the people involved and therefore possess a social reality of their own.

Systems and Associations

In this volume two associations, the family and bureaucracy, have been looked at both as abstract systems and as actual interactions, which may differ from the abstract systems. These two systems have been treated mainly by discussing their efficiency, that is, the relationship of effort expended to benefits given to different family members, especially the aged. Reference has been made to some of the system characteristics which distinguish the two methods of association. The family is diffuse, emotional, and able to deal with idiosyncratic events and activities where not much skill is required. The bureaucracy is efficient in routine activities and those which need specialized skills. Thus the two types seem complementary. It looks as if it would be promising to arrange some interaction whereby the members could have the best of both systems. Of all the chapters, that by Black and Bengtson goes as far as possible in this direction by showing how future communications systems may help in serving different members in different situations of emergency. The theoretical chapters and those which touch on theory, however, appear somewhat in a pathetic contrast with those which try to depict actual situations and conditions in a variety of contexts. Deficiencies in services do occur, some of which might seem minor but might be important within the present concern. Examples are the characteristics of the waiting rooms in France or the exclusion from benefits of some major categories in Yugoslavia such as housewives and farmers, although those benefits are guaranteed by the constitution of the country.

It is not news that actual programs do not conform to the best-planned systems approach. Thus in discussing the linkage properties we might learn from previous experience and also use other methods and theories to assess the actual status of the aged. Let us look at the two kinds of contrasting configurations, family and bureaucracy, not only as systems, but as social facts which do occur in society and are perhaps determined in part by temporary conditions and historical accidents. This kind of approach might help us then to place individuals into different spheres of influence under which they have to live and to distinguish the difficulties inherent in the situation from those that are temporary and easily avoidable. The variety of examples presented in this volume will help us in illustrating and understanding the different friction points and in assessing the possible remedies proposed for the specific problem situations.

The systems' outcomes which have been discussed in contrasting the family and bureaucracy are based on the nature of the relationship. The family relationship, being personal, endures for a long time and implies a unique emotional commitment not covered simply by system variables. In a certain sense it extends over a person's life. One cannot refuse to recognize a certain kinship relationship. One can ignore it or feel that it is not relevant for a certain act, but it is always there. The bureaucratic relationship, on the other hand, is mainly connected with an act. If there are no immediate acts to be performed or debts to be paid, there is no relationship at all. The parental relationship may be strengthened, weakened, or even abolished under certain conditions, but we must acknowledge that it is there even if we try to deny it. On the other hand, the bureaucratic relationship can be present or absent. One of the troubles with this relationship, as discussed previously, is that it has to be established anew for every need. Thus the time frame as well as the intensity of emotion are important in distinguishing the two relationships. In bureaucratic relationships one has to justify why the bureaucracy is helping a retired person who has ceased to contribute to it; a temporary link has to be established. In family relationships, however, the link is already there and the essence of the problem is what happens if it is denied for certain reasons. From another point of view, there is a qualitative difference between the two relationships. In families, the definition of obligations, affection, and aggression comes from the given relationship within the kinship structure, and thus it is established without individual effort. In the bureaucratic relationship, however, the relation is defined by the act by which the bureaucracy serves the members. Bureaucracy in general is an exchange and is always discussed in terms of its exchange features. A person has performed a certain service or has done something which gives him a certain claim on the bureaucracy, and therefore the bureaucracy will honor it.

All these aspects give the passage of time, or aging, a very different meaning for the family and bureaucracy. Within the family an aging person comes to hold a different position in relation to the existing members— from being a child to becoming a parent or a grandparent, an aunt or an uncle, or other kin relation. In the bureaucratic system, however, the relationship will exist according to a strict definition at the time. The main bureaucratic definition is through the relation of the member to the labor force. Bureaucracy supports the aged person, in general, because of his retirement; and in almost any economic system support is in direct relation to the input he has been able to contribute during his working years. In addition, there may be certain needy categories defined within the bureaucracy as deserving of support regardless of input, such as ill or handicapped persons, or, under some conditions, the aged per se. However, all these conditions are well delimited, and basically refer to some ideas of reciprocity.

Although these two sets of relationships, within the family and within the bureaucracy, depend on passing time, there is no exact correspondence between the two with regard to chronological aging. It is exactly this lack of correspondence which raises problems in many discussions of gerontology. We can look at the theoretical problems therefore as the relation of one continuous variable, namely chronological aging, to two social and discontinuous variables, namely the progression of role change within the family and within the economic sector of society. The empirical problems to which most of the chapters in this volume address themselves may be looked at from this point of view and used to exemplify the kinds of difficulties these relations provide — political, economic, and social, as well as psychological.

The Relations Between the Systems

Before assessing and choosing remedies we have to assess the diverse classes of situations in order to locate the sources of difficulties. We must investigate especially whether the difficulties arise because of the nature of the systems, because of the nature of the aging process, or because of certain peculiarities of current social change.

The general trend in society has been to substitute the bureaucratic system for the familial one. In earlier times the bureaucratic organization, the state, would provide help only in cases where the family could not. As Anderson shows, the Poor Laws and similar acts guided the care of people who were alone and whose families could not take care of them. The situation now is reversed. The family takes care of those cases which the social system, the bureaucracy of the welfare state, cannot take care of.

Bureaucracy looks at its relationship to the individual as a kind of exchange relationship. An individual first establishes a certain right to be helped; he is helped in an equitable proportion. This exchange outlook has several consequences. It leads to the pretense that the worker accumulates actual money which is returned to him after he retires. In effect, as Kreps has pointed out in Chapter 2, this fact is in most societies a convenient fiction. Old-age and social security benefits are paid out of current income and current contributions. Thus at any point in time the working population supports the nonworking. However, it is important for political reasons to keep up the fiction that payment to the aged is based on an insurance scheme. It probably would not be politically feasible to model old-age assistance methods on a family ethos. The younger people in the society would probably not support the older ones according to the present needs of the old. Thus each system has to have rules which determine how much the person has contributed either in cash or by his labor in previous times, or whether he qualifies for a special dispensation by being in a handicapped position.

There are several consequences of this attitude. One is that a tremendous amount of labor and paper work has to be expended to determine eligibility according to one of these criteria. This then puts an additional burden on the old person. The second difficulty is that some people are going to bypass the rules as established and will thereby lose any eligibility. This is true of people who have not worked during their adult lives, that is, have not done any productive labor according to the definition used at the time. As we have seen in previous chapters, the main examples of this "nonproductive" labor are agricultural work and housework for women. These are the two kinds of work which are closest to the original family context. The agricultural family is characterized by a stable procession from childhood to old age within the family context, with all members contributing over a long period of time. Therefore each person stays within the family and is supported by it. The same is true of housewives who may not earn monetary income but help in the maintenance of the household in a reciprocal relationship which is the essence of the family relationship.

Historic Changes

How extensive are these questions of one-time social change, and to what extent are they intrinsic to the relationship between the two systems? We must recognize that the difference between these alternatives is somewhat artificial. There will never be a completely stable system and there will always be some change which may render even the best-tuned mechanisms of society out of date. However, certain aspects of social change do stand out.

One is the transition from an agricultural to an urban and industrial society. The rate of change which has occurred in the last generation or so cannot continue, since if it did, clearly there would be no agricultural society left to change. At any rate, the new industrial society is better organized for the bureaucratic system, while the older farm life has been most resistant to bureaucratic change and is still based on the family system. This is true not only because of the mode of production and the fact that many social security systems do not acknowledge farm work, but probably also because of psychological factors. Traditionally the farmer has been suspicious of the workings of the state and is unlikely to enter into an exchange relationship with the state with the hope of gaining something. Thus he is handicapped in working with the bureaucracy, in approaching civil servants, and in being able to push his claims. The data from France reported by Paillat show that in small towns people do try to find somebody in the area to help them with a particular problem. These data show, probably the most of any, the importance of the linkage person, but he has to be a linkage person who is used to dealing with the bureaucracy and is known by his clientele to be able to do it. We might consider this situation, however, as temporary because of the decline in the number of farmers in the society. In addition, improved communication and education have made the differences between urban and rural populations smaller. However, it may be a vain hope that these differences will be completely erased and that the farmer will be as willing a member of the bureaucratic structure as the city worker is. A related problem here is the existence of people who have moved from the country to the city and who have lost their eligibility because of previous farm work. Here again this is a temporary situation, as the migration cannot keep going at the present rate. The extreme example might be Poland, which has in one generation changed from a predominantly agricultural to a predominantly industrial country.

Israel presents another unique problem. Because of its history a disproportionate number of old people are immigrants and have spent the greater part of their working lives in other countries. This problem may also be aggravated by the fact that the conditions under which the immigrants had lived in other countries have tended to make them suspicious of the bureaucratic system, which previously was primarily antagonistic to them. However, this extremely high immigration rate is also a temporary problem. Some of the problems we have been discussing in both industrializing and immigration countries are therefore unique problems of the present time. A solution which assumes permanency of this condition may do more harm than good.

The difficulties caused by these changes may be not only economic but psychological and social as well. Different educational and occupational experience produces different outlooks on life for people who work mainly with symbols or writing and those who work with their hands or with objects. In many countries this difference defines the middle and working classes. In general the rules are made by people who work with symbols, but they are made for the whole population, and it is very hard for people who are used to paperwork and writing as part of their daily lives to see the difficulty other people might have understanding and following the rules. Thus rules in the bureaucratic structure may be easier for people who during their working lives have been connected with written material and written instructions, or through their education have been able to be on very familiar terms with them. Again, we may postulate this as part of the bureaucratic structure itself, namely that the relationships are based on written and permanent records. This corresponds to the generally distant relationships existing within the bureaucratic structure and the fact that personal participation is irrelevant, whereas the transaction must be recorded for anybody else who might come into the position of being responsible for it. Within the family the relationship is personal and not determined by many rules. The occupations or social situations which are closest to the family system are also devoid of these formal rules and of familiarity with paperwork and written material. Again, we do not know whether increasing literacy will correct this.

Another change is a demographic development. The trend in developed countries toward longer life and fewer children per family should make for great changes in family composition, especially with regard to old people. It can easily be projected that in future generations there will be many old people without close relatives, having had too few children to assure the survival of all of them, especially if they themselves live very long. People who are brought up in a society of small families and great longevity may feel very different about family relations in general. In fact, some psychologists are foreseeing an age of "instant intimacy" to counteract the impossibility of stable relationships because of a combination of demographic and urban conditions.

Intrinsic Frictions

A variety of trends, therefore, makes the division between the two systems of family and bureaucracy less clear-cut than it is stated conceptually. Conventional statistics divide the aged into three groups according to housing: (1) those living with the family or others, (2) those living alone or with a spouse, and (3) those living in an institution. As we have seen, there are different proportions in each of these arrangements in different countries, and the trends are somewhat dissimilar. However, with modernization there seems to be a definite trend away from the first alternative with the result that most of the aged either live alone in an independent living arrangement or are confined to an institution.

We can see this demarcation as an ideal of the bureaucratic system. People are either in an exchange relationship with the state and are able to maintain their own independence in independent housing or they are really handicapped physically or mentally because of their age and thus become in a sense wards of the state. The familial relation which is symbolized by the first living arrangement is gradually being eroded. The proposal of linkage is in part based on the idea that this development is not irreversible and that some aspects of bureaucracy can be taken care of within the family. For instance, people might still be integrated into and receive benefits from the bureaucratic society but continue to live with their families.

It has been shown frequently that the lack of cohabitation does not necessarily mean a weakening of family relationships. However, it may be questionable whether the functions of bureaucracy can be assumed within the family considering specific emotional and long-term relationships, just as familial relationships are inappropriate to the bureaucratic structure. Thus in one of the countries discussed in this volume, Israel, some studies have been made showing that the last condition has prevailed. Because of the peculiar position of Jews in many countries there has been a strong familial feeling among Jews in general, and therefore some immigrants in Israel regard the bureaucratic structure as a surrogate for the family. Katz has discussed a variety of letters to government officials in Israel which use a kind of family relationship in order to obstruct the functioning of the bureaucracy. This may be an extreme case of interference.[1]

The role of the individual within the family will depend in great part on the kinship relationship and in part on the previous emotional history. These are not exactly correlated with age. Thus a young person might be a grandfather and an older person might be a sister or even a son. The obligation anybody would feel toward a person under these conditions would depend on this relationship and not on his previous contribution. Some of the papers show, however, that a lack of financial dependence on the family may improve the relationship and that the question of support, which may be the one best answered by the bureaucracy, is precisely that which interferes most with family cooperation. In modern society the family is mainly an arena for emotional relationships. The tendency toward independent lodging may be a way of removing the exchange relationships from the emotional relationships and in this way improving them.

On the other hand, the difficulties of using the bureaucracy in the family are also apparent. In the bureaucratic system everything is measured by the present time, and the personal feelings of people working for a living cannot be taken into account. The relationship here is primarily dependent on the previous labor-force situation and one's present status, whether working or retired. Again this condition does not necessarily relate much to age and even less to status within the family system. Those who have a smooth relationship with the bureaucracy will be those whose experience corresponds to the rules of the bureaucracy itself and who are also capable of and interested in following rules and filling out forms. Probably the ideal person in this instance is the person who has been a part of the bureaucracy himself. The difficulties with the bureaucratic structure occur when this exchange relationship is in any way disturbed, as we have seen in other examples in this volume.

1. E. Katz and B. Danet. "Petitions and Persuasive Appeals: A Study of Official Client Relations," *American Sociological Review* 31 (1966):811–21.

Interaction

Given their completely different configurations, how can the two systems, family and bureaucracy, interact in the most fruitful way? The two systems can act completely independently: a person may turn to his family for the emotional comfort long-term relationships may provide while allowing the bureaucratic system to pay off the rights and obligations he has accumulated vis-à-vis the larger society. But this may only be practical if both systems work at their maximum efficiency, the family giving the optimal emotional relationship and the bureaucracy providing its services with minimal complications. We have seen the difficulties many individuals encounter in dealing with the bureaucracy.

If a perfect balance between the two systems is too difficult to achieve, it might be possible to rely mainly on one of them. Entering an institution would be the prime example of completely entering the bureaucratic system while hoping for some comfort from the family. The opposite interaction is a person's living with his family and having the family take care of transactions with the bureaucracy. This arrangement is the one which is decreasing at present, possibly because it means frequently that the family will take over also the responsibilities of the bureaucracy, principally the financial responsibility.

A genuinely interactive arrangement would provide the linkage through the systems themselves in such a way that part of the functions of the family and the bureaucracy would overlap. One way, which has been proposed here, would be to integrate the family into the bureaucracy by giving some family member the function of dealing with officials and remunerating him as part of the official service. This would solve the problem of the necessity for some of the bureaucratic officials occasionally having to take on supporting roles for which the system is not equipped. Many of the problems discussed in this volume can be looked at from this point of view.

Would similar problems occur if the family as family would assume the bureaucratic role? It is likely that the payoff in this situation would be not only financial but emotional as well, in providing for leadership or dependence and a kind of emotional exploitation. We can see deficiencies in bureaucratic administration easily because they consist of obvious errors such as missing checks and low payments. The defects of the family as a means of remedying the problems of bureaucracy are more subtle and need to be researched by the psychologist. We know that the bureaucracy is often called in to remedy some of the problems of the family, such as family conflict and psychological difficulties; if the family takes on bureaucratic functions the emotional cost may be high. We have seen the deficiencies of the bureaucracy in taking on family functions. Additional research is needed to determine the capacity of the family to take on bureaucratic functions.

12. Bureaucracies and Families: Common Themes and Directions for Further Study   *Gordon F. Streib*

Family and Bureaucracy in Cross-National Perspective

The previous chapters in this volume have attempted to shed new light on an important area in which there is a scarcity of information: the interaction between families and bureaucracies in attempting to meet the needs of old people. The chapters I have selected to serve as the basis for my comments are those by Joep Munnichs (Netherlands), Paul Paillat (France), Jerzy Piotrowksi (Poland), Leopold Rosenmayr (Austria), Nada Smolić-Krković (Yugoslavia), and Hannah Weihl (Israel). These authors have outlined in a broad fashion the relationships between the family and formal organizations. In the main they have concentrated their attention on those family characteristics which distinguish the elderly as special populations, particularly in terms of their vulnerability and need for outside intervention and assistance.

The variety of information presented requires that the commentator highlight some of the major common themes, which will be discussed in the first section of this chapter. They will serve as the background for the second section, in which I will use these themes as a springboard for developing a discussion of those areas which require further study and specification.

These six gerontologists reflect different professional perspectives: two are sociologists, two are social workers, one is a psychologist, and one is a demographer. The fact that these researchers have different professional backgrounds and expertise is important in the study of family and bureaucracy, for this is properly an interdisciplinary problem. Studying the social needs and services for the aged requires a multidisciplinary perspective.

The major emphasis of the presentations is on the family structure and relations, reflecting the experience and background of the specialists involved. The problems and issues relating to the bureaucracy are relatively unexplored, and discussions of this area are generally handled with illustrative material. There is no equivalent quantitative information about bureaucracies parallel in depth to the information about the family and, interestingly enough, the problem of the linkage between the family and bureaucracy is well-nigh ignored.

One of the major advantages of cross-national studies is the opportunity to note some of the common patterns which mark the conditions of the aged in societies with different cultures, religions, and political traditions.

Demographic factors received considerable attention by the six authors as being important aspects of family-bureaucratic problems. Many of the questions of how the family may or may not serve as a linkage mechanism are the consequences of the size of the family, the number of generations involved, the living arrangements of the households, and the age and sex characteristics of the family members. Munnichs points out, for example, that the relations between family and bureaucracy are quite different when one has to deal with a three-generation family in one dwelling unit than when dealing with a single individual living alone. In the Netherlands there are over 200,000 older persons who live alone. Those among them who have no relatives are forced earlier into institutional settings. Paillat reports that in France the decrease in the birth rate is leading to an increase in the proportion of aged persons without siblings or children and an increased need for services. A special kind of demographic family problem that is especially poignant is mentioned by Smolić-Krković of Yugoslavia, who points out that in some of the countries studied there are more likely to be older persons who have no relatives as a result of devastation by war.

An area related to demographic structure is found in the attitudinal domain. Many of the investigators report that older persons prefer living arrangements that reflect "intimacy at a distance." In many societies described by the authors, the older persons, when given their choice, prefer to maintain separate households from those of their relatives. These households, however, are still close enough to those of their relatives that they may see them on a regular basis. This preference for privacy creates, as Munnichs points out, a kind of vulnerability for the older family members if they should eventually reach the state where they need constant care and attention rather than occasional visiting. Munnichs reports that in a survey of older people less than 2 percent wished to live with their children. Here again there is some cross-national variability. In Poland, for example, Piotrowski reports that although intimacy at a distance is a common preferred residential arrangement, nevertheless older people are more willing to live with children in Poland than in the Western European countries which have been studied. Piotrowski carries the analysis a step further by indicating that the social-psychological balance between the generations is similar in both city and country when a housing shortage is present. He points out that when the elderly person controls the dwelling unit, there is a potential source of conflict between the generations, especially as the size of the young family grows. One difference in the generational relations between rural and urban dwellers is that the young couple in the country can leave and move to the city if household conflict becomes too great, while the young couple in the city cannot or will not move to the country.

Rural-urban differences are another common theme. Piotrowski points out that under Polish law until recently there was no assistance for the rural aged for it was assumed that somehow relatives would be available to help the aged. The expectation that in rural areas there will be relatives to help the aged is based upon an assumption of a static society. The observations of Paillat show the results of physical mobility. The French situation described by Paillat shows that farm people may have adult children in the neighborhood, but that there is an increasing number of nonfarm rural residents. These people, who do not own a farm, may be left isolated for their children often have migrated to the city to secure employment. Thus this group of rural nonfarm elderly is more vulnerable than either farmers or urban dwellers. Smolić-Krković indicates another consequence of mobility, this time of social mobility, when she observes that families who are struggling to raise their standard of living have "no time" outside work time for fulfilling the needs of their older family members.

Another development mentioned by several of the authors is that the introduction of social services may have unexpected results. Weihl points out that the rules pertaining to filial obligation are viewed differentially by social agencies, dependent on whether the old person lives alone or with children. Weihl further states that once personnel in the welfare services have shown an interest in a person, the voluntary support system more or less disappears.

In the Netherlands filial responsibility is affected by the legal situation. Under the General Assistance Act, children are not legally responsible for their aged parents. Munnichs notes that this regulation has the consequence of obligating the state to provide economic support for the elderly. The very existence of the law, however, can contribute to the dissolution of the extended family because of the knowledge that the supportive functions of children will automatically be taken over by governmental agencies. Munnichs also points out that in those families in which the parents have been especially authoritarian the feeling of filial responsibility is diminished and children are less interested in helping their parents. Furthermore, the expressed preference for intimacy at a distance referred to earlier may constitute a convenient rationalization for the children to leave their parents alone. Thus the necessity for bureaucratic intervention may be accentuated by a combination of legal factors, attitudes towards filial responsibility, and the preference of older people to maintain their own households.

The need for intermediaries to serve as a link between old people and social institutions is emphasized by several of the authors. Paillat observes that in societies such as France a major cultural change has occurred, for no longer do charitable and religious organizations consider it their responsibility to assist the poor, the helpless, the abandoned, and the elderly. These activities have been taken over by the more impersonal, nonreligious bureaucratic structure of the state. Munnichs indicates that social advisers are needed to bridge the gap between the older person and the bureaucratic organization. In the Netherlands 55 percent of the people who visit social advisers are elderly.

At the level of direct care, a further development of modern industrialized society is noted. There is a dearth of people who are willing to act as household helpers or to assist the elderly in their day-to-day needs. Both Weihl and Rosenmayr point out the importance of having trained and well-motivated people to perform these necessary services. Rosenmayr reports that in Austria it is old men living alone who most need help in housekeeping, shopping, and care in case of sickness.

At the same time that the authors stress the need for personal help for the aged there is an indication that the elderly may not want help. Rosenmayr observes that in the village or small community the aged person may be reluctant to report his need for help to a local bureaucrat for he might fear that his problems would become common knowledge. On the other hand, the local person may be in a better position to offer assistance because he knows the person's background and living arrangements while the outsider, the "sociological stranger," would have only a segmental relationship and limited knowledge of the client.

A related problem is whether the bureaucracy has available the resources or the potential to teach personnel to provide the kinds of services that are required. Weihl, for example, indicates the problems of organizing manpower to deal with domestic service. Rosenmayr also alludes to this difficulty and asserts that modern societies should provide well-paid and at least moderately motivated personnel to help people to remain in their homes.

Still another theme universally mentioned directly or by inference is the need for a more systematic study of the nature of formal organizations and their strengths and weaknesses in solving or meeting family problems. Smolić-Krković, for example, observes that in Yugoslavia bureaucratic structures have their own imperatives, their own requirements which limit them in what they can do. These imperatives are one of the causes of the sluggishness with which the bureaucratic organization responds to human needs. Munnichs points out that bureaucrats often hold stereotyped or prejudiced ideas or attitudes about the old.

In the search for common patterns and themes the commentator must be aware of the variability in family characteristics and relations that are often related to the degree of industrialization found in a country. Piotrowski points out, for example, that in Poland a much higher percentage of older persons who have children live with them than is the case in Western countries like Great Britain, the United States, and Denmark. In part this may represent former patterns of multigeneration households, or it may be a response to housing shortages, or a reflection of a greater degree of rural life.

New Directions for Research

The opportunity to comment upon these descriptions of family-bureaucracy relationships in six different cultures challenges the reader to view the

Chart 1. *Linkages between the older person and bureaucracies*

Level I	Aged person ⟶	Bureaucracies
Level II	Aged person ⟶ Linkage mechanisms ⟶	Bureaucracies

Family:
    Spouse
    Children
    Siblings or Relatives

Family Surrogates:
    Groups or Individuals:
      Neighbors, Volunteers,
      Church Groups, Community
      Organizations, "Consumer
      Groups"

Professionals:
    Social Workers, Community
    Aides, Nurses, Ministers,
    etc.
    Ombudsmen

subject matter from a coherent perspective that will enable researchers in a variety of situations to conceptualize the common features in the problems and also to specify those aspects which have received less attention. The forms of linkage between organizations and the family have not been systematically discussed by the authors and it is therefore necessary to outline a few of the problem areas suggested by these descriptions for further study and research. A simplified scheme of the problem is shown in Chart 1.

As we see in this scheme, some aged persons can contact the bureaucracy directly as shown in Level I. However, others require the assistance of linkage mechanisms in Level II to intervene in their behalf, guide them to the proper office of the bureaucracy, help them to fill out forms for the needed services, explain the regulations, provide transportation, and the like. We are concerned here mainly with the way in which families act to provide the linkage mechanism, and thus we will not consider in detail the other possible types of linkage.

Both families and bureaucracies can be described and studied from two main vantage points: (1) structural or organizational and (2) social-psychological. There is an immense body of knowledge on an aggregate basis about the structure of families in the latter part of the life cycle. Are there two, three, or four generations? What are the age and sex of the family members? What are the levels of education, socioeconomic status, ethnicity, language, place of residence of the family members? These are family characteristics which are usually studied by demographers. Turning to the social-psychological aspects of the family, we shift our interest to the study of perceptions, attitudes, roles, identities, and personality. For example, we can speak of family members as having compliant or aggressive personalities in their contact with the bureaucracy. Or the clients or family members may hold a stereotyped perception that all bureaucratic personnel are unfriendly, cold, or hostile.

Let us now consider bureaucracies. They also have been studied quite extensively from the structural perspective: size, number of units, number of staff persons, levels or layers, nature of the hierarchical structure, goals, and communication channels. Weber and other students of bureaucracy have tended to focus on the formal properties of bureaucracies: strict rules and procedures for operation, universalistic standards of treatment, trained personnel, impersonal social relations, centralization of authority, and similar characteristics. These prototypical characteristics of bureaucracies are indeed widely present and frequently observed, but other students of bureaucratic organizations have pointed out that informal structures are also present. There are many ways in which bureaucracies deviate from the formal model in their day-to-day operations. Eisenstadt and others have referred to this as "debureaucratization."[1]

The structural or formal characteristic of bureaucracies create a variety of problems from the standpoint of the client or family members who have to deal with the formal organization. Three charges most often leveled against bureaucracies are: (1) The organizations are inaccessible because of physical location or the hours when services are available; (2) they are impersonal because they treat the patrons or clients in a cold, indifferent, rationalistic manner, and (3) they are inefficient because they are bogged down with rules, procedures, paperwork, and "red tape" which hamper the delivery of service or aid.[2]

This important question of how "efficiently" the bureaucracy serves the client, the patient, or the older person has not received systematic attention. There have been some evaluations of delivery systems. It is probably more difficult to determine how well a bureaucracy serves the family when one introduces the social-psychological dimension. But in realistic, human, everyday terms, it is this dimension the older person or his relative may remember rather than the efficiency of formal organizational structure in delivering services. For example, a person may receive service from the hospital, the branch of the social security system, or the mental health clinic, yet if he has been humiliated or rebuked or subjected to excessive delay, he may not perceive the system as satisfactory. And if he perceives the system to be resistant, unhelpful, or reluctant, he may not return to seek the services he needs. The bureaucrat, on the other hand, may feel it is his "duty" to slow down the delivery of services and perhaps to discourage the client, as a sort of natural check on overuse of the system. If the bureaucrat can make it a bit harder to receive service, perhaps he can reduce his work load.

1. For a discussion of "debureaucratization" see E. Katz and B. Danet, *Bureaucracy and the Public* (New York, 1973), p. 6ff.
2. These problems are discussed in detail in Katz and Danet, ibid., p. 34ff.

Thus it is important to emphasize that there is a wide variation in these three characteristics – accessibility, impersonality, and inefficiency – for they can range along a continuum from high to low. If a bureaucratic organization is accessible, humane in responding to clients, and efficient in its operations, there is less need for intervention by family members or others. Also, if intervention does occur, one can assume that the older person is more likely to receive the attention or service the bureaucracy is expected to provide.

In the sphere of the social psychology of bureaucracies there have been studies of the informal structures, different kinds of bureaucratic personalities, leadership techniques, and informal relations and circumvention of the formal rules.[3] Thus we have considerable information on both the family and the bureaucracy. However, the interface between the two has been neglected by students of complex organizations. It is this linkage aspect which is the most difficult and least-studied area.

We need more information on who contacts bureaucracies. A common stereotype held in American society is that it is primarily the indigent, the incompetent, and the underprivileged among the aged who contact bureaucracies. This is a gross oversimplification, for currently in the United States almost all older persons, rich or poor, must have some contacts with bureaucratic organizations. Moreover, it is essential to point out that in a nonsocialistic society like the United States there are many privately owned and operated bureaucracies, some of which are complex organizations, which the older person may have occasion to contact. Financial, commercial, and credit bureaucracies operating for profit may sometimes involve inefficiencies, difficulties, and frustrations for the older patron. The development of the consumer movement in recent years is evidence that both public and private organizations may operate in ways which are inimical to the patron, client, customer, or plain citizen. Coping with bureaucracies is often a challenge at any stage of life, but to an older person who may be in a state of declining health and energy, and who may be uncertain about his loss of independence, it poses a special problem. Thus when we ask the broad question, Who contacts bureaucracies? the answer is, almost all older persons in a complex industrial society. The subject requires further specification and may be broken down into a series of issues stated as questions:

1. What kinds of older persons are vulnerable and more likely to require intervention? The more vulnerable elderly are often those who are

3. The classic discussion of personality types in bureaucracies is found in R. K. Merton, "Bureaucratic Structure and Personality," *Social Forces* 18 (1940):560–68.

A recent careful empirical study by Melvin L. Kohn suggests that persons who work in bureaucratic organizations may be more intellectually flexible, more open to new experience, and more self-directed than persons who work in nonbureaucratic organizations. See M. L. Kohn, "Bureaucratic Man: A Portrait and an Interpretation," *American Sociological Review* 36 (1971):461–74.

poor and uneducated; persons who do not speak the language of the bureaucracy; also racial, religious, and ethnic minorities against whom there is prejudice and discrimination; the physically or socially isolated; and the physically or mentally handicapped. Persons who are vulnerable are most likely to be among the older aged and to be female. The inexorable aging process itself and the consequences of differential mortality are quite predictable. But we cannot lump all the aged together for the evidence is sound that the aged are not homogeneous, and among the very old there are persons who are very capable of coping with any organization or the most diffident and inefficient bureaucrat.

The characteristics listed here when observed as single traits in isolation may not be an insurmountable handicap in bureaucratic relationships. Usually, however, they are found in a combination of several characteristics, and a cluster of these traits tends to increase the inability of the individual to cope with bureaucratic situations. However, even when persons have several traits associated with greater vulnerability, it is possible that local community-living arrangements or collective action may mitigate or considerably reduce their inability to cope in dealing with a complex organization.

2. Under what conditions does the family assist in the intervention process? In answering this question, it should be noted that there are a variety of persons in different family structures who vary in their need to use bureaucratic systems and in their ability to cope with them. Those persons who have adult children are less vulnerable than those who have nieces, nephews, and more distant kin. Furthermore the older person who has a daughter is more likely to receive aid and attention from her than from a son — either in the form of direct aid or assistance in coping with the bureaucracy.

The second kinship factor which may affect the older person's vulnerability is whether the kin are in close enough proximity to act as intervenors. If the kin live nearby, obviously the problems of transportation are eased, whether the older person is merely contacted or transported to the bureaucratic organization if that should be necessary. Location of residence has been mentioned by both Munnichs, writing about the Netherlands, and Rosenmayr, describing the aged in Austria. Both refer to the fact that bureaucratic intervention is more necessary when older persons do not live in close proximity to their relatives. Piotrowski's chapter points out that in Poland the migration of young people to towns and cities means that older persons are often left alone in rural areas to cope with the exigencies of life by themselves.

3. What are the alternatives when there is no family or if family members are unable or unwilling to act as intervenors or mediators? In cases of short-term illness or crisis sometimes a neighbor or friend will provide the necessary help. However, for any problem that is chronic or persistent, it is less

likely that a neighbor or church member will help on a regular and continuing basis. It is then that social agencies which have a responsibility for providing assistance will be called upon for services. In fact, family members who can help in a crisis situation may also have to turn to bureaucratic agencies for assistance if the problem is chronic and the family member lives some distance away.

A very significant consideration of the intervention process involves social-psychological aspects. The attitudes that the client may have toward the family surrogate is a significant part of the context in which the intervention occurs. For instance, in many Western societies public intervention agents may be stereotyped by the client in a derogatory or negative fashion. This is because older persons, valuing their independence, autonomy, and integrity, may view the intervenor as offering "charity," "welfare," or a "handout." Although there may be a clear-cut need for assistance, the attitude toward those who may help is impeded by the social-psychological perspective the older person holds.

On the other hand, surrogates who are potential intervenors — neighbors, friends, or distant kin — pose a different kind of social-psychological threat to the elderly, isolated person in need of help. Here the intervenor may be viewed as a prying person intruding on the autonomy of the person in need. In the long run, from the standpoint of both the recipient and the community at large, it is probably more efficacious to have professionals, representing the public, give the assistance to the elderly. As Rosenmayr and Weihl point out regarding their respective countries, there is a need that the public intervenors be at least reasonably trained and moderately motivated to offer service or assistance to the needy elderly. Indeed, this is the crux of the formal organization's attempt to deal with problems which have traditionally been dealt with by primary groups.

One final point should be made: there are three stages of intervention on behalf of the older person: (1) during legislative enactment or administrative rule formulation; (2) during the operation of the agency or organization in giving service to clients; and (3) after the agency or bureau has offered support, aid, or assistance. The first stage involves lobbying or pressure-group activity. This is probably the stage of the process where the family or family surrogate will be least involved in terms of a particular family member. The second stage is the one during which intervention is most likely to take place. It is during this stage, when an agency is actually offering help or assistance, that family members may be most effective in coordinating information or service and perhaps improving the situation for the older family member. In the third area there is greater difficulty in effecting change or improving service because it involves undoing a mistake or dealing with a shortcoming or a failure to act. Bureaucratic organizations vary in their response to complaints. Perhaps the most optimistic view is that future service or activities will be more sensitive to consumer evaluation.

Conclusion and Interpretations

The linkages between families and bureaucratic structures are modern problems for they have emerged and been magnified only in industrialized societies characterized by complex, interdependent economic structures, formal organizations, and high rates of physical and social mobility.

There is a tendency on the part of some contemporary critics to view the consequences of modernized societies as a grand conspiracy, when in reality many of the problems which have emerged were unanticipated and are what might be designated as "fallout" problems. Some of the social problems of high-energy societies are analagous to the unanticipated or unmentioned consequences resulting from the development of atomic energy.[4] The physicists, engineers, and others who hailed the "harnessing of the atom" and the wonderful peaceful outcomes did not hint in 1945 that there would be vast problems latent in the use of the atom for peaceful purposes: the need to control thermal pollution, dangers of accidents, and the difficulties of disposing of huge quantities of atomic wastes. In the social and institutional spheres related to the family and old age, few persons had the wisdom and the foresight to hint at some of the consequences of modernity in high-energy societies. For example, modern medical techniques make it possible to keep senile people alive for years; the movement of families from the farm to urban centers usually means there is no "guest room" in the city apartment to house an elderly relative. Students of aging and the family now realize that both positive and negative consequences of societal change may unfold slowly. But it should be clear that some of the problems which arise are the "price" that we pay for modernity.

The chapters selected for comment show that all of the six countries considered are trying to develop the means of coping with the problems of how formal organizations meet and adapt to the problems of an aging population when the traditional family supports are weakened or nonexistent. However, there is confusion regarding what may be the appropriate norms and the most "efficient" processes which should govern bureaucracies. There is also uncertainty in the minds of both old and young family members concerning what is expected of them and what is appropriate behavior. This is true not only in the countries discussed in this chapter but also in the United States.

Family members in a modern society are often under cross-pressures. On the one hand, in keeping with traditional family norms and expectations, they may wish to assist older family members. However, in a modern society, there are also services available through formal organizations. If the

4. Fred Cottrell has written the most systematic analysis of the relationships between the technological and societal basis of aging, employing a broad distinction between low-energy and high-energy societies. See F. Cottrell, "The Technological and Societal Basis of Aging," in *Handbook of Social Gerontology*, ed. C. Tibbitts (Chicago, 1960), pp. 92–119.

family members avail themselves of these services, they sometimes feel they are neglecting their family obligations. There is also a dilemma when they decide whether they are entitled to receive such services even though they might be able to meet the needs of their older family members by heroic means and economic sacrifice. For example, a family might have to make the choice of whether to use its limited resources to educate their children or to support an aged parent. The dilemma is sharpened if the family realizes that neighbors and other citizens are receiving help for their aged parents. Some of these cross-pressures arise because many services are discretionary and are available on the basis of proven "need" rather than being based on criteria of a general social right.

To summarize, among Western societies there is a similarity of problems related to the nature and size of the aging population, the degree to which a society still has a high proportion of its work force engaged in agriculture, and the amount of social and health services which the society can afford (or will pay for). Thus, as societies move from an underdeveloped economic state to one of modernization, they face similar problems related to family and bureaucracy.[5] Indeed one can note a continuum related to the issues involved. In Poland and Yugoslavia—countries which are less industrialized than the Netherlands, the United States, or France—one sees residues of an earlier agricultural society which may mitigate the problems of the aging at present. An emerging modern society does not have a coherent system of norms and values, particularly norms and values that have appeared rather recently because of the longer life span, the change in family relations and structures, and the attempts to establish formal structures to deal with concerns which were traditionally classified as family or religious obligations.

Joep Munnichs has raised an interesting and important question when he asks, "Which is easier to change in modern societies: the bureaucratic structures or the family?" Munnichs thinks the bureaucratic aspect is more easily subject to change. I am inclined to agree with him, and I think the authors of this volume have indicated, if only in a preliminary manner, those areas which need further study and which, by research and demonstration projects, may show how bureaucratic structures in modern societies can be developed, adapted, and improved to meet the emerging problems of older persons and their families.

5. A recent attempt to develop a theory of cross-cultural aging, including a number of case studies, is *Aging and Modernization*, ed. D. O. Cowgill and L. D. Holmes (New York, 1972).

13. Family and Bureaucracy: Comparative Analyses and Problematics *Ethel Shanas and Marvin B. Sussman*

Bureaucracies and Their Activities

Bureaucracy is generally thought to be an inevitable concomitant of industrial societies. The organization of such societies, necessarily complex, is seen as spawning bureaucratic growth. The bureaucracy in its turn operates by rules which are universalistic, not particularistic; by standards formalized by law, not custom; and with trained personnel whose distinguishing mark is impersonality. The "faceless bureaucrat" is a cliché of industrial society, as contrasted with the personalized relationships assumed to exist between functionaries and clients in less complex social structures.

Lest we convey a pejorative imagery of the nature of bureaucracy, one which incorporates the notion of the "faceless bureaucrat" unconcerned about human needs, it should be made clear that bureaucracy is an honorable term. It is descriptive of a mass organization where functions are performed by specialists and the concept of the interchangeable part dominates the theory and practice of the organization. Bureaucracies have high absorptive capacities to assimilate individuals of differential skills and with varied social and cultural characteristics. In theory the bureaucracy is a democratic organization where the principle of meritocracy predominates.

Limited function and responsibility are two additional characteristics of bureaucratic structures. Coordination is obtained by developing a hierarchical triangular ordered structure of positions. Those persons located on the base or the steps immediately above have fewer responsibilities and less authority and skills, while those in the apex have the greatest authority, responsibility, and accountability.

The democratic quality of the bureaucratic organization is reflected in its recruitment policies based upon a notion of universalism. The bureaucratic ideology presumes that competence will be the most critical factor in selection; and the presence of an open, nonnepotic mobility system enables persons of skill, creativity, and ability to rise within the hierarchical structure.

According to balance theorists, bureaucracies are most competent in performing uniform tasks.[1] Such symmetrical activities require systematic

1. E. Litwak and H. J. Meyer, "Administrative Styles and Community Linkages of Public Schools," in *Schools in a Changing Society*, ed. A. J. Reiss, Jr. (New York, 1965), pp. 49–97; idem, "The School and the Family: Linking Organizations and External Primary Groups," in *The Uses of Sociology*, ed. P. Lazarsfeld, W. Sewell, and H. Wilensky (New York, 1967), pp. 522–43; idem, "A Balance Theory of Coordination Between Bureaucratic Organizations and Community Primary Groups," *Administrative Science Quarterly* 11 (1966):31–58; E. Litwak, D. Hollister, and H. Meyer, "Linkage Theory Between Bureaucracies and Community Primary Groups: Education, Health and Political Action as Empirical Cases in Point" (Paper presented at the Annual Meeting of the American Sociological Association, Montreal, 1974).

training, the use of resources on a mass scale, and great technical skill and knowledge. The primary group such as a family is incapable of successfully carrying out functions "fitted to" bureaucracies. Primary groups, on the other hand, are most competent to handle nonuniform tasks. There is no need for highly specialized knowledge and technical skills to handle these. The family or kin network consists of a small group of members, usually intimate and close, which permits easy communication and exchange and which is structurally best suited for handling nonuniform or idiosyncratic events and for reaching quick decisions uninhibited by protocol and procedure.

The family in its everyday socialization can provide the elderly person with necessary succor, nurture, and information, and can be especially influential in decision making regarding the older person's relationships with bureaucratic organizations. It can also provide an immediate and quick response to the crisis situations enmeshing elderly persons; be a buffer for elderly persons in the latter's dealing with bureaucracies; examine the service options provided by organizations; effect entry of the elderly person into the program of bureaucratic organizations and facilitate the continuity of the relationship of the aged member with the bureaucracy.

Because of its structural attributes and activities, the family is not competent to handle uniform tasks. For example, the elderly person suffering a stroke can be helped by the family during the initial attack by quickly detecting what has happened and by reporting the illness immediately to the physician. Early recognition that something is wrong can increase the probability of survival of the elderly person. But the family does not have the skill or competence to reach a diagnosis or treat the stroke. This requires the specialized training of physicians and other supportive personnel and the facilities of a hospital. The combination of early detection along with appropriate diagnosis and treatment by technically competent professionals is illustrative of the kind of linkage which is now required in complex societies if bureaucracies and primary groups such as the family are to have reciprocally profitable linkages.

The survival of any bureaucracy in a form appropriate to its tasks and conception of self as an organizational entity, relevant and powerful, is dependent on its adaptation to the demands made upon it. Bureaucracies and their functionaries may have ignored the elderly in the past, but, as this volume shows, the presence of large numbers of older persons in contemporary society means that bureaucracies must somehow adjust to the special needs and wants of these persons. In every country studied—Austria, Britain, France, Israel, the Netherlands, Poland, and the United States—functions that may have once been the unique province of the family are now becoming shared functions of the family and the bureaucracy. Where the family was once expected to look after the economic needs of its aged members, industrial societies now support the nonworking members of society through societal-wide rather than intergenerational family transfers. Where the family previously had primary responsibility for taking care of its sick elderly, specialized health services, such as nursing homes and chronic disease hospitals, proliferate to care for the sick and frail. Even in the area of emotional support, long considered the primary function of the family, the bureaucracy now provides social workers who are presumed to have the special skills necessary to assuage the desires of the elderly for meaningful human relationships.

Human Service Bureaucracies

Human services, organized into powerful and formidable bureaucracies, consume a substantial part of the wealth of any complex society. Most of the societies represented in this volume have work forces where the majority are engaged in service rather than productive occupations. A major share of the gross national product of many of these societies is expended for human services.

It would be erroneous to conclude that human service systems in their care of the aged are providing professional workers and other staff to give emotional and other support to elderly persons because of the breakdown of the family and its kin network. This is an easy assumption because of our perceptions that bureaucracies willingly pick up such unpleasant tasks as those involved in the care of the ill, ugly, disabled, and elderly.

Another equally valid orientation is that human service systems, bureaucratized and hierarchically ordered like other organizations in the society, engage in activities in the affective domain as a means of sustaining their control and enhancing their power. In doing this, such service systems are not malicious, they are merely aping the nature of bureaucratic organizations found in complex societies. Whether they are quick to undertake a new function or not is not highly relevant. The paramount issue is whether they can sustain the elitist character of their organization and maintain dominance in the superordinate-subordinate model of professional-client relationships.

There are major developments which will inhibit and in some instances stop the continuous encroachment of human service bureaucracies upon the affective territory of primary groups such as the family. The first is that most complex societies and many in third world countries have reached or are reaching their absorptive capacity to further provide monies for the establishment of new or expanded service systems. Such demands for services, and most of these do not come from clients but from the professionalized service bureaucracies, are so costly that governments and their legislative bodies are viewing these increased appeals with jaundiced eyes. They are looking for less costly alternatives, and the primary group is being given serious consideration as an alternative, or at least a complementary system, for providing a creative environment for dependent or potentially dependent individuals.

A second condition mitigating against the human service system's control over the elderly is its poor track record in handling the nonuniform tasks necessitated by everyday life, the everyday socialization which provides the affect and individualized services required by all human beings, especially the elderly. There are few reported researches indicating that institutional arrangements and the procedures used by providers of services are substitutes for primary group interaction. Consequently, while governments in complex and third world countries are developing magnificent human service bureaucracies, there are rumblings among planners and visionaries that following this American model of service developments may not be at all appropriate.

Findings by Shanas and others have consistently demonstrated that with the exception of a very few elderly persons in any society at any given time the vast majority are linked with their kindred.

The task is how to more effectively involve family and kin network in long-term care of the elderly and to do this without using the power of law and without destroying the internal dynamics of the particular family unit. Are there ways in which a society can reallocate its resources so that some of these which are now being spent in traditional services can be used more creatively, and be more consistent with the basic interests and priorities set by the elderly and their families?

One alternative would be to provide economic incentives so that families could achieve the individual and group goals they have established for themselves. If members are not goal setting, at least they should be able to maintain the functioning level to which they have become accustomed. The reorganization of human services involves further decentralization so that providers can respond even more quickly to the needs and requirements of families in the latter's familiar environment. Viewing the family and its elderly member or members as an ecosystem with the provision of general services in the household of the family and easily obtainable specialized services in centralized institutions when required is an appropriate option. It need not be a universal pattern in a society, but we insist that it be considered as an option. It would yield reciprocal benefits to both service practitioners and family members. The professional could best use his skills as an expert and consultant. He would not be required or tempted to assume complete control over the life of the elderly person and the family. Nor would the professional be "pushed" into tasks, such as providing affection for his clients, which may not be in consonance with idealized professional roles.

Similarities and Differences Among Social Systems

The reports in this volume range over time from Victorian England to prospects for the future; and over space from the Western industrialized countries – Austria, Britain, France, the Netherlands, and the United States – to the Eastern Socialist countries – Poland and Yugoslavia – and to a relatively new state – European in outlook, near-Eastern in location – Israel. In all these accounts the situation of the elderly appears to be similar. Irrespective of country, the same demographic changes have affected older people. Where once they were few they are now many, ranging from one in seven to one of every thirteen persons in the countries studied. Where once they were the parents of large families of children, they now have fewer children or none at all. Those who have adult children are likely to live apart from them, even in rural areas, reflecting a wish for privacy on the part of the generations. The wish for independence on the part of the generations is not new. It has been reported by historical demographers in both European and American studies. However, children and parents in countries largely rural before the Second World War – Austria, Yugoslavia, and Poland – do live increasingly distant from one another, reflecting the geographic mobility associated with industrialization and urbanization.

There is no evidence that these demographic changes have substantially changed the basic pattern of interaction between adult children and older parents. Emotional ties remain strong despite physical separation. In case of need parents turn to children whether or not the children live in the same household. But there is obviously more day-to-day interaction between parents and children when they live in close proximity, in the same house or on the same farm, than when they are physically separated.

The systems of government and the political philosophies of the countries studied are different, but all of them have developed systems to meet the needs of the elderly. These systems are primarily in the areas of economic support and, increasingly, the social services. In all the countries studied citizens, young or old, are viewed as having a right to the means of subsistence. The conditions under which this right can be exercised by the elderly, however, differs from country to country. In Britain and the Netherlands no liability for support of the elderly is now imposed on children, relatives, or the local community. In the United States, France, and Poland the elderly need to "earn" their support through participation in various social insurance schemes. Where support is not "earned" it is given on the basis of need. In both Yugoslavia and Israel children are required to support their aged parents if they are able to do so. Of all the countries studied Yugoslavia has the most explicit statement of the role of family and bureaucracy in relation to the elderly. Laws exist to take care of the economic needs of the elderly, the Social Security laws; to provide for the elderly, the needy, and the frail, the laws of social protection; and finally, to govern the relationship between older parents and adult children. In Yugoslavia, under the law, adult children are required to support needy older parents, a system similar to the Poor Law Provisions of nineteenth-century England, making a matter of law what may have once been purely a familial function.

In response to changing expectations on the part of both older people and society, economic support systems for the elderly are in a state of flux. The trend in the United States recently has been more and more to ensure every older person a minimum income without the stigma of a needs test. In countries where there are relative responsibility laws, it is difficult to enforce them. In the United States most jurisdictions which have such laws do not enforce them because of the high costs of administration. It is cheaper to "ignore" the law and permit the elderly person to qualify for other forms of aid.[2] Also, old people, however neglected, do not bring their children before legal authorities. The old parent would rather suffer than to admit to himself or to society that his children neglect him. It would appear that the emotional strains introduced by relative responsibility laws are destructive of good parent-child relationships, since they inject an element of threat into a situation previously personal and private.

The social service systems developed to meet the needs of the elderly are primarily in the area of health and housing, although some countries have also developed "advice bureaus" where old people can go for discussion of their problems and referral to the proper authorities. In the health areas there seems to be general agreement that services should be available so that old people can continue to live in their own homes. The need for such services is highlighted in the case of France where, as Paillat says, "Who, for example, will take care of childless couples, a frequent case in France since the decline of fertility and the death of sons in war?" The scarcity of such services, reported from every country, is emphasized in the report from Israel, where if an old person lives with a child or relative, he is informally cut off from the scarce resources of the visiting homemaker or health aide.

In all countries there has been a development of housing for the elderly, ranging from apartments and homes for the well aged to various kinds of sheltered environments for the frail and sick. Munnichs, in his discussion of the Netherlands, where almost 10 percent of the aged live in institutions, refers to the "thinning out" of the Dutch family as a factor in institutionalization, and points out that the older Dutch living in institutions are disproportionately unmarried or widowed without children. The Netherlands experience in housing is a particularly useful one to consider since it indicates how both housing and health services for the aged reflect social policy decisions. The care of the aged in the Netherlands was first assumed to be

2. D. H. Hueber, "The Effect of Relatives' Responsibility Laws on the Family" (Ph.D. dissertation, Case Western Reserve University, 1971).

primarily a housing problem, "but little by little it became seen as much more of a social problem because housing also came to mean the provision of security and care." The proliferation of institutions for the aged soon became an unacceptable drain on government resources, and the government in turn changed its emphasis to recruiting and supporting health aides, homemakers, and other personnel necessary to keep older people in their own homes.

From the papers in this volume, it would appear that when a definitive history of old people in the twentieth century is written, a general theme would have to be the emergence of the social worker as a family surrogate. In the Netherlands, for example, the social adviser is available to all citizens, but the majority of his clients are the elderly. In France the new vocation of social worker is reported as replacing the religious vocations which did charitable work with the elderly in the past. Weihl states that in Israel the voluntary help given to the elderly by the family and others tends to disappear once the welfare services have shown an interest in the person.

In every country more and more services to older people are now provided by a family surrogate rather than by family members. In fact, this must be considered a response to the new needs and the new demands made by the elderly upon society. As people become better educated, more sophisticated, and more knowing their wants and expectations rise. The elderly are no exception.

While the social worker appears to be emerging as a caretaker in the several countries described in this volume, it is worthwhile to speculate on the rationale and etiology of this emergent role, if in fact it is portentous of the future. Social work and social workers have long been regarded in most societies as a necessary occupation to act as buffers between the unwanted and the power structure. People who are unwanted, neglected, despised, stereotyped, incompetent, noncompliant, ugly, and who are viewed as being potentially dangerous to the moral and physical well-being of the body politic need surrogates and, in some instances, care. While the concerns of social workers are with the poor, deprived, and depraved, and, for some, their identities and sympathies may be with clients, their professional training and practice ideology identifies them with establishment interests.

Whenever a category of individuals increases in number so that it expresses itself through a group process or by individual response to existing conditions and situations, e.g., retirement at a mandatory age and the "problem" of what to do with this group, the concern of elites and of those who are in human service systems becomes how to "handle" this situation. Social workers are both "pushed" and "pulled" into the arena. They are pushed because few other professional colleagues want to do anything about the situation of the aged and aging individual; and they are pulled because in taking over this "problem" they carve out a new functional area for themselves and can bargain more effectively for power and rewards from those professions higher in the human services work system.

The use of professionals in affective domains may be only a temporary measure during a developmental period when policy makers, planners, government officials, and other administrators and elites use traditional patterns of human service system organization to cope with growing problems. It is obvious even to the lay person who has to pay the high costs of such services that the provision of emotional support and other interpersonal needs can be ably performed by the highly trained social worker, but this may be a waste of taxpayers' money. One does not need professionals to provide everyday types of interactions, including everyday socialization. One does not need professionals whose training has created specialized cognitive styles, techniques of problem analysis, methods of communication, and perception well suited to handle those cases which may be "two standard deviations from the norm" to handle idiosyncratic daily events.

An area in which social workers could indeed be of great service for the elderly and other members of families and kin networks would be in employing their expertise as advocates and organizers for the elderly. Social workers could use their tremendous capabilities in turning disparate older individuals into viable social groups. Such groups in turn could effect transformations in current patterns of providing financial and economic supports and services so that these are more appropriate to the requirements of the elderly and their primary groups. In some instances social workers can function in the traditional roles of ombudsman, employed by the bureaucracy but representing the interests of workers or clients. In the ombudsman role, they can present grievances to the administration of organizations and institutions for their consideration. Another possible role for social workers would be to utilize their skills in the organization of elderly groups and their families for effective lobbying and political action aimed to eliminate discriminatory policies, legislation, and programs affecting the elderly, and to create those programs which will establish economic, health, and social maintenance as a right for all rather than as a privilege.

Still another role for professionals would be to serve as managers and administrators of the interests of elderly persons and their families. Politics, policies, and programs may be so modified in a number of societies so that resources are now made available to the elderly to be used at their discretion. If this occurs there will be a great need for competent administrators and consultants to help old people "buy" the needed services and means for their maintenance and to enable them to enjoy a quality life. While providing resources to a dependent social group and permitting it to establish its own priorities and to use its options autonomously may appear to be a radical change, it is much in keeping with the ideologies of free choice found in all societies. Professionalized human service systems can be made more responsible with reference to the needs and preferences of their clients through negotiating what they will provide, thus moving professionals and clients towards a relationship of greater parity. The roles of advocate, organizer, administrator, and ombudsman are proposed as more salient roles for social workers dealing with the elderly than the provision of emotional and other affective supports, which can be most effectively provided by members of family and kin networks, and, if not by them, by less professional persons.

Prospects for the Future

The question of the aging and the aged is now a priority item for international consideration. Problems currently faced by old people in developed countries may not as yet have arisen in developing countries but with increased industrialization and urbanization, combined with demographic changes, the role of old people in society is everywhere in a state of flux. Responding to these felt needs, the United Nations convened its first Expert Group on Aging in the spring of 1974. Several of the special concerns of the expert group are relevant here.

The Expert Group felt that all national and international programs for the elderly should have as their ultimate goal the improvement of the quality of life for older persons. Both the family and the bureaucracy would agree that the improvement of the quality of life is a desirable end for all members of a society, whether young or old. The basic question, however, is how is the quality of life for any age group, in this instance the elderly, to be improved? The Expert Group asked for the provision of adequate environments, health services, social welfare services, leisure-time activities, educational opportunities, and the right to work for older people. The Expert Group, like many other advocates for the elderly, was reporting the need for more supportive services for the sick and frail aged; the need for social welfare services for old people with problems; and, as a forecast of the future, the need to develop time-filling activities, including work, for those older people who, subsistence assured, seek to improve the quality of their lives.

It is apparent that despite references to the important role of the family in old age, basically the experts were outlining a social plan for aid systems, which by their very nature, could only be bureaucratic. One sees here another foretelling of the emergence of shared functions between the family and bureaucracy. Bureaucratic aid systems, however, as Rosenmayr points out, do not necessarily mean that those who receive aid are victims of the system. They can instead be its initiators, developers, and guides. A calling of the bureaucracy to account for its action is also possible where strong advocates are involved. The family can serve as that advocate for its kin members. Or these advocates can be professionals working with the elderly, or, as may already be seen in many countries, old people themselves.

It may be that the taking over by bureaucracy of the functions of economic support and health care of the elderly will serve to create better relationships between old people and their adult children. What the family can best supply its aged members is affection, and those special exchanges of services unique to each family constellation. As Talcott Parsons has said, "The family can thus be seen to have two primary functions, not one. On the one hand it is the primary agent of socialization for the child, while on the other it is the primary basis of security for the normal adult."[3]

Endemic to all relationships between individuals, or those between an organization and an individual, or between organizations is continuous by-play, sometimes referred to as power moves, to enhance one's status, position, and attendant rewards. "Take-over" is part and parcel of any individual or group strategy. It is a component of exchange theory as illustrated in the first chapter of this volume, but one takes over only to the extent that the other party in the transaction will have received sufficient rewards to maintain the relationship. On a macrolevel it is difficult to conceptualize that any system or group can take over functions completely and absolutely. In bureaucratic organization–primary group linkages there are gray areas which produce conflict, confrontation, confusion, and ambiguity. There is every indication that this territorial overlapping will not cease because of the continued efforts of primary groups and bureaucratic structures to obtain a preferred position in their relationships.

Exacerbating this condition of overlapping domains between bureaucracies and families is the information implosion which is providing neatly packaged units of data easily acceptable and not too difficult to comprehend. One consequence is the questioning of the aura of the expert and demystification of the professional role. In some quarters, in fact, there is a "revolt of the client" against the professional.[4] As ordinary folk are discovering that a good deal of their treatment by professionals contains a large component of placebo, they are questioning if there is any justification for complying with the superordinate position in the superordinate-subordinate model of treatment currently being practiced. This model of treatment, heavily oriented in concepts of pathology, presupposes that the client who is in a subordinate position takes on this compliant role in exchange for being cared for or cured of his or her ailments. In this process the client is con-

3. T. Parsons, "The Normal American Family," in *Man and Civilization: The Family's Search for Survival*, ed. S. Farber, P. Mustacchi, and R. H. Wilson (New York, 1965).

4. M. R. Haug and M. B. Sussman, "Professional Autonomy and the Revolt of the Client," *Social Problems* 17 (1969):153–61; J. Pilati, "The Hospitals Don't Belong to the People," *The Village Voice*, February 6, 1969; A. Gartner, ed., "New Ideology of New Careers," *New Careers Newsletter* 3 (1965); E. H. Van Ness, "The Regional Medical Program in Heart Disease, Cancer and Stroke," in *Utilization of Rehabilitation Manpower in the Community Setting* (Mankato, Minn., 1967).

trolled not only in relation to the particular problem that brings him to the professional but in every other aspect of life.

As the diffusion of knowledge increases, the growing perception is that perhaps too high a price is being paid for the professional services being rendered. Increasingly more clients of human service systems are perceiving much of professional activity as a case of meddling and as an invasion of their privacy. Client populations are not trying to do away with professionals and their expertise; they still want their services but much more as consultants and experts performing particular functions. A relationship closer to parity between client and professional would remove the all-controlling feature of the current service model and reduce the dependency of the client upon the professional.

In sum, there is no reason why bureaucratic organizations serving the elderly cannot perform the uniform tasks for which they have been specifically organized, and why primary groups such as families cannot perform and perform well the nonuniform tasks to which their structures are most suited. The case materials and data presented in this volume which question the role of bureaucracy and the bureaucrat indicate some of the dilemmas of contemporary bureaucracy and demonstrate the need for corrective influences on the extreme isolation and exercise of power found in the contemporary linkages of bureaucracies and families.

There is a need for increased sensitivity to clients and a willingness to listen on the part of human service systems and their functionaries. Listening and communicating are the beginnings of much more effective and coordinated relationships. The promise of a more symbiotic and balanced exchange between primary groups and bureaucratic organizations serving the elderly is predictable. In our judgment such a development in the coming decades can only improve the quality of life for the elderly person who needs both the bureaucracy and the family to enhance his survival and life style.

Index